FRENCH LAUGHTER

FRENCH LAUGHTER

LITERARY HUMOUR FROM DIDEROT TO TOURNIER

WALTER REDFERN

OXFORD
UNIVERSITY PRESS

OXFORD

UNIVERSITY PRESS

Great Clarendon Street, Oxford OX2 6DP

Oxford University Press is a department of the University of Oxford.
It furthers the University's objective of excellence in research, scholarship,
and education by publishing worldwide in

Oxford New York

Auckland Cape Town Dar es Salaam Hong Kong Karachi
Kuala Lumpur Madrid Melbourne Mexico City Nairobi
New Delhi Shanghai Taipei Toronto

With offices in

Argentina Austria Brazil Chile Czech Republic France Greece
Guatemala Hungary Italy Japan Poland Portugal Singapore
South Korea Switzerland Thailand Turkey Ukraine Vietnam

Oxford is a registered trade mark of Oxford University Press
in the UK and in certain other countries

Published in the United States
by Oxford University Press Inc., New York

© Walter Redfern 2008

The moral rights of the author has been asserted
Database right Oxford University Press (maker)

First published 2008

British Library Cataloguing in Publication Data

Data available

Library of Congress Cataloging in Publication Data

Data available

Typeset by Laserwords Private Limited, Chennai, India
Printed in Great Britain
on acid-free paper by
Biddles Ltd., King's Lynn, Norfolk

ISBN 978-0-19-923757-9

1 3 5 7 9 10 8 6 4 2

Acknowledgements

I owe a debt of gratitude to Terence Cave and John Parkin for their cross-talking with my parrots, to Geoffrey Bremner dialoguing with my Diderot, and to my wife Angela for keeping step by step with me throughout my enjoyable research and writing of this book.

Thankfully, I have no need to express gratitude to any body for financial assistance, as I sought little and obtained zilch. Far more importantly, I do want to thank from the bottom of my semi-bionic heart all the hundreds of unpaid workers whose ideas I have hijacked. Whenever conscious, I have admitted debts. The fact remains that this book is my personal statement on humour, whether French literary, or everyone's. Some might think that I have made things difficult for myself by selecting authors perhaps not primarily known for their humour. I have done so because of a lifelong and profound conviction that humour can be found in the less likely places.

Parts of Chapters 4–9 were previously published in: John Parkin and John Phillips (eds), *Language and Power* (Lang, 2006); *Language and Communication*; Jane Taylor et al. (eds.), *The Anatomy of Laughter* (Legenda, 2005); *French Studies*; John Parkin (ed.), *French Humour* (Rodopi, 1999); and the *Modern Language Review*, respectively. I wish to thank all these editors for permission to reproduce such material.

W. R.

Contents

Abbreviations

Place of publication for works in English is London and for works in French Paris, except where stated otherwise.

Bach.	Vallés, *Le Bachelier*, in *Œuvres*, ed. R. Bellet (Gallimard, 1990), ii
CDW	Beckett, *Complete Dramatic Works* (Faber, 1990)
CP	Vallès, *Le Candidat des pauvres*, in *SEP*
CS	Tournier, *Des clefs et des serrures* (Chêne/Hachette, 1979)
CSP	Beckett, *Collected Shorter Prose* (Calder, 1988)
DFMW	Beckett, *Dream of Fair to Middling Women* (Calder, 1996)
Dis.	Beckett, *Disjecta*, ed. R. Cohn (Calder, 1983)
EC	Tournier, 'L'Espace canadien', *La Nouvelle Critique*, 105 (1977), 52
Enf.	Vallès, *L'Enfant*, in *Œuvres*, ed. R. Bellet (Gallimard, 1990), ii
Exp.	Beckett, *The Expelled and other Novellas* (Penguin, 1980)
First	Beckett, *First Love* (Penguin, 1995)
Inn.	See *Unn./Inn.*
Ins.	Vallès, *L'Insurgé*, in *Œuvres*, ed. R. Bellet (Gallimard, 1990), ii
GJ	Tournier, *Gilles et Jeanne* (Gallimard, 1983)
L	Tournier, 'Une logique contre vents et marées', *La Nouvelle Critique*, 105 (1977), 47–50
M	Tournier, *Les Météores* (Gallimard, 1975)
Mal.	Beckett, *Malone Dies*, in *Molloy, Malone Dies, The Unnamable* (Calder, 1959); French version: *Malone meurt* (Union générale d'éditions, 1951)
Merc.	Beckett, *Mercier and Camier* (Picador, 1988); French version: *Mercier et Camier* (Minuit, 1970)
Moll.	Beckett, *Molloy* (New York: Grove, 1970); French version (Union générale d'éditions, 1963)

Mur.	Beckett, *Murphy* (New York: Grove, 1957)
Proust	Beckett, *Proust* (New York: Grove, 1931)
RA	Tournier, *Le Roi des aulnes* (Gallimard, 1970)
SEP	Vallès, *Souvenirs d'un étudiant pauvre* (Éditeurs français réunis, 1972)
TC	Tournier, 'Treize Clés pour un ogre', *Le Figaro littéraire*, 30 November 1970, pp. 20–2
Unn./Inn.	Beckett, *The Unnamable* (New York: Grove, 1970); French version: *L'Innommable* (Minuit, 1953)
V	Tournier, *Vendredi, ou Les Limbes du pacifique*, postface by Gilles Deleuze (Gallimard, 1967)
VD	Tournier, *Vues de dos* (Gallimard, 1981)
VP	Tournier, *Le Vent Paraclet* (Gallimard, 1977)
VV	Tournier, *Le Vol du vampire* (Mercure de France, 1981)
Watt	Beckett, *Watt* (Calder, 1963)
Worst.	Beckett, *Worstward Ho*, in *Nohow On* (Calder, 1992)

Interpréter un texte, cela revient toujours à évaluer son humour.
Un grand auteur, c'est quelqu'un qui rit beaucoup.

Gilles Deleuze

Is there anything of Mr Clemens except his humour?

Anon

Promises, Promises

Let us, then, brace ourselves for the ordeal.
Louis Cazamian

In many critical studies of writers, scant attention is paid to their sense of and their exploitation of humour. Though she had her day, it is a Cinderella subject. Each essay in this book results from an intuition, a partial observation, that the author has, not as a sop or an optional extra, some variety of humour organic to his work. I have settled, like a bee or an incubus, on literary texts which are triggered, energized, and sustained by humour, and not texts where humour pops in and up incidentally. Intuiting more widely, I began to feel that the authors chosen, while each monolithic, could be usefully placed in juxtaposition with other practitioners. We are, none of us, and least of all writers, insulated monads. My authors are special cases, but of course turn out to be other than unique, to have things in common.

As a teacher, in any class I have ever taken, even if the topic was tragedy, and leaving aside any laughter directed undercover at me and my efforts, if I failed to raise at least one laugh or smile I knew that I had failed as a teacher. How on earth could pedagogy, or literature, be proof against such a constant occurrence in extracurricular life? In work, I have always wanted to show humour at work.

'Let sleeping dogmas lie', wrote Anthony Burgess, punning twice in four words.[1] I never apologize for puns, because that is a knee-jerk response, a cliché. Puns will crop up here and there in these essays, for, being packed with meaning, puns are concentrates that should not be watered down. My overall ambition has been to castrate that emasculating adverb 'merely' from 'playful'.

Humour attracts much snobbery and hypocrisy. Metaphors commonly applied are: spice, leaven, comic relief. For many it stresses

overmuch the allegedly low sides of human behaviour. Some even feel
they are above it, and see it as fit mainly for children and vulgarians.
Laughs are mouth-farts which well-bred people do not emit. Many
talk of 'using', 'inserting', or 'introducing' humour, which restricts it
to the status of an adjunct, instead of seeing it as central, inherent,
crucial. In many ways, in fact, humour (think of our own laughter
surprising us) employs us as a conduit, like much of language itself.
Some of humanity's finest minds and imaginations have championed
and proudly practised humour. In Genette's view: 'Le plaisir comique
est, tout autant que l'émotion tragique, source de plaisir esthétique'.[2]

This book does not sport the backbone of a theory. It is looser-
limbed than that. Held together by its covers, it is a rhapsody. It is, to
divert a word, more of a polygraph than a traditional monograph. If
I needed or wanted to call in heavyweight bouncers to eject readers
alleging that this book is shapeless, I could name Pascal, Diderot,
Melville, and many another. My alternative title, Cross-Talk Acts,
promises only variety, not homogeneity, or classical unities. All I will
say in self-defence is that 'acts' in the music-hall are not the same
as 'acts' in a well-oiled play. I will not, à la française, 'chercher la
petite bête', nor be meticulous over nomenclature and demarcation-
disputes. I leave nitpicking to sociable chimpanzees. I am more
taken with reconstruction than deconstruction. Eclectically, jackdaw-
fashion, I use any theoretical lead or commonsensical view of what
constitutes funniness that suits my variegated purposes. Humour is not
happy to be confined to tramlines. What tickles my meninges may
well leave a reader cold. All books are messages in bottles launched
from one-seater desert islands. Where this one makes landfall, and
what reception it gets are way out of my control.

The keyword 'humour' will resurface, in its own name or another
garb, here and there in these pages. Rather like a performing seal
claiming its right to fishy rewards. To put that differently, the reader
needs to supply on many pages 'This is an instance of French literary
humour', without my pressing the loud pedal all the time. As the
unapologetic streetwalker of Prévert's poem/song has it: 'Je suis
comme je suis [...] et n'y puis rien'.[3] I dislike definitions, so often
the kiss of death. A nod is as good as a wink, and the reader is
no blind horse. I cannot josh or bully you into agreeing with me
about comedy, humour, funniness. I hope in all this to treat readers
as grown-ups—who still stay loyal to the child in themselves. I feel

blithe about what I say, but I do not imagine ever that I say anything incontrovertible.

You my readers are engaged in a cross-talk act with me. Why my alternative title? First, my cultural foundation is essentially popular; high literature was a latish development. For this book, I have searched, thought, and laughed, high and low. Secondly, the title is a baggy way of embracing various goods. I should really use as a title that phrase of many comedians 'That reminds me ... '. In other words, I work by loose connexions. As the brain is made up of neural networks, association of ideas is all we have. I have always been fascinated by such associations and their neighbours, simile and metaphor. Humour depends heavily on the surprising (but, at its best, seemingly inevitable and fruitful) associations of ideas previously kept distinct. Loose connexions are the opposite of tight-arsed, puristic, academic closure. The opposite of *strictu sensu* is *sensu lato*. I do not relish, as a father or a writer, being strict. I speak broadly. Much humour is a matter of fleeting analogies, quicksilver pairings. 'Humours' were once bodily fluids; now much humour takes the piss. All the same, the real devil, at whose horny feet I often kneel, is the demon of analogy and the possibility of *false* connexions.

Most ancient jokes spell out far too much and end up long-winded, not as in those very knowing shaggy-dog stories, but out of a kind of pedantry. More charitably, folk then were in less of a hurry than we moderns. The modern shaggy-dog is wilfully infuriating. It is a relief to get to the point, or rather the crowning pointlessness. Is brevity, then, the soul of wit?

In my usage, 'humour' enfolds comedy, wit, satire, derision, laughter, various rhetorical ploys (hyperbole, digression, irony), and wordplay in its multitudinous forms. That, would say Alice, is an awful lot for one word to mean. I concur but remain, like Humpty, unabashed and ready to pay it overtime, until I fall off my wall. As humour is so capacious and variegated, to talk of it, or with it, is to mix registers, which, besides, comes naturally to me.

The three main time-honoured theories of humour are: (1) surprise, but humour can just as easily confirm expectations (e.g. racist jokes) as unseat them; (2) incongruity, but some jokes slot together perfectly and have no corrosive internal contradictions; and (3) superiority, but in self-irony, for instance, how can one be superior to oneself? A joke can be, like a mathematical theorem, beautiful. Most humour rests on mistakes or successes: subwitting or outwitting. Witticisms, jokes often come as unbidden (if not subconsciously unprepared) as slips of the tongue, or as poetic images. And both jokes and poetic images can be unparaphrasable, mysterious, in their effectiveness.

When I first disembarked in the USA, I saw a van bearing the legend 'Snap-on Tools'. I reflected: for those of us males with hang-ups, or letdowns, about sexual dysfunction, the get-up-and-go Yankees have thought of everything, including stand-in peckers (more firmly attached than dildos). Humour, however, is not a snap-on tool. It is the organ itself, with all its faults and failures (I could not tastefully say 'warts and all'). The laws of levity are made to be broken, or at least elasticized. Humour sometimes employs the barge pole, to distance the target, sometimes the shepherd's crook, to corral all of us in the same flock, to dunk all of us in the communal sheep-dip.

Humour can be a weapon of, or a response to, rhetoric. This stamping ground of clichés, this mounting of stylistic high horses, is intrinsically laughable. All rhetoric has designs on us, and so we need the resistance-movement of humour. Within their own force-field, rhetorical ploys are busily at work in texts critical of what Plato called the 'pretty toys' of this operation. Rhetoric's masterstroke is, at times, to be sceptical of itself, like certain Jewish jokes. Need it be said that we all speak rhetoric fluently?

Back to the alternative title. I enquired through Francofil (the profession's *téléphone arabe* or bush-telegraph) how to find a French equivalent to 'cross-talk acts'. Apart from the feeble 'duo humoristique', I garnered nothing that would dissuade me from my guess that the French tradition, here at least, does not name what it does not have, or only rarely has. Why, then, arrange shotgun-marriages between several leading French writers? Well, French culture is heavily incestuous. Writers cannot simply ignore predecessors or contemporaries. More profoundly, they have a strong sense of tradition, of all being engaged in a common, if superior, enterprise. By analogy with 'lettres (or 'lectures') croisées', I would propose 'monologues croisés'. These can operate within a single *œuvre*: one work by an author facing up to, contradicting, extending another one (take Gide, please). In an actual double-act, the straight man is as indispensable as the star: as sounding board and comeback.

When a schoolboy, I wrote an Elysian encounter between Shakespeare and Molière, which deliberately shot itself in the foot when the latter expostulated that he could not understand a word of the Bard's English. We cannot force conjunctions, or, if we persist in trying, we have to make them work and pay their way. In wanting to call this book *Cross-Talk Acts*, I wished to avoid any suggestion of an Elysian encounter between the writers that I compare, contrast, and occasionally pair. A more apt locale would be the music-hall stage where each one performs his number, solo or in cahoots, for our amusement and our edification (a common rough pun for 'education'). Comedians are great teachers. Their lessons teach us student readers to think differently, laterally.

My engineered encounters here will not often be a direct face-to-face. One writer will pop up in the discussion of another, like a jack-in-the-box, or a heckler from the audience. I gladly admit that many of the dual routines are conducted sotto voce. Even solo stand-up comedians rely on cross-talk—either a false or a real dialogue with the audience, or invented dialogues in which the soloist plays both or several parts, 'does the voices' (like Rameau's Nephew's imaginary orchestra). Maybe humour always relies on some sort of dialogue or dialectic. Viewed differently, all jokes are comic monologues: most tellers detest interruptions. They are would-be dictators, and the listener's only assigned function is to register the point of the joke and to laugh. In a cross-talk act, of course, two budding dictators strive to gain the upper hand. Humour is political, depending on power-relationships. Then there is composite humour, as in rumour and joke-cycles, that everyone can mount and ride. This is less cross-talk than the talk of the town. Humour, clearly (!), is gregarious and selfish, solipsistic and social. These contraries are still couples. As Dominique Noguez has said: 'L'humour est peut-être narcissique, il n'est pas solipsiste. Pour en faire il faut être deux'.[4] These tensions keep it taut. Finally, cross-talk acts are as much about to-and-fro aggression as choruses of opinion. Comparison is as much about making distinguos between apparently unrelated things as is pulling them together. Even plagiarists have a bone to pick with those they cannibalize.

Plagiarism might seem like robbing Peter to pay Paul, but I prefer the notion of all hands to the pump. Many of those I have burgled have, by an act of anticipatory plagiarism, scooped me. Thus, in the last resort, no one person is responsible for the ideas expressed in this book. It is a communal endeavour, or a collective crime, and Napoleon thought the latter guilt-free. This is meant to be an interactive book, in which readers are invited to collaborate on scriptwriting for the cross-talk acts featured. Besides, all of us readers are authors' foils, but not necessarily their stooges.

I should explain about the riffs, a term borrowed from jazz. These are more general and briefer forays not specifically centred on French literary humour. I wanted to evade parochialism, umbilicism, and to remind readers of the more universal reaches of humour. I hope that they aerate the book. They are also, of course, leftovers, but fry-ups can be extra tasty, can't they? I trust, too, that they chip into the cross-talk motif.

Lastly, to be merrily racist, as much humour is, a few generalizations about French literary culture. The French language is still today less slap-happy, more stiff-necked, and has greater pretensions to poshness than English. (Strange, the myth of 'la raideur anglaise' with which Jules Vallès for one sported so productively.) Victor Hugo had to labour mightily to champion the mixture of genres which comes so naturally to the English. The British Academy is a very different beast from the Académie française; it is not prescriptive about language. French intellectual inbreeding is the curse of hyperconscious traditions. 'Incest more common than thought' was previously said, in an unconsciously revealing headline, in an English context. Incest, cross-talk, osmosis must be interrelated. Such incest, in France, is often of the intensely hostile variety and, like hypochondria, is a key national sport, at least among among the chattering and scribbling classes.

'Humorist' for a long time connoted 'eccentric' in English culture. The word 'humour' itself was an early instance of the cross-Channel shuttle. As far as words go, these two traditional enemies have long lived in each other's pockets. However auto-pilot is English antagonism to our neighbours, who of course pay us back in kind, surely any nation that prides itself on its sense of humour must acknowledge that the enemy must be understood, the better to counter him; and that, in an ideal world, understanding another people's humour might also help to see that people as more fully human, and less of a foe or monstrosity.

Just as I believe that Voltaire's dictum ('La plaisanterie expliquée cesse d'être plaisanterie')[5] is approximately right, so I have not laboured in this book the terms of my title. I prefer to encourage readers to make the connexions, comparisons, and contrasts which I only occasionally make myself, though I believe I have provided some materials for such shuttles or Chunnels.

Here endeth my unapologetic apologia.

I

The Laughing Philosopher: Diderot

Like Walt Whitman, Diderot has the chutzpah to contradict himself without feeling any disabling anguish. What else but a rare sense of humour could better accommodate such contrary but enriching temptations as he pursued? So often with Diderot we have to resist being pulled back into that dread academic reflex and balancing-act: 'On the one hand … on the other'.

If his works depend greatly on humour for their sustenance and dynamism, Diderot the social animal, too, led a frequently ludic life: *mystification*, that intellectual version of horseplay, taking over others' works in order to remake them, dreaming up elaborate and long-term japes or relishing those he witnessed, often at his own expense. If Democritus is traditionally known as the laughing philosopher, should not Diderot share this crown? He must have been wonderful company (that collective noun suits the plural Diderot to a T), but often he must also have been a serious pain in the neck. Michel Delon puts it admirably: 'Romancier dans sa vie avant de l'être sur le papier'.[1]

His exuberant sociability ensures that his two major fictions, *Le Neveu de Rameau* and *Jacques le fataliste*, depend on cross-talk acts and needle-matches. Each participant acts as the foil to the other, as a very proactive straight man. The French equivalent for this role is *un faire-valoir*, which points up the contrast which makes each interdependent and interesting, because each is resolutely what he is, like Bouvard and Pécuchet. This lively reciprocity guarantees that, despite appearances, neither seems definitively *un automate*. They keep each other going.

On top of the cross-talk act of social superior and inferior in these texts, in *Jacques le fataliste* we hear cross-talk multilogues, especially in wayside inns, with everyone present chipping in with their sou's worth. Finally, Diderot enacts frequently a cross-talk act with himself and, by extension, with his readers. As Yeats said: 'We make out of the quarrel with others, rhetoric, but out of the quarrel with ourselves, poetry'.[2] Despite his egopetality, Rousseau produces mainly rhetoric. Never a solipsist, Diderot constructs dialogues with himself, split in two, with warmly imagined readers, and with others in the same *limonade* or trade as himself, past or present.

In this essay, I want to investigate how humour fits into and inflects Diderot's thinking.[3]

Les Bijoux indiscrets

Diderot first tried his hand at fiction in *Les Bijoux indiscrets*, a pseudo-oriental yarn, featuring a magic ring and its exploitation of female genitals, which it forces to tell the truth about their amorous experiences. In it, Diderot turns innuendo into a full-frontal means of enquiry. He was not only a Socratic midhusband, but also a philosophical commercial traveller.[4]

The historian of sexual humour, Gershon Legman, states that the device in this text ('pudenda loquens') is known in erotic folklore typology as the 'sleeping dictionary'.[5] (There is a parallel tradition of 'mentula loquens'. No doubt not a few women would throw an etymological Bailey bridge between *mentula* and *mentiri*: to tell lies.[6]) Such cunnilingualism is picked up by the collective authors of *The Vagina Monologues*: 'If my vagina could talk, it would talk about itself like me; it would talk about other vaginas; it would do vagina impressions'.[7] Such a performance would display what the body has in mind.

There is no doubt at all that *Les Bijoux indiscrets* is sexist, but gladsomely so, in that the sexual objects, the objectified sexes, can think and talk, so that a kind of dialogue is set up. It is not the one-way traffic of that oxymoron, pure pornography. Diderot might also playfully counter charges of male chauvinist piggery by stressing that the women in his story, who anyway enjoy the harem life, are already prisoners before his fictional experiments on them. Besides, despite the induced but accepted compulsion to spill the beans, they had previously relished the highly satisfactory compulsion to engage in the acts that they later have to confess. The Sultan, it is true, has a manic curiosity, but Diderot himself, however enamoured of his own fecund *faconde*, was constitutionally incapable of the dictator's monologue. For his part, Mangogul uses his magic jewel as a thumbscrew and a lie detector. He conducts an extortion-racket, an extortion designed to elicit an informative racket. The talkative vulvas do not laugh or tell jokes, but the very idea of loquacious genitalia is itself the joke.

Of course, the vaginas do not utter solely sexual indiscretions and infidelities; they discourse also on rhetoric, philosophy, history, gambling, and the theatre. In fact, Elaine Russo points out, the only woman to talk of desire is the one lesbian, who discloses her thoughts through her mouth. Russo also stresses that the ceaseless chatter of the *bijoux* begins to pall on Mangogul, and that he himself grows boring and misogynistic.[8] Despite his *libido sciendi*, he often falls asleep while listening. Do any of us pay rapt attention to others' tales of their sexual exploits? Even a highly sexed reader may well cool down in the face of unremitting pornography. Sade might have reflected on such matters. The keyhole perspective of the voyeur or eavesdropper can give you a crick in the neck. Russo has the grace to allow that Diderot was very well suited to sympathizing with the voluble vulvas, as he too was 'forced to give vent to an irrepressible desire to speak or publish impertinent material, and must suffer the consequences of his embarrassing chatter: censorship or imprisonment'.[9]

On one page of *Les Bijoux indiscrets*, Corneille is attacked for acting in effect as a ventriloquist manipulating dummy characters. Throughout this novel, the vagina is presented as a mouthpiece, or blowpipe, or more ludically again, a pea-shooter.[10] In French, *bijou* can refer to either female or male genitals, unlike 'crown jewels', exclusively male, in English. Whether sexist to some degree (and who of either sex is not?), Diderot must have realized that to make a penis into an informative organ would have given rise to (or subsided into) much repetitive, uninspired boasting. Some women may be orthodoxly chatterboxes, though many are truly and naturally eloquent through whatever outlet. There is no etymological link between 'vulva' and 'divulge', though there is between 'vulva' and 'voluble'.

As Stephen Connor reminds us, ventriloquism can be proactive or passive: speaking through another, or being spoken through by him/her. 'In the intermediary ventriloquism of *Les Bijoux indiscrets*, a voice is given to another, but now it is the unwelcome and unsolicited gift of her own voice'. In effect, a poisoned gift. 'Here, the genitals are the site of the self's own self-division; the self is taken to be self-haunted, possessed by itself'. Finally, for Connor, 'Diderot gives us, not merely the voice of the jewels, but the attempts on the part of various agencies to make them speak different kinds of truth on their own behalf'.[11] It is, then, the urge to interpret, the antagonistic mess we all make of any phenomenon, that is the real target of Diderot's comic verve. As Montaigne said of human bookishness: 'Nous ne faisons que nous entregloser'.[12] This is of course what social intercourse is all about.

In the novel, the favourite Mirzoza gambols with the idea of reducing people to their essentials. This is a variant tactic in Diderot's recurrent teratology: monstrification for the sake of a new slant can take the form of enlargement or, as here, shrinking, streamlining:

Les danseurs seraient réduits à deux pieds, ou à deux jambes tout au plus; les chanteurs à un gosier; la plupart des femmes à un bijou; les héros et les spadassins à une main armée; certains savants à un crâne sans cervelle.[13]

Diderot thus shows equability and, as elsewhere, indulges his love of pushing ideas to extremes, like a comedian. This is a form of lateral thinking, of redesigning the body. It is an essentially comic idea, rather like the children's game of 'Têtes folles', where the body's constituent segments can be redistributed so as to create zany hybrids. It is, of course, a serious game. In his *Lettre sur les aveugles*, Diderot proposes that, if a blind man were to construct a human model, 'il placera l'âme au bout des doigts'.[14]

According to Aram Vartanian, 'only Diderot among the *philosophes* spoke of sexuality with an enthusiasm similar to La Mettrie's'.[15] In a posthumously published essay on painting, Diderot pens a long, wonderfully rhapsodic lament-cum-indictment against the sex-denying tendencies of Christianity. It is a just-so story:

Si la Madeleine avait eu quelque aventure galante avec le Christ; si, aux noces de Cana, le Christ entre deux vins, un peu non-conformiste, eût parcouru la gorge d'une des filles de noce et les fesses de Saint-Jean, incertain s'il resterait fidèle ou non à l'apôtre au menton ombragé d'un duvet léger; vous verriez ce qu'il en serait de nos peintres, de nos poètes et de nos statuaires.[16]

In this joyous rewrite of the Judaeo-Christian story, he includes even-handedly homosexuality. Is Diderot's interest in writing *Les Bijoux indiscrets*, or mine in discussing it, prurient? Christopher Ricks, for one, gladly confesses to bringing a 'critical concupiscence' to his readings.[17]

A text can get a reader going. The hospitable vaginas in Diderot's tale may, reassuringly, be edentate, but they are never off-putting or seeking to put the male off his stroke. Moreover, this novel is a microcosm of the author's extremely communicative universe, where bodies speak volumes, pontificate, fly kites, and proliferate. The best adjective to form from his name is 'didérotique'.

Le Neveu de Rameau

'Je sais aussi m'aliéner'.[18] It is tempting to translate this both as 'to go mad' and 'to split myself in two'. The two states have more than a nodding acquaintance. Le Neveu de Rameau, an antiphonal exchange or cross-talk act, is a wonderful example of how a heavily allusive text, full of references to eighteenth-century figures and events unknown to the vast majority of its readers, can still speak to us, seem relevant, entertain, and enlarge our imagination and sympathy. For instance, it has an important place in the opera-war called 'La Guerre des Bouffons'. It is itself a verbal and intellectual war, between two opposed buffoons: the blatant clown, Rameau or LUI, and the largely owl-serious straight man, MOI. They beg, not always politely, to differ. In this extended, confrontational interview, how much of the Nephew's spirited juggling of opinions and manic physical posturing is dreamt up on the spot to counter or indeed best his cross-examiner, through love of being thought 'different', or simple bloody-minded-ness?

The real-time nephew of Rameau was also like his uncle a composer and theorist of music. Like his nephew, the uncle, Jean-Philippe Rameau, got himself sacked from positions when it booted him, by behaving obstreperously. He too had his Bohemian days, when he composed sketches for the trestle-theatres at fairs. He became estranged from Rousseau and the Encyclopédistes. He was not genial or companionable. In short, he was as much of a mixed bag as his fictionalized younger relative. The Nephew hardly profits from any nepotism. However parasitic he is in general, he still has to make his own way, a very sinuous one. Diderot has reinvented him for his own good reasons.

Diderot consistently applied what we now call 'negative controls'. In his own words: 'Quand on établit une loi générale, il faut qu'elle embrasse tous les phénomènes, et les actions de la sagesse et les écarts de la folie'.[19] What overarching theory, what ethical system, could adequately contain, restrain, or retrain the Nephew? He does not escape mortal coils—otherwise he would be uninteresting—but he wriggles out of pigeonholes, except those he chooses to squeeze into himself. Yet neither he nor Diderot has a butterfly mind, rather: a kangaroo one. *Le Rêve de D'Alembert* demonstrates persuasively that, even in delirium, there are hidden associations, a narrative thread. Its general lesson is: 'Notre véritable sentiment n'est pas celui dans lequel nous n'avons jamais vacillé, mais celui auquel nous sommes le plus habituellement revenus'.[20] The semi-rootless Rameau has a home-base or a bolt-hole in himself.

Le Neveu de Rameau is subtitled 'Satire seconde'. In early classical use, 'satura' was a discursive composition in verse treating of a variety of subjects and, later, a poem in which prevalent follies and vices were assailed with ridicule. The root is *satur*: sated. Rameau certainly gives us a bellyful of himself; he is all but too much. The governing idea is medley, pell-mell. As Juvenal wrote: 'Difficile est saturam non scribere'.[21] How often, in the face of blatant abuses or idiocies, has anyone felt this? Why 'Satire seconde'? This could imply 'au deuxième degré': tongue-in-cheek, ironic. 'État second' means 'spaced-out', trancelike, as the Nephew is in his frantic mimes. *Le Neveu de Rameau* is a medley, a sausage, often suspect as to its ingredients or provenance, possibly injurious to health, but oh so satisfying to consume.

The common argument that critics of others' practices cannot evade the phenomenon they attack—thus Rameau hypocritically castigates hypocrisy—is based on the notion that 'it takes one to know one'. The absurd end of that line of blinkered logic would be to maintain that Herman Melville was a cetacean, or that Walt Disney had adopted mousehood. So what is left for the satirist? Ross Chambers suggests discrete, devastating thrusts, 'hit-and-run' tactics, for if the critic attacks from a fixed, systematic ideological position, he/she can be dismissed more easily as trying to gainsay one false system with another.[22] To this end, mimicry can be self-protective clothing or colouring. It can reflect the choice of operating, as Mao advised, like a fish in water; camouflage can secrete subversion.

In his *Salons*, Diderot voices a vivacious complaint about Michel Van Loo's portrait of him, and its freezing of his mobility of face and body.[23] No wonder the Nephew's equally protean physical and psychic self excites MOI's amazement. This text is an oscillating work. Does it, like a manic comedian, never settle? LUI probably believes that only mud settles down. The epigraph from Horace ('Vertumnis, quotquot sunt, notus iniquis') tips the wink. Vertumnus was the Roman god of the seasons and therefore of change. Rameau will be a shape-shifter, a quick-change artist. While captivated by LUI's changeability, MOI shows, in saying 'Mes pensées, ce sont mes catins', that he too is on the move in his intellectual skirt-chasing.[24] Diderot himself thinks erotically, but not everyone can catch fast women. The staidly bourgeois MOI is unlikely to want to grapple with whores, though he savours the idea of it. LUI is a male whore, and the *idea* of him is entertained by MOI. This *philosophe*'s alternative activity, watching chess-players (an orderly world, in contrast to the Lord of Misrule) sees him again tagging along, a camp follower. LUI's moves fascinate him, and he is breathless at keeping up with this moving target, this human perpetual-motion machine. Rameau, then, irrupts into MOI's rather cosy world. He buttonholes the sage: 'Un composé de hauteur et de bassesse, de bon sens et de déraison' (p. 4). LUI is an amalgam, an oxymoron, a living paradox.[25] He is his own alter ego: 'Rien ne dissemble plus de lui que lui-même' (p. 4).

Though a disrupter of social conformity, he knows that he is dubious. When he quotes Virgil: 'Quisque suos patimur manes', he is probably aware that this line has a wobbly meaning.[26] Its elements include spirits, ancestors, and punishment. He may interpret it as referring to his uncle, whose success he himself suffers from. He excels, all the same, at repartee, the essence of the cross-talk act. He propounds an ambivalent view of geniuses: they are unscrupulous, antisocial, but unique. For MOI, they bring long-term benefit to mankind. Rameau is clearly not a genius, but a painfully frank man with a highly developed talent for the second-hand and second-rate (his mimicry). Diderot regularly uses 'contrefaire', with its suggestion of parody and fakery, for this talent. When LUI lists his traits ('Vous savez que je suis un ignorant, un sot, un fou, un impertinent, un paresseux, ce que nos bourguignons appellent un fieffé truand, un escroc, un gourmand' (p. 18)), he partly turns demerits into merit marks. By presenting them en masse, he attenuates their potency; his bark, in general, is worse than his bite. No wonder that MOI marvels at such self-cancelling pell-mell by exclaiming 'Quel panégyrique!' (p. 18).

Relating how he lived at one stage 'comme un coq en pâte' (p. 18), the Nephew recognizes how he blew his chances by speaking out of turn, thus exceeding his social pigeonhole. In general, he never euphemizes, beats about the bush. He turns everything into a pantomime—in the French rather than the English music-hall sense. Thus he acts out his imaginary begging of the offended hostess to take him back in. Though there are limits to his self-abasement, some days he would nevertheless kiss her arse. His social talents include that of pimp/middleman. A variant on the physical mime-show is an imagined dialogue with another: a two-part soliloquy, in effect. Does his candour make him 'strip himself' for the MOI figure, as Champfleury argued?[27] Rather does not his recourse to irony ensure that he piles on extra layers, to keep himself warm?

He amuses, and flummoxes, MOI, who cannot get his head around such slipperiness. When LUI acts out his own emotions, he sounds, or rather he is, hammy, like Russian silent films. I am reminded also of gurning, and of South Indian Kathakali dancing, in both of which the face is contorted grotesquely. French uses 'le gag' almost exclusively for physical comedy, and rarely for one-liners, throwaway jokes. This is to heavily privilege silent comedies. The Fall, Baudelaire might have said, leads to pratfalls. Russian silent films use the body as semaphore (cf. the Monty Python version of *Wuthering Heights*, where the lovers signal soundlessly to each other with flags). Of course, Diderot himself, in his theatrical or pictorial writings, was something of a sucker for overdone expressiveness. Impersonation, besides, is likely, like a parody, to overdo things, for it latches on to stereotypes, the most easily reproducible aspects of who or what is being taken off (De Gaulle's long nose). Taking off is more often than not humorous in intent; MOI notices the 'éclats de rire' of those watching Rameau's performance. Even ham-acting, however, can be engrossing and enjoyable. In the Nephew, we witness the intimate cross-fertilization of language and gesture. Just as rhetoric is verbal gesticulation, so bodies speak volumes. Logically, LUI talks to his body as to an interlocutor.

He recognizes that he is a Proteus with stiffening joints, a premature stiff before the final rigor mortis. Like someone cracking his knuckles, his recounted efforts to make his fingers supple enough to play are excruciating. When he imitates playing a violin, his honesty makes him, even in dreamland, mime miscues. MOI is so carried away by the simulated authenticity that he too can hear the silent sounds emanating from the imitated violin. Sensibly, he decides that it is beside the point to pity this sublime lunatic. There are obviously degrees of mimeticism, from the base (when LUI acts the worm) to the sublime (when he imitates a whole orchestra). Naturally, in miming, Rameau is performing, not creating, and indeed he is imitating a performance. So he is at three removes from the real thing. The fact remains that he is serious in his musical impersonations. This is his contribution to culture, as much as he can manage. It would be a mistake to call it deadpan, for he is so close to paroxysm. The contrast between the spectacle and what it means to him is comic, or tragicomic, or jocoserious.

Diderot claimed that at the theatre he would stop up his ears, when he knew the play well; he reacted just as passionately to what was then the dumb show of the actors as when he sat normally.[28] On the page, Diderot puts Rameau non-stop on stage. Whatever he utters, he acts out (like people who gesticulate when phoning). He improvises, though much of the groundwork for his numbers must have been laboriously built up over the years. He treats MOI to silent comedy with his mimodramas, and raucous comedy in his simulation of a one-man band. All in all, Diderot was deeply magnetized to gestures, finding them much of the time more truth-telling than words, despite the fact that a thespian is etymologically a hypocrite, i.e. one playing a part. In his influential *Paradoxe sur le comédien*, he distinguishes between 'le comédien imitateur', capable only of mediocre execution, and 'le comédien de nature'. Rameau melds the two: he is a natural imitator; he cannot help it.[29] He remains *un cabotin*. Too often for his own good, he puts all his cards on the table. Despite his love of irony, he can be too upfront. In *Paradoxe sur le comédien*, Diderot argues that the true actor does not feel, but calculatingly copies to perfection, the emotions called on by his role. As against that theory, the Nephew becomes what he has in mind. This is Method Acting carried to extremes.[30] Nevertheless, cold calculation sits ill on Diderot. After the blind and deaf-mutes, Diderot, renowned for his physical mobility and gesturing, moves on to a man reduced much of the time to his body, but what a loquacious body, how articulate its sign language. He possesses funny bones.[31] If, however, you were in his company for long, he would become as wearing as a hyperactive child.

Some cultures gesticulate more than others, which often place inhibitions on flamboyance in any form. Gestures are a shorthand and a reinforcement, replacing or backing up speech with movement. They are yet another code needing to be registered and cracked. At the ballet, or watching Japanese films, I have signally failed to break the gestural code. They can be blatant, or they can talk double, like irony.

The Nephew hogs any stage. What of MOI? Rameau thinks he can prove that no one, especially MOI, despite his or her pretensions, can be truly 'holier than thou'. We are, in his summation, all in the same communal tub, muddying the water, scratching each other's backs, lounging sybaritically, fighting for the elusive soap, and ready to drown our sorrows. Diderot implicitly asks through the Nephew the crucial question: when will what I think of myself, and what others think of me, coincide? To sum up the Nephew, you would have to paraphrase and reconstruct everything he says or does. He is an expanding compound noun, a polymorphous perverse. MOI, contrariwise, likes to talk in clear, single nouns, which he opposes often automatically to Rameau's discourse. Towards the end, MOI counterpunches with his apologia for the sage who is exempt from the universal pantomime so picturesquely evoked by LUI, and not posturing but pondering. More often, though, the *philosophe* is guilty of pedantry and priggishness. Perhaps he represents Diderot's recognition that his plays, if not his fictions, were a misjudgement on his part. Moralizing is not art, which of course does not mean that art is immoral; it is differently moral.

Like the archetypal parrot, LUI is raucous, utters awkward truths, has reprehensible habits, and is made dependent on people for food and shelter. All in all, MOI is a comic's feed, or *comparse*: a walk-on part, except that MOI is always physically present in the text. The Nephew is concerned less with the general principles invoked by MOI, though he does himself generalize like mad, than with personal convenience, that *vespasienne* where all can relieve themselves without having to spend a sou. As part of his general performance, Rameau makes out that he is more obtuse and prosaic-minded than he in fact is. This is part of the act, a smokescreen. In reality, MOI's failure to convince LUI of very much indicates a stout and intelligent resistance on the part of the spasmodically wise fool. Though each interlocutor comes equipped with his own agenda and existential baggage, they do interact and affect each other, even if neither sincerely hopes to radically change the other. No doubt the devil has the best tunes.[32] Still, the apparently dry puritan talks animatedly about the pleasure he gets from female charms, and the fact that LUI has problems getting his host to laugh proves that MOI can at times resist LUI's snake-charming spiel.

Rameau expends great energy in his pantomimes, even the one which impersonates Bertin, an *automate*. Like a comic, he claims to make himself, his theories or his enactments up as he goes along. In social terms, he is a parasite, that is: someone who needs to be humorous in order to survive; comic skill comes with the job. Besides, the parasite is of necessity a comic figure, for his betters can all easily afford to look down and laugh at him. Although the Nephew belittles the arch-sponger Tartuffe, it is not for his hypocrisy, but for his ham-acting which blows the gaff on his plotting. Michel Serres asks: 'Qui saura jamais si le parasitisme est un obstacle [au fonctionnement d'un système] ou s'il en est la dynamique même?'[33] Indeed, LUI claims that he is a 'wondrous necessary man':[34] 'C'est qu'on ne pouvait se passer de moi, que j'étais un homme essentiel' (p. 65). He forgets that we are all dispensable, and ultimately dispensed with by death. While he lives, he sees himself as a vital cog, or the lubrication, of the social mechanism. As a hanger-on, he does of course have to sing (or, more accurately, act the goat) for his supper, via his party pieces. As he lives by his wits, he simply has to be more realistic than the comfortably off *philosophe*. As a result, he has suffered the indignity of being the butt of the host's condescension or outright malevolence. Cadgerdom has ever provided only a precarious livelihood. The Nephew has to be versatile, hence his seeming often to be several people at once, a multiple personality. The freeloader has been around at least as long as the philosopher. We all start off, in the womb, as parasites. If this social figure were indeed superfluous to requirements, it would have long since become extinct.[35] Paradoxically, like the overpaid chairs of multinationals, parasites are non-productive, yet thought to be generative. Finally, how parasitic is all literature, all criticism? In terms of language, purists have always fretted over the amount of parasitic words in many discourses: tautologies, quotations, allusions, borrowings—infections of all kinds, foreign bodies in the text. *Finnegans Wake* houses such parasitism ad nauseam.

Though he often behaves as a wild man, Rameau is irremediably socialized, excessively so, for he cannot envisage a society structured differently from the one all round him. He despises it, yet plays along with it: 'On m'a voulu ridicule, et je me le suis fait' (p. 61). Yet his gaffes are his saving grace, as shown by the ribald Italian phrase which gets him booted out of Bertin's house ('I'm sitting here like a prick between two balls/dickheads' (p. 63)). He consoles himself that he is nonetheless special, a cut above other pauper clowns; 'Je suis rare dans mon espèce', a portable lunatic asylum (p. 65). While he admires outstanding criminals such as the Renegade of Avignon, he himself is merely a petty delinquent.

What he can achieve is an extraordinary rendition of an entire opera, with one-man orchestra and dance-troupe, a frenzied performance and a multiply schizophrenic feat. He becomes so totally what he has in mind and memory that he appears quite mad: 'Saisi d'une aliénation d'esprit, d'un enthousiasme si voisin de la folie qu'il est incertain qu'il en revienne' (p. 83).[36] Nobody, least of all women, needs telling that hysteria is as much a male as a female phenomenon. Rameau's mimes are unscripted, spontaneous until MOI tries to capture them in words.[37] Leo Spitzer does his damnedest to emulate Diderot in a dynamic essay, which focuses on the rhythms of this section of *Le Neveu de Rameau*, governed as it is by mental and corporeal agility.[38] He notes acceleration, impetus, excitement, vibrations, breathlessness, and urgency, leading to a final relaxation (p. 140). It is, naturally, the rhythmic cycle of coitus, orgasm, and detumescence. This is self-propelling prose, as can be seen in the tenses selected by Diderot. Not the definitive past definite, but the nervously active imperfect (so suitable for the defective Nephew), the graphic present, and the proliferating present participles. I imagine the key criterion to apply to Rameau's show is lastingness. In the age of cinematography, LUI's act could have been recorded on film, whereas in his own era he can extemporize but not perpetuate. His creator, like Nabokov's Humbert Humbert, has 'only words to play with'.[39] With them he orchestrates comic hyperbole.

According to Spitzer, Diderot shared the belief of Nietzsche and Thomas Mann that the basic feature of the artist is apishness: greed, sensuality, amoralism, mimicry (p. 185). In Diderot's own words 'La singerie dans les organes'.[40] I doubt that any of the three writers was being conventionally moralistic. The beast and the genius overlap. The very dubious hero of *Le Neveu de Rameau* is, in the social menagerie of his epoch, a performing chimp, whereas the self-righteous MOI tries to act the wise owl. Spitzer, borrowing Nietzsche's term for Wagner 'Schauspieler seiner selbst', calls Rameau 'this Protean actor-of-himself' (p. 185).

His performance is crazy expressionism. When he comes to, he is amazed by the amazement of his audience. Diderot conceived of passions as cords/chords. Is the Nephew too highly strung? Such desperation derives from his plangent recognition that he lacks the true creative ability of his uncle. You are born either with a silver spoon in your mouth, or with clay feet and fingers like bananas. Indeed, the very name of Rameau is a millstone round his neck (p. 99). Yet his innate sense of humour makes silk purses out of sows' ears: 'Aussi sommes-nous gueux, si gueux que c'est une bénédiction' (p. 100): a wonderfully ironic idiom, where the word for 'blessing' connotes fullness ('in spades'). He is plenteously poor. He can sound, like Jacques, fatalistic: 'De maudites circonstances nous mènent; et nous mènent fort mal' (p. 103). On the permanently vexed question of freedom versus determinism, what the Nephew embodies is the belief that we can be free sporadically; we can enjoy purple patches of liberty. His climactic mime illustrates this sustaining credo, or illusion. The worm can turn. But what of the universal pantomime of manunkind, 'le grand branle de la terre', our round dance? (p. 105).

The text terminates with a pirouette, and a punchline: 'Rira bien qui rira le dernier' (p. 109). That old proverb does not add, as it might, that he who laughs first (at himself as much as at others) makes it harder for anyone to deride him for good. Self-criticism and self-love (necessary for survival) are inextricably twined or twinned. LUI's laughter is a pre-emptive strike. Laughter does, literally, have the last word in this text but, more importantly, also the first word, in that humour informs, colours, and dynamizes the whole caboodle. Outside the text, he who laughs last is often the slowest to see the joke/point. That punchline makes me wonder where the punch lands. Perhaps both LUI and MOI, in future meetings, will go on finding each other funny (amusing/peculiar), and fascinating. As Iris Murdoch pretty pompously puts it: 'Nothing is more educational, in the end, than the mode of being of other people'.[41]

Rameau claims, finally, to be incorrigible, and MOI has to philo-sophically agree. The intermittently ignoble savage is never at a loss for words. Like Diderot, like Jules Vallès, Rameau is fragmented, dispersed, yet all of a piece. A sport like him can illuminate and show up the norm, as this unclassifiable book expertly demonstrates. It is strange, but refreshing, to see how Diderot, so often settling for the inconclusive, can make disappointment a fulfilling experience for the reader, and Rameau's failure a success. The Nephew is a consummate failure, which is what all clowns aspire to attain. Closure, one of those words that buzz annoyingly in the ear, whether applied to texts or to mourning, slides off Diderot.

Admirers of *Le Neveu de Rameau* have included Goethe (who translated and championed it); Marx, who spoke of Diderot as his favourite prose-writer; Hegel, who saw the Nephew as a divided consciousness, a symptom of a sick society; Bernard Shaw; and Freud. The Nephew bursts his imposed bounds. The setting, a famous coffeehouse, could not have realistically contained his frenetic pantomimes, which would have wrecked the crowded joint.

What a desperately sad world it will be when he who laughs last has finished laughing.

Jacques le fataliste

Avant la lettre, the guiding spirit of this disconcerting shaggy-dog novel is pataphysical: if I say one thing, the opposite is just as likely to be true.[42] This fits a picaresque novel very well, for who knows what travel will throw up? It positively encourages adaptability, provisionality. Anyone can quote Diderot at one moment, on the footplate of one train of thought, then quote him at another contradicting himself. In this unstable scenario, Jacques and his Master are adept at making life more congenial. In Diderot's special arithmetic, direct ratio (p. 34) segues to indirect ratio (p. 365).[43] Much of his maker inheres in Jacques: the compulsive talker, the stirrer-up of trouble yet a man eager for reconciliation, ribald, lover of paradox and of practical jokes, and the floater of contradictory ideas.[44]

Jacques le fataliste is a road or a buddy novel, but perhaps not true picaresque, because neither protagonist makes a living by roguery, as distinct from (in Jacques's case) roguishness. It takes place on the high road and in wayside inns, and it offers a graphic view of the

underside of eighteenth-century French society, not only *le peuple*,
but also the behind-the-façade behaviour of the allegedly respectable
classes. *En passant*, it illustrates poverty, food-shortages, a largely
lawless countryside, graft, and inequity.

The title raises the spectre of fatalism, the doctrine that all is
foreordained; we are programmed for life. Diderot introduces a
twist. Just as he was fascinated by abnormal people, exceptions to
the general run (the blind, deaf-mutes, Rameau's Nephew), so he
sees inconsistencies in human behaviour which modify or belie the
doctrine of fatalism, even while paying it lip-service. Does not Jacques,
like the lady, protest too much? Perhaps, simply, we enjoy some of
our compulsions—sex, eating, exercising our wits often for nefarious
ends—and so feel free while under their sway. And loathe others:
social position, onerous duties, death, and so experience these as
bondages. In fact, because of all these qualifying factors, 'fate' comes
to a large extent to coincide with character; it becomes internalized
and thus more personal. For instance, Jacques has a compulsion to
talk volubly. Can he be a total robot if he enjoys 'free speech'? To
use the obvious pun, Jacques is determined to be a signed-up fatalist.
He talks as if he wholeheartedly believed in his (borrowed) credo, but
acts as if none of it were true, that is: he acts impulsively. He pays
formal homage to the Higher Authority, but is often bolshy to the
earthly one.

As Arthur Koestler observed: 'The very concept of determinism
implies a split between thinking and doing; it condemns man to live
in a world where the rules of conduct are based on As-Ifs and the rules
of logic on Becauses'.[45] Philosophers in the late twentieth century
eventually worked out, they think, that unadulterated free will, the
opposite of fatalism, would be the most amoral state imaginable.
The very word 'determined' is ambiguous, of course, because it also
means resolute, full of willpower. Diderot's variable stances on the
subject include this: 'On est fataliste, et à chaque instant on pense,
on parle, on écrit comme si l'on persévérait dans le préjugé de la
liberté [...] On est devenu philosophe dans ses systèmes et l'on reste
peuple dans ses propos'.[46] Jacques inverts this pattern, for he is a man
of the people and he philosophizes, a homespun thinker. It is hardly
surprising that it was a former employer of Jacques who instructed
him in the doctrine of fatalism. No doubt he wanted to keep his
ebullient servant in his place, at heel. Thus Jacques has acquired it

parrot-fashion, and so applies it indiscriminately, like Pangloss with his optimism.

Surely his refrain of 'Tout est écrit là-haut' is meant as an author's joke. As any newspaper or conversation displays, we all have recourse to ideas of fate or bad luck at the least excuse. Doing so *is* an excuse, a laziness, an alibi. We pull together things that do not belong together. We look for patterns, formulae, classification. Diderot mocks this clichéic habit, which is a self-fulfilling prophecy: whatever happens will have had to happen. The catch-all doctrine of fatalism naturally works most plausibly after the event. It is 20/20 hindsight.

Fatalism leaves out chance. We speak, all the same, of the play of a mechanism and the fickle finger of fate, as if even destiny were inconsistent and ruled, in its turn, by Sod's Law. Chance means anything is possible; destiny that nothing can change from the programme. Once we allow for (or, for the statistically in-clined, factor in) chance, is all hell let loose? Chance could still be thought of as deterministic, in that it dictates to us. But there is no superhuman power in charge of chance. Happenstance: the very word contains the seeds of happiness, or at least good fortune (*hap*).

Despite the temptation to offload all responsibility on to Destiny, Jacques resists the 'Oriental' solution of passivity and amoralism (if we are not to some degree accountable for our actions, the buck stops nowhere; it is free-floating).[47] Something cussed in him makes him act as if he had elbow room for initiative. In addition, the people he meets are unique and incorrigible. We may all be shackled, but we are various and, even within ourselves, we fluctuate. Jacques's alertness to the whole question reduces its awesomeness. Is his refrain a case of Kierkegaard's attributed dictum that life can be understood only backwards, but must be lived forwards? The refrain from the past is meant to justify his present conduct and state of mind. But life keeps proposing new challenges to him, and his refrain comes to seem like a mantra, wishful thinking. What better space for manoeuvres than a leisurely journey?

He experiences omens about gibbets and funerals. At first it appears as though all we can safely prophesy is death, and that death is perhaps what servant and master are travelling towards, with so much gusto on the way. Diderot, however, instinctively rejects forecasts, for they would hogtie the future instead of leaving it open. Maybe the undoubted mysteries of life are beneficial, for they jolt us awake, and prevent us from being mere automata progressing in a straight line. Besides, those omens, those apparent warnings from Fate, often have prosaic explanations. The horse that insists on bolting towards scaffolds is found to have once belonged to a hangman. Horses can be as mulish as their human masters. Fatalism is the humour of resignation rather than of protest. Such resignation is not limp. For Diderot, truth could spring only from antagonism, which is one of the main reasons why he persists in antagonizing the reader. Within the text, dialogues are running battles, though all the participants are generously ready to listen to other people's opinions and stories, and to react with compassion or moralizing indignation.

As company (*cum pane*) and compotation are major joys of community life, the relationship of the co-travellers is a crucial element in the whole narrative. Like Bouvard and Pécuchet, their camaraderie outlasts their frequent quarrels; even their respective horses are good mates. The Maître is a prompter, secondary but indispensable. He can behave like a kid at an English pantomime, bursting to intervene, to warn the performers, and to rewrite their script. He does of course have his tics: 'Il regardait à sa montre l'heure qu'il était sans le savoir, ouvrait sa tabatière sans s'en douter et prenait sa prise de tabac sans le sentir' (pp. 294–5). He looks, therefore, and is several times called, 'un automate'. So might say anyone observing any of us at many unguarded moments. 'Ô combien l'homme qui pense le plus est encore automate!'[48] His snuffbox is his version of Jacques's *gourde* or hip-flask: two addictions and sources of consolation. Even though Jacques listens attentively to his superior's account of his love-life, this is unarguably small beer and passably tedious, in comparison with the inferior's rumbustious counterpart. On occasions Jacques falls asleep, or pretends to, though this may be yet another insolent leg-pull on his part. The Master complains that his servant anticipates his narratives and thus spoils them. It is understandable, if unfair, that Jacques sees him as *un automate* (p. 33), and declares his graveside oration on Jacques's former master to be worthy of a parrot (p. 65). For once in their cross-talk routines, the Master then counters by explaining, like a schoolmaster who has planted a deliberate mistake to test his class, that he had delivered a ridiculous spiel in order to take Jacques's mind off his grieving. Of course, Jacques, self-confessedly 'un animal jaseur' (p. 216), has a name, as common as muck, that in its diminutive form is the stereotypical French equivalent to the English 'Polly' for a parrot.[49] Just as, according to Jacques, 'chacun a son chien' (p. 232), so we are all each other's parrots, and Jacques, his Captain's repeater, should be the last to speak of his present master's psittacism. He himself resembles the adroit beast who can parrot a lesson, but then proceed to do his/her own sweet thing.

The socially superior master is the existentially inferior of the pair. He is largely passive in the face of his servant's energy. No doubt elements of Diderot inhabit him as well as Jacques: the proneness to meddle, the often theoretical moralizing, the fascination with individuals more animated than himself. As so often in *Don Quixote*, the valet instructs the employer. As a revenge for the servility to which Rameau's Nephew was so often constrained, Jacques exerts a not always subtle tyranny over his master. When he loosens the straps on the other's horse, causing him to fall off, he is, in effect if only locally, writing down his master's fate, scripting his life-narrative.

The couple row and are reconciled by the innkeeper's wife, acting as arbitrator. The shifting balance of power between them modifies further the central question of freedom. Clearly, Diderot had in mind Don Quixote and Sancho Panza—two clashing temperaments which are strangely complementary, in the compatibility of dissimilarity, better known as 'opposite poles attract'. Bouvard and Pécuchet offer a variant take on this Laurel-and-Hardy pattern. Diderot has split himself in two again; the two parts quarrel but stay together. He gives the pair a shared past as well as present, and that provides a solid basis despite disagreements.

In an inn, fed up with being bossed about, Jacques eventually agrees that, while the Master has the formal right to issue commands, the servant will in future have the acknowledged right to be insolent and capricious. He accepts the role of subordinate (he submits to Destiny), but claims the privilege of bloody-mindedness. This is the let-out or sanity clause in their contract, and at the same time it is the clown's or wise fool's charter. Jacques distinguishes between 'les titres' and 'la chose'. The master has the abstract title, but the servant is the real thing (p. 229). All this has much less to do with the coming French Revolution than with a throwback to the medieval Feast of Fools: licensed topsy-turvydom. Thus Jacques's stipulation is ultimately conservative, a fool's licence, spasmodically applicable, and not socially incendiary. It is mainly to do with a kind of free speech. Jacques, anyway, believes that he is of the people by his gift of the gab and that, together with making love, gasbaggery is the only pleasure the poor can afford. He had, in any case, been gagged as a child. This gag has been, maybe cornily, interpreted as a symbol of the censorship against which Enlightenment *philosophes* had to struggle. His coined proverb, like all proverbs, works only in certain circumstances: 'Jacques mène son maître' (p. 230).

The third party in the discourse of this book is the narrator, whose autonomy is repeatedly stressed by Diderot. He can, at a few strokes of the pen, prevent Jacques being killed by inventing fortuitous help for him. There is a refrain, surpassing Jacques's one about fate: 'Il ne tiendrait qu'à moi' (p. 80), or 'qui m'empêcherait?' (p. 336). The author is the true master of all ('Quelle autre couleur n'aurais-je pas été le maître de lui donner?' (p. 47)). As the author is a sort of god, he can even rewrite the productions of other god-artists (Goldoni, p. 133). Furthermore, this novel suggests that artistic mastery, of time, plot, or narration, parallels human mastery over, or at least collaboration with, Fate (cf. Nietzsche's concept of 'amor fati'). The ostensible story we wait for, Jacques's amorous exploits, is kept dangling before us like a carrot. This suspense resembles children asking on a long journey 'Are we there yet?' We are still children. Diderot dangles that carrot, and we, asininely, follow it. In intercourse, too, delaying tactics have their part to play.

The anecdotes we do get furnish vital evidence in the whole enquiry into liberty. For they concern stratagems, attempts to outwit others or Fate, e.g. the two captains' passionate scheming to stay together, or Gousse's crazy plan to rob himself. Initiative, however, cuts both ways. Jacques is beaten and mugged after generously helping a poor woman. In more general socio-economic terms, the riches of the upper classes are shown as founded on exploitation. In today's terms, a big firm practises capitalist robbery, but employees steal from it whenever possible. Is there anything consoling in this tit-for-tat? If life is experienced as a game of Snakes and Ladders, nobody can feel entirely safe.

Kicking against his professed credo, Jacques is brave and warm-hearted, unlike a robot; he routs single-handed a gang of brigands. The philosophy of fatalism suits his easy-going nature. It is essentially vague, and therefore accommodating, like an old suit or a loyal horse. Jacques's fate is in fact once handily defined as his horse, his accoutrements, his master. These are all things or beings close to him, touchable and modifiable. By a series of hints and minor modifications, Diderot gradually whittles down the suprahuman concept of fatalism to more manageable proportions. This novel begs to be read between the lines. It requests audience-participation. How else to get the point of the sustained joke?

The fourth party is the reader. A recurrent and pointed joke is that we readers often itch to rewrite the novels we read. We want alternative encounters, different outcomes, especially happy or happier endings. The imaginary reader shunted into the text and accosted by the narrator is something of a stooge, who presents largely conventional objections to the goings-on, and thus allows the master of ceremonies to score points off him. To some extent, like the Master, the reader too is an automat. No doubt we readers are often in a rut as we journey through a text; we have our unexamined habits and expectations, which deserve a thorough shaking-up. *Jacques le fataliste* re-educates us not to be so impatient, not to count on congenial solutions.

Among the tactics used by Diderot to counteract the clichés of traditional fiction are digressions (designed to stop the onward march of predictability). Diderot dances eccentric steps. He hears a different drummer but, of course, a drummer, on the high road or a byway, remains a drummer, and thus a call to a different order. No one escapes some kind of drumming. Humankind is a tradition-seeking animal. Even when a writer wants to invent his/her variant tradition, he/she can become embroiled in their own waywardness, or others can appropriate and solidify it, or irregulars are, anyway, beholden to predecessors, e.g. Sterne to Cervantes, Xavier de Maistre to Sterne. This is a kind of freemasonry, which is naturally just another form of bondage.

Diderot frequently counters the hypothetical reader's putative complaint that a given character (for instance, the hostess using the word 'hydrophobe' (p. 148)) could not have uttered such a thing, by belligerently reminding us that anybody might say anything. Playing games with the reader presupposes an agonistic set-up. You rarely play games against yourself. The author's game also encourages a reader's sense of humour to come into play. (So many critics are thus bad readers because humourless.) The overall strategy aims at a *captatio benevolentiae*. By seemingly alienating us, the author entraps us. At heart, Diderot meets us, in that marvellous idiom, halfway. He knows we are never wholly passive. Even in an armchair we are on the move, like the text itself, or any humorist. We may be targets, but moving targets. We are cliché-experts, and we are aware that the jest's prosperity lies in our shell-like.

We should remain equally alert to the laughter *between* characters in the text as a crucial part of their social interaction. Like a comedian, Diderot is alive to his audience, plays off it and to it. In spite of the critique of the lazy reader, hostile to challenges, he basically respects us, for he thinks we deserve a better class of fiction than that often served up to us. Sterne (he will come back) wrote sagaciously on this whole matter:

No author, who understands the just boundaries of decorum and good breeding, would presume to think all: The truest respect which you can pay to the reader's understanding, is to halve the matter amicably, and leave him something to imagine in his turn, as well as yourself [...] I do all that lies in my power to keep his imagination as busy as my own.[50]

So, the relationship is dialectical. There is precious little, in Diderot, of the elitist, even sadistic, pleasure taken by some authors in defeating the reader, by private jokes, persistent red herrings, etc. On the contrary, Diderot acts very like the host who says 'I don't want you to get drunk', while plying you with booze. Diderot does not want readers to be, in Vallès's term, 'victimes du livre', like Don Quixote earlier or Emma Bovary later, but he cannot resist trying to cast a narrative spell over us, to inebriate us with his own potent brew.

Jacques and his master match this author–reader relationship. Listening to his servant's story about his war-wound, convalescence, and the problems in paying the medical bill, the Maître is so caught up in the narration that he talks in the present tense, as if the past were happening this very moment. 'J'étais à demain', he explains when Jacques yanks him back to the real present where Jacques is safe and sound (p. 108). This shows the mesmerizing effect of narratives, and implicitly invites the reader to feel a similar excited involvement. If the pair duplicate the reader–author relationship, it is a working one, reliant on give-and-take. Finally, apart from the (very few) contemporary readers of *Jacques le fataliste*, Diderot always kept in mind future readers. In 1746, he used as an epigraph to his *Pensées philosophiques* Persius' 'Quis leget haec?', which presumably secretes both hope and doubt.

The profusion of anecdotes prove that anybody can be a storyteller or dramatist. Anecdotes are mini-novels, condensed plays, like the best jokes. These multiple narrators remind that we all depend on narratives for sustenance, enlightenment, and enjoyment. Mother wit, on show in these anecdotes, is a variety of wit. Survival and revenge need some of the qualities of a strong sense of humour. In them, we see wit not as an embellishment or a consolation, but as a driving force.

The long episode of Mme de la Pommeraye is like a Marivaux play gone berserk. It starts in a familiar way. Wounded in her ego by a lover ceasing to love her, after she has sacrificed her serenity and reputation for him, she decides on vengeance. From virtuous, she wills herself destructive. She resolves to trash his life by striking him in his most vulnerable point, his self-esteem. To that end, she buys a girl and her mother, and engineers matters so that Arcis falls in love with the girl. After the wedding, Mme de la Pommeraye makes sure that he is informed of his new wife's previous vocation as a prostitute. Her monstrous plan has apparently worked. Arcis is at first disgusted, frantic with despair. But then the tables slowly turn. The girl, who was not ingenuous in agreeing to the scheme, really loves Arcis. By a pathetic appeal she convinces him of her love (this is one of those sentimental tableaux Diderot was so fond of in English novels and in paintings. For once, it is expertly calculated). The irony is, of course, acute: by her vile plan Mme de la Pommeraye has helped Arcis to happiness.

This anecdote is clearly not a time-filling digression; it is closely connected to the testing of determinism in the whole novel, because it demonstrates in dramatic form a human, or passably inhuman, attempt to outwit a cruel fate. As the finale is a turnaround, the likelihood of programming anything successfully is put into question. Which is worse, a man's thoughtless neglect, or a woman's retaliation? Jacques criticizes the woman, the Master is typically undecided, and the narrator herself, the innkeeper's wife, rather awed (pp. 208 ff.). In this text, Mme de la Pommeraye achieves a greater measure of sublimity in evildoing than she had ever reached when virtuous. Is virtue boring, as would-be seducers are forever suggesting? Why expect constancy in human beings when the physical world about them is mutating non-stop? Diderot loves describing changing weather.

Mystification (cruel practical jokes elevated to a fine art) is a prime mover in this episode, and again in that of le père Hudson, which is connected to the first by being related by Arcis, whom Jacques happens to meet. A reprobate cleric's orgies are discovered. Not content with hypocritically protesting his innocence, he contrives to get his accusers condemned on the very charge of sexual perversion they had brought against him. Unlike the previous anecdote, the plan of this immoral humorist to reverse the situation succeeds. Fate can be escaped. At the end, the narrator speculates what kind of child might result from the union of Hudson and Mme de la Pommeraye: 'peut-être un honnête homme? Peut-être un sublime coquin' (p. 257). In their icy self-control, both these villains are great actors, or authors penning their own scripts telling how to manipulate lesser creatures.

In Diderot's fiction as in his essays, he gives a varied account of women's otherness. He varies between sadistic delight in humiliating them (see *La Religieuse*), and feeling humble and adoring. Generally, he sees women, like Racine, as raw nature, ready to burst out of its pretty veils if excited, scorned, or menaced. In the social terms of his era, Mme de la Pommeraye, as a woman, is initially in a position of inferiority in relation to Arcis. In this respect, her situation resembles that of Jacques vis-à-vis his master, another link between anecdote and main story.

Other attempts to best Fate fail, for example Gousse, who tries to defraud his wife by robbing himself, but is then robbed by his mistress. Clearly, only those with a real talent for crime or evil should engage in them. In this way, over-rigid moral standards are shown to be riddled with ambivalences, just as traditional artistic practices are undermined. In the anecdotes, the reader listens to an oral transmission, which often takes the form of a relay race (see p. 119). Though interrupted umpteen times, the Hostess always picks up her lengthy narrative about Mme de la Pommeraye at the exact point where she left it. One anecdote can cut across another, as in a competing comedy team, for example the tale of the two captains and the Mme de la Pommeraye episode. Diderot makes no attempt to justify his plethora of very detailed narrated stories, which nobody would have been capable of remembering or recounting. Jacques and his master habitually interrupt each other; anecdotes dislocate, or rather syncopate, the main story. Interruptions, however infuriating to the interrupted one, are the life and soul of social discourse.

There is an obvious link between joking, lying, and narration, and 'telling stories' captures this overlap. You narrate something supposed to have happened when you know all along that it never did, or happened differently or less intriguingly. It is a verbal construct, a castle made of cards/words. You lead the receiver up the garden path.

Virtual reality is the hallucination of heaven, the peyote vision, the dionysiac stupor. It is the play, the novel, the film, the radio mystery, the panorama, the pastoral symphony, the soap opera, any system devised for losing ourselves in another world.[51]

Reading is a kind of self-brainwashing, with a little help from our more creative friends.

The great trump card of fiction in the whist with philosophy is that it can afford to be, it needs to be, far less systematic. It can display humans behaving unaccountably instead of logically, or pursuing a very idiosyncratic logic. In *Jacques le fataliste*, Diderot brings overarching philosophical disputes down to earth. Fiction supplies philosophy with examples, concrete cases, narratives, physical contexts, rhythms, and colour, which are hardly ever achieved by philosophers' imaginary situations involving A or B, or even Tom and Dick. From their own angle, no doubt, most philosophers employ their pitiable little fictions because they mistrust the less than systematic exemplarity of proper fictional instances.

It may be that the motif of 'C'était écrit là-haut' alludes to the author's writing-down of his personages' destinies, the author's rather than God's creation. If the author can be viewed as the deity of his fictional universe, then he is, here, an ironic, ludic god (but so perhaps is the supposedly real one). At one moment, the narrator claims to be in complete control, at another to be at a loss which way to turn. Of course, honest writers know that they are never in total charge of the text they sign. The plot can spurt off in unplanned directions, characters can sprout new and surprising facets, or a minor character can commandeer centre-stage. Most true writers are surely sometimes amazed at what their fingers compose. If everything went exactly to plan, authors would bore themselves stiff.[52]

Throughout *Jacques le fataliste*, the narrator's chief tone is wiseacre and cocky ('Que vous importe?' (p. 3), What's it to you?). Within the text, Jacques and Master share a (mainly one-way) joking-relationship. Jacques is funnier because freer than his more constipated boss. As it is a relationship of some duration, there is less time-wasting in tactfulness, and they can indulge in banter, mutual insults, teasing and horseplay. Insolence, a major component of humour, figures strongly throughout. Truth itself cannot forgo humour (p. 21). *Jacques le fataliste* is a good-humoured book, like the well-tempered clavichord. Diderot's *obiter dictum* on the harpsichord inspired René Crevel's brilliant *Le Clavecin de Diderot* (1932).

Diderot's novel is, partly, a *conte philosophique* that mocks the grand narrative of fatalism by determinedly substituting grand stories which, often ambiguously, celebrate human freedom. How not to see this as a humorous solution? The plots are humorous. They can be visualized as Diderot cutting up the book of life to release arresting shapes and comic figures—not randomly, as they all hang together like chads. The descriptions of gestures and verbal exchanges are often exaggerated *à la* Dostoevsky, but remain vital because of the rapidity of notation. Some have felt that Diderot's best plays are his novels. Tearing of hair, arm to brow, wringing of hands: Diderot knew of course that, as well as speaking volumes and telling more truth than words, gestures can be pure ham, physical cant (see p. 245).

Though *Jacques le fataliste* smacks of Voltaire's *Candide* in its eagerness to deride *l'esprit de système*, Voltaire's philosophical tale merely opposes theory and practice in mechanistic succession. Diderot's much superior fiction makes them coexist in a partnership. Jacques is never forecastable after the fashion of Voltaire's jerky puppets. At the end, Candide is something of a wreck in a refugee-community. According to any of the three alternative endings, those 'Pourrait être continué' so dear to Gide, Jacques is still alive and kicking, and never moaning, as in effect Candide does: 'Stop the world. I want to get off'. Although he never puts it this way, Jacques's basic attitude is: what you lose on the swings you gain on the roundabouts, and vice versa. Whereas Candide finds a modus vivendi only at the finale, Jacques enjoys life throughout his adventures.

Jacques is an improvement on Rameau's Nephew, who is more of a thoroughgoing fatalist. He uses his own name proudly although it could not be more common, and he does not need the dubious gift of mimicry. He can simply be himself. He has the volatility of the Nephew, but with a far less hysterical core.

This novel has an undercurrent of mystery. There is the never clarified enigma of the Castle. A symbol of inequality? A paradox?

A red herring? (pp. 29–30). Diderot's Château is a light-hearted precursor to Kafka's Castle. As a *mystificateur*, Diderot resembles a child hiding who more than half wants to be found. He did not, nor would have wanted to, possess Kafka's implacable powers of mystification. Diderot rejects allegory as a played-out form. Despite the wish for certainty, life can never be explained away in neat philosophical or even scientific formulae. Why then do many of us readers thirst for clear solutions, labels to paste over messy situations? We want quick answers. Diderot lived in a more leisurely age, of months-long *mystifications* rather than one-liners and sound-bites, when the rat-race was run at a slower pace.

In his treatment of fictional time, Diderot frequently shunts the past into the present, and features dreams or omens which obey no orthodox chronology. Throughout, and rather coquettishly, the narrator stresses that his text is not 'un roman' or 'un conte', but truth. Read this as a truer picture of people and the world we live in than is usually provided by literature. The narrator watches, and invites us readers to watch, a new reality as it grows under his pen. He does value us, for he tells a bad young poet to go into commerce; we deserve the best. Appearances turn out often to be deceptive, so we need to be put on our guard. In tune with the common Enlightenment recourse to irony, veiled allusions, Trojan horses used to hoodwink the enemy, Diderot, loving *mystification*, practises demystification. He loves pulling the wool over our eyes so that, when he whips it off again, we can concentrate on seeing more clearly than before. This autocritical novel wants to teach us to be critical. His self-aware (rather than embarrassedly self-conscious) fiction is two things in one, a bargain, like the pun. It *is* a novel, by any definition of that baggy term, because it tells a story, or umpteen stories; it has striking characters, vivacious dialogues, dramatic situations galore. It is also a reflexion on the novel-form. This second aspect leaves some readers cold. They complain that such matters are too technical, mere shoptalk. But surely all of us should want to be aware of what we do, and why and how we do it—to live thinkingly?

Just as Diderot wrote an intriguing *Paradoxe sur le comédien*, so *Jacques le fataliste* has been called 'un paradoxe narratif sur le roman'. It is an early example of the autocritical novel (if not the anti-novel), in that it incorporates its own commentary on itself, like *Don Quixote* or *Les Faux-Monnayeurs*. In *The Art of Fiction*, Henry James expressed his sniffy displeasure at novelists who blow the gaff on their own artifice, by asides, parentheses, or other forms of intrusion, such as the admission that their story is all make-believe. 'Such a betrayal of a sacred office seems to me, I confess, a terrible crime'.[53] A stress on foregrounding, to contradict the master, or schoolmarm, no more rules out hidden depths than foreplay precludes full intercourse.

Like Montaigne, Robert Burton, or Sterne, Diderot offers pointed digressions. Coincidences, with which Diderot is also profligate, are the apparent opposite of digressions: connexions versus disconnexions. The syncopated narrative does not break the traditional spell of storytelling. Rather it continues it by other means, for the reader is proactively engaged, caught up in the suspense. His people are errant and aberrant. The quantity of amorous episodes increases the amount of freedom within determinism, for love, in all its forms, chooses and enjoys its captor. Sexual desire, in the shape of 'bagatelles de la porte' or prolegomena to coition, teases the reader. When Jacques describes the slow ascent of Denise's legs and reaches the knee, the master breaks in to protest that there cannot be much further to go. Jacques ripostes that Denise had unusually long thighs. Such teases are not coy, as they narrate mutual pleasure and benefit; they are genuinely priapic and vulvic (pp. 279–80 and 369). As for the seeming euphemism of 'lending an ear' (pp. 27–8), while the ear is a fairly minimalist stand-in for the vagina, no doubt, much sex is preceded by verbal seduction, encouragement, begging; and thus the ear is intimately caught up in the whole process. In addition, an exploratory lover will try all orifices. More so even than in *Le Neveu de Rameau*, Diderot parallels in *Jacques le fataliste* the rhythms of lovemaking, including by-play and foreplay (pp. 283–5, 27–8). Repeating Montaigne, the narrator assertively defends the verb *foutre*: 'Je vous passe l'action, passez-moi le mot' (p. 294). Exploiting the French idiom, we could say he calls the pussy a pussy. 'L'art d'écrire', wrote Diderot, 'n'est que l'art d'allonger ses bras'.[54] Sexuality in this novel is to be conceived in its widest, wide-openest sense. Diderot reroutes in advance Baudelaire's dismissive 'La foutrerie est le lyrisme du people'.[55]

Although its characters tend to go in for snap judgements, this novel in fact suggests the pitfalls in conclusively judging anyone or anything. The shapely anarchy, the wilful discontinuity, of its form *is* its message. The anecdotes are often more gripping than the central thread of the journey, and the journey, with its wayside halts, more vitally interesting than the ultimate destination. Details are more engaging than theories. God and literary codology (and the two have more than a passing likeness) lie in the details (and they are not more boringly honest elsewhere, either). If life is a big joke for God or Fate, it can, on its way to the grim end, be a rich joke for participants. The very repetition of Jacques's purloined slogan is comic, a parrot's refrain or *scie*. We are always at the mercy of something or someone, but does that amount to 'Fate'?

A thoroughgoing fatalism would install a desperate sameness, the lowest common denominator: subjection. *Jacques le fataliste* offers variety, a miniature of life's rich tapestry. In various ways, everyone is an exceptional being. 'L'univers ne me semble quelquefois qu'un assemblage d'êtres monstrueux'.[56] Diderot views monsters no more pejoratively than Malraux speaking of 'le fou, le monstre incomparable, préférable à tout, que tout être est pour soi-même et qu'il choie dans son cœur'.[57] Opposites cohabit, or wrestle for supremacy: good/evil, truth/falsehood, master/servant. The only way to cope with the ceaseless and puzzling flux of life is to keep the mind as elastic, to be as open to possibilities, as we can.

The quintessential novelist, Montaigne, scoops Diderot: the inter-mittences of the heart, the labile self, the indispensable humour—for how can *sagesse* be otherwise achieved? Like Montaigne, Diderot's sense of the comic is organic and everyday. When Montaigne plays with his cat, like Diderot with his reader, he wonders in all amazed seriousness whether she is toying with him or he with her. Perhaps it matters less than a tinker's fart who or what is the *magister ludi*, so long as the experience—what we laughingly call or call laughingly life—is engrossing, rewarding, and entertaining.

Just as Jacques lifts his earlier master's slogan, so Diderot debonairly and very selectively plagiarizes *Tristram Shandy*. Or was it the other way round? We should not confuse plagiarism and eclecticism. Diderot had of course already tackled the question in the shape of parasitism in *Le Neveu de Rameau*. The intricate question of plagiarism (nowadays euphemized as 'intertextuality') crops up several times in *Jacques le fataliste*.[58] In the plots and subplots, there is a good deal of stealing or attempts to steal. Many writers have a potential criminal record in the area of plagiarism, but what they filch the better ones make their own: the outcome has a value-added component. Diderot certainly had a green-fingered knack for fructifying his grafts. Besides, he and Sterne were in large agreement. 'A pretty story! Is a man to follow rules—or rules to follow him?'[59] Who is to be the master?, as Humpty Dumpty asked pertinently, if a tad fascistically. Surely neither author would have been unduly concerned about suffering or practising plagiarism, and would have shared a hearty laugh at the naivety of such a charge. Take one instance. It is a groin wound for Uncle Toby and a knee wound for Jacques, as for Corporal Trim. Thus Jacques is fittingly more akin to the plebeian than to the bourgeois. While a groin injury might well hamper sexual activity, a knee injury—even though knees can be exceedingly useful in congress—is less inhibiting. One of the several productive features of plagiarism, as of pastiche, parody, or twisting for reuse in general, is that it helps to keep alive a tradition and creates continuities. Thus Diderot not only eclectically gallicizes Sterne by mentioning him by name in his novel, but adds to his fame. You do not plagiarize the forgettable. Besides, like jokes, ideas feed off others' ideas. If we borrow words (such as 'humour') from alien cultures, why not borrow jokes or ideas similarly? Probably it is the *shape* of a joke or idea that strikes a chord beyond national boundaries.

Both *Tristram Shandy* and *Jacques le fataliste* are the kind of books that say, in effect: 'You will not get what you want, but what I want'. Both authors refuse to be unthinkingly consumed. To that end, both issue frequent reminders, like stand-up comedians referring to their script, that we are indeed reading a book.

Jacques le fataliste is self-confessedly 'une rhapsodie' (p. 293), or patchwork, or, again, because of its capriciousness, a capriccio. Both novels are proud to be shaggy-dog stories, lengthy jokes. Both might well echo Valéry's remark: 'Rien de plus ambulatoire qu'une idée fixe'.[60] 'Nothing is more walkabout than a fixed idea' is not a bad summation of *Jacques le fataliste*. Both of them are in hock to Rabelais, not only for their earthy humour, but also for their lively scepticism about speculative systems. Both possible plagiarists expect to be rumbled, and positively want alert readers to laugh with them at such nonchalant light-fingeredness. Diderot chose his scouts well: Lucretius, Rabelais, Montaigne, Spinoza, Sterne. Surely the most important thing about plagiarism hangs on whether the text taking off from another uses it as starting blocks or a trampoline, rather than a millstone. Both authors were blithe plagiarists, and true originals.

Ironically, Diderot was among the upholders of the 'natural rights' of authors in the very polarized debate about intellectual property of ideas, against the defenders (including Condorcet) of the utilitarian concept of the 'public good', or fair shares for all. Strange, when one of Diderot's favourite verbs was *se répandre*: to share your goodies round. He alternated between invading other people's business and offloading his offspring cuckoo-like into others' nests. Both are active in *Le Rêve de D'Alembert*. In general, he leapfrogged, an act in which the support of another is needed, as in dwarfs on the shoulders of giants.

Sterne and Diderot, who met, probably recognized each other as a sisterly soul. There can be honour among thieves. Is it merely paradoxical to suggest that it was their very independence of spirit that drew them together? Or dialectical dependency, or in terms either would have relished more: you scratch my back and I'll scratch yours (in the typically medicinal French equivalent, swapping senna and rhubarb).

Even if we go blasé, and claim that Diderot tells us not much new, and that commonplace observation informs us that no human being lives invariably according to his/her professed beliefs, *how* Diderot embodies this datum is what matters. A shaggy-dog story is rambling, inconsequential, and often has a bathetic or pointless ending, after a big build-up. Is this true of *Jacques le fataliste*? Or is it, as *Tristram Shandy* boasts of being, a cock-and-bull story? Is it a joke about telling jokes, a metajoke?

If Flaubert is often saluted as the novelists' novelist, *Jacques le fataliste* is, for some at least, the novelist's novel. Although it is a novel about novels, among other things, it is not a matter of purely in-house, closed-circuit concern. Most people consume some fiction, if only in tabloids or soaps. It is the expectations, good and bad, of any reader that Diderot focuses on. Among writers who have especially admired this novel are Stendhal and Kundera ('That banquet of intelligence, humour and fantasy').[61] Although writers praising other writers' work may undoubtedly be seeing themselves through a glass brightly, they are, after all, 'de la limonade', and have hands-on experience, unlike critics.

La Nausée resurrects the lesson of *Jacques le fataliste*: order is false, and posthumous; reality is ambiguous. Roquentin will settle for the (artificial) order of artistic creation, at the end. *Jacques le fataliste* finishes up in the air, 'en suspens'. Nietzsche was ravished by the sense of insecurity, of ground moving under your feet, of unstable identities, afforded him by this novel. If you want any more, Diderot signs off, you can sing it yourself: 'Reprenez son récit où il l'a laissé et continuez-le à votre fantaisie' (p. 373).

Diderot Overall

Whatever the weight of countless determinisms on us, whatever hopes Diderot entertained that human beings and their society were modifiable through rational organization, perhaps his deepest conviction was that we are all, in the last resort, incorrigible. We are Luddites putting spokes in the wheels and pulleys of 'l'homme-machine'. Our senses and our appetites pull their weight in any equation. A recurrent motif in his thinking is that most humans have largely one-track minds and are thus to some degree mutilated. Hence the stress on pairings, even of opposites ('les extrêmes se touchent'). LUI/MOI, master/servant, dialogues everywhere. On a wider canvas, federations, as with the team collaborating on the *Encyclopédie*. Let us put our heads together, in every possible sense: amorous embrace, intimate conversation, even envisaging a two-headed 'monster'. All of this is typical of the gregarious speculator. A true encyclopaedist, he worked hard and long to bring together discrete individuals and disciplines, using osmosis, cross-referencing, and borrowing terms and criteria from one area in order to apply them to another: one of the busiest thinkers ever. In the fullest sense, he was an ideas-man. The son of a cutler, he made nothing with his own hands, yet imagined many apparatuses. He did not paint, but he proposed subjects to painter colleagues. He enjoyed little or no political clout, and yet he told Catherine ll how to run Russia. He wanted to reform drama, but had no experience of stage-managing or directing a play.

Diderot has to have the last word, and the last laugh: 'Je ne saurai qu'à la fin ce que j'aurai perdu ou gagné dans ce vaste tripot où j'aurai passé une soixantaine d'années, le cornet à la main, *tesseras agitans*'.[62] He never abandoned taking part in the universal lottery.

Riff on Laughter

I want to perform a riff on laughter, as it affects any of us and not just in the special world of literature. Literature can be graphic, as in graphic description or the graphic present, but not, except at a remove, visual or auditory like real-time laughter.

Why do the French tend to entitle books or special issues of journals on humour 'Le Rire … '? You can see why 'Comédie' is ambiguous, as it also connotes 'stage-play'. Do they really think humour and laughter are interchangeable or indivisible? Or is it a xenophobic snub? Laughter is not entirely at anyone's beck and call. It can be ordained, coaxed, or wrung out of us, but we cannot, if we are to laugh genuinely, as distinct from faking it, as some women do an orgasm, will it.

The nun and saint Hildegard of Bingen compared laughter to seminal ejaculation. She writes excitedly while making this likening, but then has second thoughts, and castigates laughter as low and disgusting. In her first view, the body is shaken by the movements of copulation and, at orgasm, laughter produces tears just as the phallus emits sperm. All these events bestialize man; such laughter is Original Sin.[1] Against this opinion, let us posit lovers who giggle, chuckle, or chortle out loud (or out quiet) at the climax of their greatest intimacy, or even sob with joy. They would hardly expect an intruder to join in the merriment, for it is essentially private.

We can surely laugh, also, when on our own. In more cases than not, however, we then want to share our funny discovery with others. Quickly, we set up a triangle: me, what triggers my laugh, and my audience for the re-enactment/retelling. Within limits, therefore, laughter is social. It can be contagious, as it often is between psychotics, but equally well between friends, family, or even perfect strangers. In this, it resembles yawns, which also leave the mouth agape. A chief function of social laughter is to disarm, to charm, to make ourselves liked.

Bergson's view of laughter as a correctional facility sees it as punishment: gelastic lynching, or at least tar-and-feathering. Charles Bovary's first day at school provokes the hostile class to hoot at his name which he mangles, and turn his advent into a charivari or uproar. As well as being joyous, even carnival can exert censorship of the odd ones out, and be life-threatening. Look at the idioms: to laugh someone down or to scorn, to laugh in someone's face, to laugh out of court—all acts of exclusion. On a more casual but still important level, we can laugh something away, debonairly.

One man's cry of anguish can be another's sneer or bellow. The French film *La Quête du feu* shows laughter originating among early humans when a falling rock glances off the hirsute head of a Neanderthal sitting, with others, round a fire. They did not yet have bananas. This scene suggests that laughter comes naturally. The victim of the mishap, between the rock and a hard place (the ground) elicits the same *Schadenfreude* as we post-Neanderthals enjoy in similar circumstances. We laugh at another's pain which is spared us.

In *Les Mots*, Sartre describes his child self grimacing to himself in the mirror, for his own punishment and benefit. It is a combination of self-attack and aggression against unseen others. It goes against the social norm of presenting oneself at one's best and in a non-threatening manner. 'J'étais horriblement naturel'.[2] Sartre junior was practising the art of gurning, self-monstrification, nowadays often presented as a comic competition as to who can pull the most grotesque faces. By extension, the word 'gurning' now modulates into 'ham-acting'.

We can naturally often grimace and groan because of physical pain, or, if we suffer from that knee-jerk malady, on hearing puns. This is 'le rire jaune', laughing on the other side of your face, the sickly grin. Near or past death's door, our face can exhibit rictus, the death's head:[3]

> Webster was much possessed by death
> And saw the skull beneath the skin;
> And breastless creatures underground
> Leaned backward with a lipless grin.[4]

'Showing teeth' is used as a synonym for laughing by some theorists, e.g. Anthony Ludovici.[5] The rictus might be a sign of death-throes, but we can in life, less lugubriously, be in the throes of laughter. Among classical figures said to have died laughing were the painter Zeuxis, the comic writer Philemon, and Chrysippus, a Stoic philosopher—the last two convulsed on seeing an ass eat figs.[6] It might well be thought that laughing ourselves to death is not a bad way to go. Nietzsche, for one, thought: 'Truly, it will be the death of me, to choke with laughter'.[7]

It is not clear whether Diderot was being a wet blanket when he defined laughter as 'une espèce de toux dont la cause est dans l'esprit'.[8] A widespread theory and folk remedy urges that laughing can be therapeutic, and affect positively the circulatory system, the respiratory apparatus, the brain, or even the immune defence.[9] Therapists have called it 'stationary jogging', though no doubt its more humourless practitioners turn it more into a treadmill. It can certainly help mightily to preserve sanity. Only the maddening laugh relentlessly pursuing the monomaniac Clamence in Camus's *La Chute* saves him from full-blown lunacy. This laugh, satanic or otherwise, acts as the true judge's gavel, cavilling, and keeping some semblance of order in Clamence's world of false judgements. Overall, *La Chute* itself often seems like a bad joke, an excruciation, and its elaborate oscillations between heights and depths a metaphysical quip or conceit.

If we are not a party to its cause, witnessing other people laugh is not always a pretty sight; laughter easily disfigures the face. (As a control experiment, we should cross-check our own dials in the mirror.) Possibly, such uninvolved distaste is kin to the Western etiquette of not opening your mouth when chewing food. In addition, laughing out loud can seem a form of boasting or other instances of uncongenial showiness. 'I'm laughing' conveys a certain invulnerability, like 'I'm alright, Jack'. We may feel left out of a sexual secret or joke. He who laughs last has just thought of a dirty meaning; it is a dirty laugh.

We cannot survey laughing without allowing in the nay-sayers, those whom Meredith (after Rabelais and Pliny the Elder) called 'age-lasts'. At their worst, these gainsayers are constipated party-poopers, sniffing at other people's frank enjoyment. To some, loud laughter is as obnoxious as triumphant farting, self-satisfied belching, or explosive sneezing, especially in a confined space such as a lift or a dinner-table. Such guffaws are felt to be antisocial, gross, as in Lord Chesterfield's notorious advice to his son: 'In my mind, there is nothing so illiberal

and so ill-bred, as audible laughter'.[10] Beyond mere decorum, laughter
has been feared over many centuries as a sign of madness ('le fou rire'),
loss of self-control. Laugh and the world laughs with you, says the
saw. Sometimes, laugh, and other people want to know what is the
matter with you. There is the vacant smile of the mentally challenged, that is: all of us on occasion. Laughing at nothing is a very
troubling concept, as is laughing out quiet. Expectably enough, 234
occurrences of the word 'rire' have been counted in Hugo's *L'Homme
qui rit*. While laughter can be a response to grotesque spectacles, it
can also appear to non-participants as grotesque itself. In *L'Homme
qui rit*, Gwynnplaine provokes widespread laughter by his automated
cachinnation, a variation on Tourette's syndrome, the foul-mouth
disease. He is condemned to laugh and mocked because he laughs.[11]

A refusal to laugh, a categorical 'That is not funny', are potent
weapons in the squashing of a humorist's project. Such apparent
killjoys may be fighting a rearguard action against incontinence, or the
purely negative kind of mockery. There is a very understandable fear
of anarchy, all hell broken loose. Empson wrote, a little vaguely: 'You
don't have madhouse and the whole thing there'.[12] Laughter has often
been equated with the gainsaying, destructive Satan; and Baudelaire
dated it from the Fall. There is, indeed, much to be said against many
forms of laughter, which include: the forced, the hypocritical, the
false. As virtually everything else can be faked: passports, certificates,
female orgasms, playing dead when cornered by a bear, grief, famous
paintings, currency, or alibis, why not also laughter? Perhaps the most
cowardly sort is dutiful laughter, chiming in, though this can be a
variety of tact. The listener is under pressure. Nervous laughter results
from stress or panic, and is no funnier than wetting your pants. We
can forget to signal our amusement, if we focus too exclusively on the
serious point embedded in the witticism. Or we can boast a mouthful
of teeth like a neglected graveyard ('rire à belles dents'—if only!).
Finally, we may not like the comic messenger him- or herself, just as
we may refuse to cheer when the opposition scores.

Less confrontational than laughing or refusing to laugh is the smile.
It is more non-committal, while retaining its own multivalences:
vacuous, idiotic, sadistic, enigmatic, condescending; we can smile
gamely. The smile makes less fuss, is more discreet and, at its most
sincere, more civilized. (The tough-guy injunction 'Smile when you
say that' keeps the periodic antagonism of the laugh.) We are egged

on to smile, not laugh, for the camera. A smile, of course, is mute, but it can speak volumes. As such it can resemble soundless laughter, often accompanied by quaking but not exploding. We can, similarly, laugh up our sleeve or, in French, under our cape (and the smile, in French, is a sub-laugh).

Laughter, then, is not necessarily noise. It can be, like reading or farts, silent, or dumb, like insolence. More often, however, it is the physical manifestation, the in-your-face display, of being amused by or amusing another.

We know, and professionals remind us, that you often have to work for laughs, and need to milk them vigorously when you draw them out. Even if writers cannot make us physically see or hear laughter, they can wring ours in response out of us.

The French, when laughing aloud, may say: 'C'est à se les [les testicules] mordre'. I have never laughed to that extreme, and feel that the legendary beaver who, at bay, castrates himself ('Castor a castrando' is the old derivation) is being supremely self-defeating.

2

The Question
of Humourlessness (Rousseau,
Sade, God, and Brisset)

'We are not amused' is the celebrated squelch attributed to Queen Victoria. Not being amused can clearly, as here, be wilful, or, elsewhere, involuntary. I am fully prepared to accept the idea of unconscious humour, though reluctant to believe in unmeant humour. Unless words really do our thinking for us, surely we are, in some way, responsible for what we emit. In a book about humour, I must make space for its antonym, if not necessarily its opposite, humourlessness. It will seem perverse to make Rousseau and Sade cohabit, given that, in an unspoken, or rather private, cross-talk act, Sade took great delight in mocking Rousseau's utopian thinking at every opportunity. It is strange, too, that two of the most passionate writers of the eighteenth century should be so lacking in humour. It is in addition bizarre to import from the late nineteenth and early twentieth centuries a genuine sport, Jean-Pierre Brisset. The reasons for this choice may become less mysterious in due course. Need I add that even humourlessness can be funny, as in the myriad of jokes about slow-witted Germans who fail to get the point of a joke.

Rousseau

In *Émile*, Rousseau disrecommends La Fontaine's *Fables* for juvenile reading, as the young would be corrupted by such immoral *moralités*. He ignores La Fontaine's humour, without which the poet would be a tinkling cymbal. In the same vein, Rousseau castigated stage comedy in his *Lettre à D'Alembert*. The core of his problem with humour, however, lies in his less than self-critical exaltation of his precious self. He is the first major writer to make a protracted song-and-dance about feeling and being different from everyone else. In this, of course, he speaks for us all. 'Suis-je donc seul sage, seul éclairé parmi les mortels?'[1] This is the diametrical opposite of classical self-estimates. No wonder that Rousseau is commonly held to be the grandfather of egopetal Romanticism. 'Cet homme ne ressemble à nul autre que je connaisse; il demande une analyse à part et faite uniquement pour lui'.[2] He puts himself beyond the pale, but demands special considerations: empathy, not condemnation. He sounds like the pathetic concentration-camp inmate in Camus's *La Chute*, who begs to be treated differently from the mass of prisoners, because he alone is innocent. Rousseau, too, is always a special case. Surely a sense of humour reminds us that we are not fundamentally different from or superior to anybody else. Rousseau's view of himself is curiously static. Nature made him what he unendingly is. In his social thinking, too, he wants to stop the clock. He had a persecution-complex because, of course, he was widely persecuted. The fact remains that he calls to mind the American comedian's joke: 'I told my psychiatrist that everyone hates me. He said I was being ridiculous—everyone hasn't met me yet'. He was plentifully laughed at; he became a favourite Aunt Sally or butt.

As a boy, he mooned his butt to passing females, and ever afterwards went on exposing himself to other people's indignation or mockery: a *tête de Turc*, or whipping boy. He was forever making an exhibition of himself. Jean Cocteau wittily commented on Rousseau's obsession with his bottom: 'Le postérieur de Jean-Jacques est-il le soleil de Freud qui se lève? J'y distingue plutôt le clair de lune romantique'.[3] Though Rousseau often states his surprise at hostile reactions to his exhibitionism, perhaps it is all an act, either at the time or in retrospect, like the class clown who both plays up to negative expectations and seeks attention. When Rousseau portrays himself as ludicrous, perhaps he is annexing what so many fellow *philosophes*, those practitioners of hostile incest, thought of him: a boor, silly and clumsy (as in Freud's equally gauche 'roux sot' joke).[4]

It is true that he is capable of and quite often practises the more bitter, joyless forms of humour: polemical satire and sarcasm. Even those who detect a sense of humour in him tend, however, to find it ponderous. It is not so much a matter of lacking wit, the pursuit of snappiness, for that is given to few. It is a more profound dearth: a sense of proportion, which is not just boring common sense, but an awareness of your impact on others; and an unawareness of your own inflated self-valuation. Humour is not always quick. Think of the 'slow burn'. It needs, however, to know when to hurry the pace, to put the foot down. Rousseau rarely manages this change of gear.

Much of Rousseau's philosophy is just plain daft and laughable. In *Émile*, the young pupil is taught practical geography by being abandoned by his tutor in a dense forest with instructions to find his own way home. (That might work with SAS trainees.) The lad is taught moral courage by the tutor's looming up at his window in the dead of night, dressed in a sheet and moaning horribly. Rousseau's instinctive actions can be just as comically misplaced. In the *Rêveries du promeneur solitaire*, he recounts po-faced how, on a walk, a Great Dane came charging at him. Jean-Jacques attempts to leap vertically, Nijinsky-fashion, to let the huge dog pass underneath him (Nijinsky also ended as a paranoid schizophrenic). Expectably, the hound flattens him and knocks him unconscious. Imagine an animated cartoon, and you will get the picture. Typically, he then tries to make us ashamed of our tittering (he once ordered us not to be taken in by this monster, who was also a human being) by embarking on a description of a mystical epiphany on regaining consciousness: the 'Totum simul' of perfect congruence with his environment. A moment of grace after failed gracefulness. A key term in the *Rêveries* is 'dédommagement', compensation: a kind of pension granted to the ageing self. The whole text tries to turn loss into gain—psychological capitalism.

In the *Confessions*, Rousseau can at times recognize that the joke is, rightly, on him, as when he remarks on the asymmetrical breasts of the Venetian courtesan, who coolly advises him to give up sex and take up trigonometry.[5] Segments of the *Confessions*, where he resurrects incidents from his childhood, are comic, both the event and the telling of it. But that was relatively easy: we are more forgiving to children. He found it far harder to laugh at himself when older. The ability to acknowledge his own ridiculousness is less palpable in the description of Rousseau conducting the cacophony of his first illiterate musical composition.[6] To be charitable, I should add that this catastrophic performance also betrays a protest that many of us might own up to, a protest against having to learn and obey rules. Michèle Crogiez links such rare instances of humour not with Rousseau's cult of frankness, of taking his pursuit of the truth with high seriousness, but with the *récits* of *Les Confessions*.[7] 'Dirons-nous, à titre d'hypothèse, que Rousseau craint de ne pas être pris au sérieux s'il donne dans l'humour?' (p. 220). Rousseau suffers from the conviction, 'opposée à celle d'Erasme par exemple—que [la vérité] est mal servie par la plaisanterie' (p. 221). Despite his anti-classical championing of the unique self, Rousseau clings, for his rhetorical principles, to the classical criterion of unity of tone (ibid.). Diderot thought differently, and his rich sense of humour enabled him to accommodate himself to Rousseau, whereas the largely humourless Genevan failed to appreciate the genius of Diderot.

In his essays, Rousseau is so obsessed with legalistic sanitary cordons, *garde-fous*, that he downplays the social value of laughter. He does see the utility of popular fêtes, but any exhilaration therein must be harmless; no hair is truly let down. Bergson's killjoy emphasis on the policing function of public response to private eccentricity is direly reminiscent of Rousseau's totalitarian wheeze, in *Le Contrat social*, of the implacable judgement by public opinion on those who violate the norms. Rousseau should have been the last on earth to plug such repression of the individual. Presumably, the laws he dreamt up did not apply to himself. A self-chosen martyr like Rousseau not uncommonly has an undernourished sense of humour. Especially in old age, he was frequently a solitary. Do hermits have to provide their own audience, their own receivers? If so, they must split themselves in two, like people playing chess against themselves. If so, would this be true humour, authentic self-irony? Or would a recluse still, ultimately cheat, like us lesser mortals? After all, the perfect punchline would be suicide (even stand-up comedians can 'die' on stage). Rousseau gives practically no indication of such laughing to or at himself on his solitary walks.

Women justifiably object to the frequently expressed male assumption that they have no sense of humour. As Frances Gray points out, 'humourlessness is a double burden, rather like barrenness in the Old Testament, a failure both social and personal. And, like barrenness, it's assumed to be primarily a women's problem'.[8] Rousseau, who worshipped various women during his life, late in life adopted a long Armenian robe (a kind of caftan) with silk sashes and fur trimmings, and announced that he had thought and written as a man, to public disapproval; henceforth he would become a woman. It reminds me of

T. E. Lawrence dressing as an Arab in order to parade his alienation from Europeanness, and to show his conviction that, in an age of futile luxuries, simplicity of dress (as long as it was a striking simplicity) was the only way of distinguishing himself from the mass. Or, to put that another way, the only manner of being natural was to choose eccentricity.

In *A rebours*, Huysmans writes of Des Esseintes: 'Il vivait sur lui-même, se nourrissait de sa propre substance, pareil à ces bêtes engourdies tapies dans un trou, pendant l'hiver'.[9] Rousseau ups the ante in his version of this mood: 'De quoi jouit-on dans une pareille situation? De rien d'extérieur à soi sinon de soi-même et de sa propre existence; tant que cet état dure, on se suffit à soi-même, comme Dieu'.[10] Much of his rhetoric, particularly in its hyperbolic moments, is quite delectably suspect, and therefore unknowingly comical. The *Rêveries* themselves seem to exist less in time than in a time warp. As for the *Confessions*, Camus's Clamence for once speaks the simple truth with unforked tongue when he says of loaded texts like his own: 'Quand [les auteurs de confession] prétendent passer aux aveux, c'est le moment de se méfier, on va maquiller le cadavre'.[11] Against that charge, we should also warn ourselves that Rousseau's undoubted deceitfulness, his bad faith, are also ours. By his example, he brings home to us the specious self-justifications each of us practises, often without even noticing.

Take masturbation, towards which I would hate to be judgemental, for, as Woody Allen argued, 'it is sex with someone I love'.[12] For his part, Rousseau emulates his contemporary, the Swiss physician Samuel Tissot, in the fearful indictment of manstupration. Tissot's *Onanisme* was originally published in Latin, which is so user-friendly to young lads and lasses. In *Émile*, Rousseau has the tutor sermonize his pupil: 'Il serait très dangereux qu'il apprît à votre élève à donner le change à ses sens et à suppléer aux occasions de les satisfaire; s'il connaît une fois ce dangereux supplément, il est perdu'.[13] In *Les Confessions*, he expands, still euphemistically, on this theme: 'J'appris ce dangereux supplément qui trompe la nature et sauve aux jeunes gens de mon humeur beaucoup de désordres aux dépens de leur santé, de leur vigueur et quelquefois de leur vie'. Thus, while alarmist, he at least recognizes the temptation, though he must stamp on it:

Ce vice que la honte et la timidité trouvent si commode, a de plus un grand attrait pour les imaginations vives; c'est de disposer pour ainsi dire à leur gré de tout le sexe, et de faire servir à leurs plaisirs la beauté qui les tente sans avoir besoin d'obtenir son aveu.

Masturbation is therefore an imaginary rapist's charter. He himself was 'saved' by living with Mme de Warens. As he adored her, he could not defile her even in his mind, though the 'stimulants' (seeing her all the time, sleeping in a bed she had slept in, surrounded by objects evoking her) were acute, such that a reader visualizing these goads would think Rousseau must have been 'à demi-mort'.[14] Fortunately, like all prohibitions, joyless anti-onanism campaigns excite the targets' imagination and encourage the urge to outwit the nay-saying authority. Like euphemism, they publicize what they hope to ban. The writer Rousseau might have reflected that a frequent link has often been thrown between masturbation and reading or writing: equally solitary and self-gratifying activities. As we will see with Sade, there is a fine line between pedagogy and pornography.

Rousseau is on record as laughing heartily in company, and he was adept at caustic rhetoric in print. It is humour he lacks. As Robin Howells remarks on *Rousseau juge de Jean-Jacques*: 'There is no wit in this exercise, either in the sense of comedy (the issue is too desperately personal), or in the sense of opening a closed system to an outside point of view'.[15] If, as Isaiah Berlin once said, 'Rousseau was the first militant lowbrow',[16] he would have benefited from relaxing more than he did into humour. Even amid Nature, he was too prone, like Dr Johnson, to consider mountains as rather uncouth objects. All in all, he saw humour as *ruinous*:

Il analyse lucidement combien l'humour exige du lecteur qu'il se mette à distance du raisonnement, exactement comme les bons mots au théâtre qui, s'ils font apprécier les talents du dramaturge, ruinent inéluctablement l'illusion théâtrale.[17]

Rousseau had no sense of that distance that would have got him out of himself. Though it is easy to laugh at him, we should realize that in so doing we are so often laughing at ourselves.

Sade

On Sade, I will be, unlike Sade, mercifully brief. In George Steiner's view, 'eroticism, covert or declared, fantasised or enacted, is interwoven with teaching, in the phenomenology of mastery and discipleship. This elemental fact has been trivialised by a fixation on sexual harassment'.[18] Sade, that 'fanfaron du vice', only too clearly wants to teach his readers a lesson, to impose a countereducation.

Sade shares Jean Sareil's opinion that 'rien n'est plus fatal à l'érotisme que le rire'.[19] I would replace 'fatal' by 'essentiel'. What a strait-laced sex-life he envisages. Is not sex spasmodically but regularly comic, for everyone except the most mechanical, brutal, and agelastic performers? Of course, sex in Sade's writings *is* largely mechanized. While citing Sade honestly acknowledging that 'la médiocrité de mon talent ne me [permet] pas d'en apercevoir les limites', Philippe Sollers remains convinced, provocatively, that 'tout ce qu'écrit Sade est humour'.[20] Sade's self-judgement shows the true unregenerate having it both (or all) ways, like his epic fuckers. Against Sollers, we can quote Sade instructing libertines to keep a straight face: 'Le moindre rire [... dans les parties de débauche] sera une des fautes les plus graves et les plus cruellement punies'.[21] He thus divorces pleasure from laughter. Though he recommends in one text: 'Ne renversez point leurs idoles en colère: pulvérisez-les en jouant', in *Justine* M. de Bressac, who inevitably has designs on the girl to whom he is pontificating, claims that a punning Jesus cannot be taken seriously, and that his supposedly divine play of words on Peter/*petros* is pure linguistic legerdemain.[22]

It is conceivable that Sade was laughing non-stop at any velleity towards idealism, all the idols that dumb humans sacrifice to. It is, however, equally conceivable that Sade pens involuntary self-parody (of which any of us, naturally, is capable), like any obsessive. Repetition, monotony, proliferating lists are all inherently comic because absurd, as we will see with Huysmans. Undeniably, there is cruel, gloating, triumphant, sarcastic laughter everywhere in Sade's texts. It is a key weapon in the lust for domination over another. In Laclos's near-Sadean *Liaisons dangereuses*, both Merteuil and Valmont dread being thought naive or ridiculous (absolute tyrants would not care). Finally, they turn their vengeful irony on each other, transmuting words into acts. On the other hand, Valmont's one-night stand with the courtesan Émilie reveals her as hardly a victim. She lends herself gladly to the double-meaning missive that Valmont writes to the prudish Mme Tourvel on her naked commercial back. This is desecrating but enjoyable wit. *Les Liaisons dangereuses* operates by irony and innuendo: Sade mainly by the full-frontal attack. The former is probably what sets the imagination and the pulse racing. In his lengthy incarceration, Sade masturbated copiously in real time and on paper (his books, as the French say, are to be read with one hand). In anti-onanism texts, the mind (the imagination) mattered as much as matter (emission). They got that much right.

We come back to Steiner: 'Eros and language mesh at every point. Intercourse and discourse, copula and copulation, are sub-classes of the dominant fact of communication'.[23] Steiner, like Sade, takes himself very seriously.

John Phillips provides a fair-minded, if very English, summation on the question of Sade's humour:

> There are many instances in the libertine novels of an intended humour that takes a variety of forms: satire, parody, and black comedy are regular features. However, the reader will often encounter passages whose comical effects are probably unintentional. For example, there are numerous descriptions of sexual prowess and genital size, the excessive character of which seems ridiculous rather than arousing. Humorous responses to Sade are by no means new—the nineteenth-century English writer Swinburne and his friends roared with laughter as they read him aloud to each other.[24]

We have seen in Rameau's Nephew, and will see repeatedly, the humour resident in hyperbole: Huysmans, Vallès, Céline, Sartre's relentless magnification of Roquentin's philosophical epiphanies. In *La Philosophie dans le boudoir*, young Eugénie is an ultra-fast learner. Within one day of debauchery, she dons a dildo to rape her own mother, while being sodomized herself by her new mentor, Dolmancé. Here is her ecstatic résumé of this production line: 'Me voilà donc à la fois incestueuse, adultère, sodomite, et tout cela pour une fille qui n'est dépucelée que d'aujourd'hui! ... Que de progrès, mes amis'.[25] Phillips remarks on the 'comic acceleration [as in cartoons] of behaviour [...], the use of ellipsis, which [involves] incongruous juxtapositions'. When he analyses the 'many tableaux representing sexual geometrics', I am reminded how the trigonometer Rousseau might have let his hair down and added to the figures. On the Sadean surfeit, Phillips concludes: 'For the modern reader Sadean horror is fundamentally unrealistic, and it is principally this aspect that distances one from it'.[26] In other words, if you can abstract the homicides, torture, and sexual excess, and concentrate on the telling, the sequences of words, all will be well. But this is like switching off the sound in a talkie. Phillips avoids using the bargepole, but still employs a kind of tongs to handle the filthy material.

Religion

The Enlightenment did not scoop the mockery of religious obscurantism, but it made such retaliation sexy.[27] Sermons rarely make us roll in the aisles. 'There is no humor in heaven', says Pudd'nhead Wilson, which is surely one of the many good reasons for not hungering to ascend there.[28] The Devil has not only the best tunes, but also the sexiest body. For Diderot, the arbitrary Christian god was more concerned about damage to his orchard than about any scrumper who broke his neck: 'Le Dieu des chrétiens est un père qui fait grand cas de ses pommes, et fort peu de ses enfants'.[29] Many have vented anger at the divine sense of priorities, and especially at the Almighty's automatic use of the veto, which renders negotiation pointless. No wonder God takes little interest in us for our own sakes, our special needs. Does he even look at us? He sees only Himself, for He thinks that we are He, made in His own image, in an original, plagiaristic act of self-idolatry.

For many centuries, and to grossly oversimplify, the Church's policy was that wit, on appropriate occasions, was all well and good, but most likely to be bred by the elite of humanity, whereas comedy, and especially laughter, were low, and all that the great unwashed were entitled to. Much the same could be said of the status of sexuality. The bestial inferiors were known to be addicted to sex, but the upper crust believed that it had to officially disapprove of such behaviour, while of course practising it behind the façade. The more liberal ones knew they relied for their own comforts on a working class. Laughter was more or less diabolical in inspiration. The Old Testament offers several instances of the Deity laughing at the defective or sinning individual. It is part of the power scenario: despots belittle. You would have to have a heart of stone not to laugh, at some point, at Job's concatenation of travails. How anyone, all the same, could trust such a double-dealing deity, from whom no sane consumer would buy a used cart, eludes me. Job declaims the great bellyaching complaint of all time. *Job* is the most vexed text, and Job the most vexed human, in the Old Testament. Is his thirsting for explanation and justification of his countless woes ever satisfied by a vivisecting God? Is the problem of pain ever solved?

When suffering or angry humans counter-attack God, is it mainly atheists and agnostics who comfort themselves, like Heine, with the thought that 'Dieu me pardonnera, c'est son métier'.[30] In *Endgame*, Beckett writes: 'The bastard. He doesn't exist'.[31] This captures perfectly our schizophrenia on the subject. God's mockery of his erring children betokens a lack of humour. Humour, as well as being brutal, can also be forgiving towards humans' sins or crimes. Nietzsche could believe only in a God who understood how to dance on light feet, though he acknowledges that Zarathustra is laughed at by the uncomprehending crowd. The lesson he teaches, joyfully, is that we should not kill false idols by wrath but by laughter (a variation on Sade's iconocataclysm): 'Come, let us kill the Spirit of Gravity'.[32] He must have had God in mind when he wrote this epigraph to his *Gay Science*:

> I live in my own place,
> Have never copied anyone even half,
> And at any master who lacks the grace
> To laugh at himself—I laugh.[33]

He knew full well that laughter does not have to be kind, only truthful: 'Laughter means being *schadenfroh* [gloating], but with a good conscience'.[34]

Jean-Pierre Brisset (1837–1919)

Religion, sex, and philology come together in an eccentric and fascinating orgy in the writings (largely self-financed) of Jean-Pierre Brisset, who will provide us with a further and different slant on humourlessness, and a twist on Rousseau's quietist spiritualism and Sade's materialism. Sade hated God, Rousseau dreamt up a civil religion, and Brisset deified frogs.[35] Brisset also chimes into the eighteenth century in his obsession with the origins of language (Rousseau, Court de Gébelin), and his anti-Catholicism. Looking forward, he was also a self-taught man, but how unlike Sartre's pathetic Autodidacte. Above all, he made free with the corseted

French language, in a pre-Surrealist fashion. Truly, 'ce vieillard est un carrefour'.[36]

Gérard Genette, much given to word-juggling and other forms of Genettique engineering, said:

L'humour est un assez sûr chemin vers la folie: on commence par faire l'imbécile *cum grano salis*; sous ce couvert insidieux, on finit par le devenir sans autre grain que, justement, celui que désigne l'expression 'avoir un grain [to be touched]'.[37]

Brisset's work is encyclopaedic in that his alternative system embraces the whole of human evolution.[38] A swimmer observed from above looks like a frog splayed out. From this founding analogy stems a long and intricate account of developing man from prehistoric days to the twentieth century. Brisset works, for his arguments, entirely from puns and etymologies. Evolution is linguisticized. God remains mainly abstract, and is often referred to by the mathematical symbol pi. The Roman Catholic Church Brisset comprehensively loathed, all who sail in her and all that she stands for.

How ludic are the umpteen puns in the writings of this man who was, and was not, *un fou littéraire*? Nobody in their right mind should need persuading of the importance of play for the development and homeostasis of children, adults, nations, humankind, and the animal kingdom. Certain linguisticians, and a moment's thought by virtually anybody, recognize that a principal mainspring of language is play: joking, messing about with words, coining them, trying it on with them, parodying others' uses and idiosyncrasies, mocking superiors, telling stories (in both senses), and so on. Lucretius's theory of the *clinamen* (swerve, sidestep) inscribes play in the very fabric of the universe. Play can, obviously, be intensely serious: witness any child or athlete. One specific form of linguistic play, black humour, may derive its name from the 'black bile' which allegedly breeds melancholy, but also creativity.[39]

Maria Yaguello takes over, possibly from André Breton, the notion that Brisset knew not what he did. In her anthology, *Les Fous du langage*, she grants that some of the excerpts have 'une valeur poétique ou esthétique, souvent involontaire (c'est le cas des élucubrations d'un Brisset, par exemple)'.[40] In his *Anthologie de l'humour noir*, Breton cites Hegel's concept of 'objective humour', and links it with 'le hasard objectif' of Surrealism; both are aleatory.[41] Could Brisset's placing of frogs and humans in the same evolutionary basket be such 'hasard objectif', or a deliberate policy?

'Hasard objectif' is that rather comfy set-up whereby the non-human world plays ball with our innermost desires by donating joyous or startling coincidences. The Surrealists' stated preference for the gratuitous made them favour unpointed, capricious puns, which are quite alien to the demonstrator Brisset, but which they delightedly found in the baroque conjunctions of Raymond Roussel. Surrealists often suffered from the oneupmanship which, perhaps inevitably, per-verted group attempts at spontaneous creativity, collective dreaming or raving. Yet there was possibly more fruitful freedom in team games like 'Cadavre exquis' (a more fragmented variant of 'Consequences') than in 'automatic writing'; collective aleatoriness was conceivably more productive than solo arm-chancing. 'Hasard objectif' pushes the idea of puns as *objets trouvés*, windfalls, ready-mades. 'Le hasard', nevertheless, had to have its hand forced, be channelled. Surrealists claimed to have the sublime gift of serendipity.

Before excerpting fourteen pages of Brisset's texts, Breton elects to talk of 'la décharge émotive de l'expression de Brisset dans un humour tout de *réception* (par opposition à l'humour d'*émission* de la plupart des auteurs qui nous intéressent' (p. 308, Breton's stress). This polarization would appear to make Brisset's humour more passive and stereotypically feminine. Breton then compares Brisset, as Marcel Duchamp had done earlier, to Douanier Rousseau: 'Le désaccord flagrant qui se manifeste entre la nature des idées communément reçues chez l'écrivain ou le peintre de ce primitivisme intégral est générateur d'un humour de grand style auquel le responsable ne participe pas' (ibid.). How can a humorist be responsible and uninvolved? Objective humour begins here to sound curiously like the verdict of 'objective guilt' prevalent in Stalinist Russia's show trials.

Breton celebrated less pickily the sexual core of Brisset's writing: 'Avec lui se développe, sur un fond pan-sexualiste d'une grande valeur hallucinatoire, et à l'abri d'une rare érudition, une suite d'équations de mots dont la rigueur ne manque pas d'être impressionnante (A.B.)'.[42] The heavily eroticized verbal universe of Brisset is well caught in Breton's admittedly pretty pompous enthronement of wordplay: 'Et qu'on comprenne bien que nous disons: jeux de mots quand ce sont nos plus sûres raisons d'être qui sont en jeu. Les mots, du reste, ont fini de jouer. Les mots font l'amour'.[43] The Surrealist game of 'l'un dans l'autre' suggests both the telescoping action often found in punning, and a miniature analogue, or ersatz, of the sexual act. Robert Desnos's punning spoonerism : 'Rrose Sélavy n'est pas persuadée que la culture du moi puisse amener la moiteur du cul' does not stop him engaging in mock-apology elsewhere: 'Pitié pour l'amant des homonymes'.[44] For his part, Brisset never begs forgiveness, even jokingly, for his dynamic puns.

Breton, above all (where he placed himself), always sounds so schoolmasterly, so would-be papal; he preaches his prejudices, indoctrinates his *doxa*. He rejects and fears pathos. Brisset is clearly the odd man out among the varied linguistic energumens of Breton's anthology. As Pierrsens so rightly says of Breton's formula, 'humour de réception': 'Tout l'élan dévastateur qui anime l'entreprise de Brisset est tout à coup désarmé, torpillé, désormais inoffensif—ramené au rang de *curiosité*, ou de trait d'esprit'. Just as Sartre dismissed Surrealism as glorified schoolboy japes, so Pierrsens condemns Breton's attempted confiscation of Brisset: 'Notons qu'ainsi le surréalisme ne pouvait qu'être fasciné par toutes les manifestations d'insubordination, mais condamné à les contempler comme spectacle, comme frisson'.[45]

Brisset's humour would be more palpably conscious if he possessed a sense of irony, for irony would have acted as a corrective to his lust for symmetries of meaning in all he surveyed. It would have been not so much deconstructionist as arresting: sceptical brakes. Irony lodges the tongue firmly in the cheek. (The English concept of 'tongue-in-cheek' transfers none too happily to the French 'pince-sans-rire'.) While Brisset was conversant with several tongues, and never lacked supreme cheek, he never brought them into contact. Irony, nevertheless, is deadpan humour, which is what I find in Brisset. To cannibals, Swift's 'Modest Proposal' that the starving Irish should eat their babies would be neither blackly amusing nor ironic, for it would make them smack their chops. Brisset is totally un-ironic. He always says what he means, and this has the uncanniness of true candour. Neither is he euphemistic. Given his antipathy to dead (but they won't lie down) languages, he would be the last person to say 'Excusez mon latin'. Although he is upfront, indeed full-frontal, he is more often than not decorous (e.g. referring to the genitals as *nudités*). This matters little, since the actions he describes are plain as a pikestaff, even if the terms he uses are at times ever so slightly obfuscatory.

How aware is he of his deviation from the norm? Could he have said, like the child commenting on her own coinage: 'I said oddly, diddle I?'[46] In Blavier's view, 'Brisset ne change pas l'écriture, mais seulememt bouleverse, *ludiquement*, les acquis actuels de l'étymologie courante; il y a chez Brisset invention de contenu théorique, mais non invention de fonctionnement. Brisset n'est pas métalinguistique'.[47] Play, however, can be commentary, and clearly can convey an attitude towards expression. Koegler attributes the generally low esteem in which punning is held to

its close similarity to the loosening of association and 'clang' associations found in the unconscious and openly expressed in schizophrenia. Society protects itself against the threat of being reminded of unconscious processes by downgrading the pun as a form of humour, thus limiting its use.[48]

Are pun-machines, such as the eighteenth-century socialite Marquis de Bièvre, the wordsmith James Joyce, or the psychoanalytical theorist Jacques Lacan, any less linguistically mad than Brisset? Bièvre was a living legend in his era, who became trapped in the role of paronomasiac automat, and who probably kept a stock of puns ready for insertion into conversations on the appropriate cue. His play *Vercingentorixe* features a pun per line. Likewise Brisset: punslinger at pun-point, dancing on a pun-head, for him life was a ceaseless pun-fight. Though he could hardly write a line without punning, the only record we have of him punning orally was when, challenged to play on 'Israélite', he came up instantly with 'il sera élite'.[49]

Unknowingly, Brisset practised anticipatory plagiarism, as pata-physicians are wont to say of those who scoop them. On occasion, he sounds like Lacan: 'Le diable est un père sévère criant: Persévère! C'est aussi un *père vert*, le vieux pervers'.[50] Unlike Lacan, Brisset believed puns to be so fundamental that they could not be restricted to the unconscious; he gave them full light of day. They are built into language: 'Ce langue à jeu, ce l'engage, ce langage'.[51] (Gender is labile in Brisset.) Whereas the oligarchy of Orwell's *Nineteen Eighty-Four* wanted to derealize and empty language, Brisset wished to cram it to bursting. To see meanings, whole layers of them bifurcating every-where, is puntheism. This credo sees puns playing, in the history of humankind, at first possum and then passim. On the threshold of the century of the Absurd, this certain faith in the total reliability of words singles out Brisset.

Elliott Oring favours the concept of 'appropriate incongruity'.[52] That is: there can be an internal coherence in jokes, even if the elements are heterogeneous. Such tactics defy logic, while having a logic in their own special context.

Some respondents are ready to see Brisset as a humorist, but only so as to belittle or domesticate him: a harmless joker. They refuse or fail to see that his humour is consubstantial with his message; the vehicle and the load are inseparable. Some of those who do congratulate him on his suggestive genius, his poetry—all of this somehow *malgré lui*—are saying in effect: 'Out of the mouths of babes and sucklings', but they forget the full quotation: 'Out of the mouths of very babes and sucklings hast thou ordained strength' (Psalms 8: 2). Yet Brisset's inventive rewrite of linguistic evolution (from croaks to words) always includes an element of confidence-trickery (the pun as 'catch'), as in this etymology of *blague*: 'Beux l'ague, bois l'eau, blague. La *blague* consistait à offrir une boisson trompeuse, contenue dans une vessie devenue la blague à tabac'.[53] Like an adept comedian, Brisset at times offloads dirty-mindedness on to his audience: 'Il faut, antique pourceau, que l'on te mette le nez dans tes ordures' (p. 313). In a more relaxed mood, he can be, simply, charming: 'On s'asseyait dans son assiette et on y mangeait. La première assiette fut la partie du corps ainsi nommée, laquelle, lorsqu'on était assis dans la terre glaise, y dessinait sa forme. Chacun se trouvait bien dans son assiette' (p. 316). Sometimes, it is unclear how much is idiosyncratic association of ideas, or how much literalization of idiom, as in this passage: 'Le roi régnait d'abord en obligeant ses sujets à le lecher et relécher. Le roi, qui est un oint, est donc un membre léché. Le vrai roi est l'homme qui est ou doit être bien léché. Les ours mal léchés [uncouth creatures] ne sont pas des hommes'.[54] Is this uncertainty as to comic intention a case of undecidability, or at least suspension, as in Lewis Carroll: humour as the grin without the cat?

For Réja, Brisset's humour was 'une joyeuse fumisterie, mais poussée terriblement loin;—quelque chose comme de l'humour à très longue détente'.[55] Brisset's work has certainly been a delayed-action bomb, whose ticking went largely unnoticed by his contemporaries. His humour is a mixture of the ingenious; he is skilful at discovering, inventing, adapting, contriving (and 'ingenious' comes from *ingenium*: wit), and the ingenuous (from the root 'free-born'). For me, he is fully aware of the quirkiness of his own investigatory wordplay, as in this on

Esau: 'Le pelu plut tant qu'il plut, mais quand il devint méchant il ne plut plus'.[56] Although there were coincidental, ready-made puns in his home area—the nearby village famous for its frogs, and its inhabitants nicknamed 'les grenouillards'; Brisset's birthplace, Noës (and the sons of Noah built Babel), Brisset knew in fact that he had to work for his plays on words: 'On ne découvre que ce qu'on cherche'.[57] He knew in his bones that he was originating a counter-history of the world, but he no doubt preferred to live, imaginatively, in his alternative reality, which was certainly more substantial than some forms of our contemporary (virtual) reality.

All told, I take his humour as an instinctive pre-emptive strike. He was getting his retaliation, against those who said he was just plain mad, in first. As a former ranker and then officer, besides, he must have been very familiar with dumb (or loquacious) insolence. His humour is jocoserious, and cannot be labelled, dully, as 'involuntary'. It is deadpan, the humour of a man sure of his way-out beliefs and of his own value. He has more affinities with pataphysics than with Surrealism, and is fittingly fêted on 25 *haha* (30 October) his birthday.

What variety of cross-talk have Rousseau, Sade, God, and Brisset been conducting between them?

Humourlessness seems to be the lack of an inner-directed sense of humour, for which no amount of outer-directed savage indignation can compensate.

There are benighted souls who think that ludic and serious are polar opposites, or reciprocal exterminators. It is possible to be serious without being owl-solemn.

Riff on Dreams

I remember few of my dreams. I must have an overzealous board of film censors. You do not hear much about amusing dreams. Freud does talk about jokes and puns extractable from dreams, but po-facedly finds them pedantically serious. In *The Interpretation of Dreams*, against any disparagement of their evaluation, he quotes as the other extreme F. W. Hildbrandt's *Der Traum une seine Verwertung für's Leben* (Leipzig, 1875):

There emerges from time to time in the creations and fabrics of the genius of dreams [...] a brilliance of wit such as we should never claim to have at our permanent command in our waking lives. There lies in dreams a marvellous poetry, an apt allegory, an incomparable humour.

Part sniffily, Freud is somewhat taken by this 'enthusiastic eulogy', this rhapsodic account. He was convinced that in dreams absolutely anything is possible. 'In waking life', however, he confessed, 'I have little claim to be regarded as a wit'. He goes on: 'The reader can convince himself that my patients' dreams seem at least as full of jokes and puns as my own, or even fuller'.[1]

In 2000, in Nashville, I was hospitalized for a couple of months while surgeons cleaned out lungs, and repaired a very faulty heart as far as they could. I dreamt profusely for once in my life, and remembered the weird dreams, which were clearly, or muddily, something to do with institutionalized sleep-patterns, the disorientation caused by four total anaesthesias in rapid succession, and the liberal supply of morphine. I felt as if I were relearning to sleep. After one major operation, I swore incredulously but adamantly that I had not yet had it. I was, in fact, still on a boat, my dream-conveyance.

A couple of American friends took me in for convalescence for a further four weeks. While in their home, I dreamt they were running an oneiric cat-house. They rented feline sleeping space. It was a cats'

Valhalla, yet the beasts were invisible. Did cat-house have its other meaning of brothel? In the hospital I had dreamt of coaxing the least attractive nurse of the mainly pretty team into bed with me. Within a stone's throw from dying, it was as if I wanted either to die laughing, or to laugh while dying, uncontrollably, come hell or high water. Perhaps I was dimly recalling Iris Murdoch's intriguing proposition: 'The novel is a comic form. Language is a comic form, and makes jokes in its sleep'.[2] Perhaps it is not surprising if hospital dreams twist and confuse everything, when, for example, staff dress men in backless frocks for weeks on end. As Freud said: 'The realm of jokes knows no boundaries'. Logically, then, he must be catholic in his collecting: 'We do not insist upon a patent of nobility for our examples'.[3]

In your dreams, you can lay to rest the heavy burden of good taste.

3

Huysmans: Back-to-Front, and Backpacking

A rebours

In his mock interview, that joke that many an author has toyed with pulling: writing your own review, Huysmans mentions among the subdued claims to fame of his *A rebours* 'une pincée d'humour noir et de comique rêche anglais'. This is putting the reality of that text too mildly: the pinch is more of a sly punch. Even so, the spoof reveals unusual honesty in its wry conclusion that the author is incapable of writing a true *chef d'œuvre*.[1] No doubt Huysmans's fictional stately home (only a 'maisonnette', according to its imaginary owner, Des Esseintes) has received too many visitors in the last century or so, but there remains much to be said about the varying kinds of humour that are built into it. Is what is back-to-front, *à rebours*, essentially comic? It is certainly so in its unseating effect on the reader, who is made to face the rear of the horse, although, as with all things, you get used to it.

The last of his line, Duke Jean des Esseintes, decides to begin his elaborate experiment in pickiness by rejecting his aristocratic forebears, his social coevals, and the world of men of letters. His *table rase* will be stocked differently. What he dreams of as a bolt-hole is 'une thébaïde raffinée, un désert confortable, une arche immobile et tiède où il se réfugierait loin de l'incessant déluge de la sottise humaine'.[2] He wants none of the self-denying conditions of the ideal hermit. In fact he will take self-indulgence to inordinate lengths. In its interior, at least, the house would be, in every sense, a folly. He insists that, before this new venture, he had indeed wanted to 'se singulariser', by (for example) preaching a dandiacal sermon to his assembled suppliers, or organizing an entirely black banquet: tablecloth, food, served by naked negresses

(p. 16). In effect, he is no longer, in his own eyes, a dandy, because he now cares little for making an impact on others, like the classic self-showman Beau Brummell. Dandyism can take other forms.

There is something inherently comic about the dandy, often called 'popinjay' (from 'papagay': parrot), because frivolous and 'precious', if socially valueless, or at least unproductive. No doubt the exotic, or impeccably dressed, dandy intends this gear as an insulation, a buffer-state against the loathed majority. No doubt, too, that any proponent of the Hobbesian theory of humour as superiority would detect silent laughter at others' expense in the dandy's whole enterprise. The dandy differs from the snob. For the latter hides what he is up to, whereas the former parades himself.[3] The snob depends on others for his values, while the dandy pursues autarky. In theory, the dandy does not need a gallery to which he has to play. If Beau Brummell spoke of his clothes as self-advertisement (the bruiser Norman Mailer entitled one of his books *Advertisements for Myself*), such a catwalk parade would suppose people lining the streets in order to register and marvel at his gorgeousness. Against this, the true dandy should want neither to be admired or loved nor to displease, for why try to impress in any way those you profess to despise? Ideally, he is sterile, like the mule with which he shares stubbornness. Although Des Esseintes has given up vestimentary dandyism, he cultivates what Roger Kempf calls 'un travail à rebours'.[4] As he seeks solitude, the merest thought of spectators he dismisses as too publicly showy, and vulgar. Although the dandy is supposed to show discrimination, Des Esseintes is in fact given to the pell-mell in his overburdened decor, and, like the Sorcerer's Apprentice of the legend, always risks losing control over his proliferating objects. Baudelaire recommended impassivity for his version of the dandy. Des Esseintes is excitable, and neurotic. As Rae Beth Gordon says of the cult of neurasthenia in the later years of the nineteenth century: 'The shocks of the modern urban environment had a greater impact on the neurasthenic's nerves than on his unaffected contemporaries'.[5]

All the immense care that he takes over his experiments seems maniacal, and therefore comical. He chooses a project, or makes a wager, that he will live henceforth against the grain, against Nature. No doubt there is something rebellious about going so wilfully against the current. But a solo rebellion makes little sense to anyone but martyrs. His backfiring, like farting, is a traditional ploy of comedy,

which habitually turns things round or upends them. Because of its
perversity, he resembles in this a person who elects to walk only
backwards. When filmed, no retrogressive perambulator preserves
dignity. Des Esseintes makes a fetish of the ersatz. His aquarium,
with its mechanical fish and changing coloured water, enables him to
imagine himself on board a ship. Strange how the spendthrift duke
so often economizes in this way. The dose of wilful self-delusion,
of cheating and defeating himself (a classic comedy turn), is heavy.
He aims to justify it by worshipping artifice but, beyond that, by
fabricating an alternative and better imaginary realm: 'Le tout est de
savoir concentrer son esprit sur un seul point, de savoir s'abstraire
suffisamment pour amener l'hallucination et pouvoir substituer le rêve
de la réalité à la réalité même' (p. 30). The term 'hallucination', and
the shift from 'savoir' to 'pouvoir' show how much will and self-
inducement are involved. Huysmans works by paired opposites, and
so his artificial creation counters nature, 'cette sempiternelle radoteuse'
(p. 31). He will not see until near the end to what extent his search
for constant newness is itself highly reiterative. Can it be other than
a *blague*, unintentional or otherwise, to maintain that no womanly
shape can outclass that of a steam locomotive? (p. 32).

When he launches his eclectic but exhaustive and fatiguing survey
of literature through the ages, Des Esseintes, in effect, delivers a
pickled harangue, an Augean dropping of names. A catalogue of
favourites can pass, but a litany of dislikes, of anybody famous or
not, tends to sound merely peevish, and therefore laughable.[6] Can
we take them altogether seriously? Such jeremiads are the humour,
as old as the hills, of pedantry. *A rebours*, like its author, suffers from,
while rejoicing in, a surfeit of culture. Des Esseintes opinionates
non-stop, as he tramps through or leaps over hundreds of years of
literary production, or casts it aside peremptorily. Petronius, a comic
genius, is spared the guillotine, and against the duke's usual tastes,
it is his expert vulgarity that is warmed to, a kind of far more
energetic and even life-affirming naturalism. Des Esseintes does not
altogether favour brother-souls. Of Tertullian, Huysmans says that
'ces idées, diamétralement opposées aux siennes, le faisaient sourire'
(p. 44). At the same time, Petronius himself, as author, is distant,
armoured behind his 'langue splendidement orfévrie' (pp. 41–2).
Seeking novelty, albeit in the ancient, breeds such neologisms, one of
the multiple avatars of wordplay. Des Esseintes travels further lexically

than topographically. He would love to be a hapax, an existential nonce-word. Unashamedly, *A rebours* is a snob's book, though today an untutored teenager could assemble an intertextual universe of rock music that would baffle most older people. It is a palimpsestic or, in Anthony Burgess's coinage for James Joyce, a 'palincestuous' text, a high-class glory-hole.[7] Even the duke's walls are Morocco-bound.

Des Esseintes's perverseness strives hard to make the superfluous central. When he overcoats a tortoise in precious gems, he is trying to remake nature. These stones are in fact a mixture of genuine and fake, which engenders 'une harmonie fascinatrice et déconcertante' (p. 58). For whom? Can the duke amaze himself? In a foretaste of the bleak ending, the beast refuses to play ball: it moves. His owner's touch, here, is lethal, for in no other way can he affect nature.

With his liqueur mouth organ, Des Esseintes moves on to more potently self-parodic and ludic territory. In this experiment, he aims to create an osmosis between taste and sound. Defended by poets, but medically an illness or psychosomatic idiosyncrasy, synaesthesia is traditionally difficult for non-synaesthetes to credit. Cross-breeding senses, or talking at cross-purposes: the space for humorous error is increased. Talking like a madman, Des Esseintes plays 'interior symphonies' on his revamped harmonica. Yet his claims are not so different from any mortal's readiness to make analogies between music, moods, senses, places, etc. Though he would hate to admit this, he is rehearsing 'le démon de l'analogie' by which we can all be seduced. His contraption is an oxymoron and a conceit. He performs on his tongue 'de silencieuses mélodies, de muettes marches funèbres' (p. 64), and thereby beats Proust's soundless madeleine. Huysmans's honesty makes him qualify his hero's amazing claims. The product is mixed: 'D'approximatifs et savants mélanges' (p. 64). Finally, the epiphany achieved is unpleasant. Whisky summons up agonizing dental work on his gums (though as Graham Greene said, toothache makes you feel incontrovertibly alive). Presented deadpan, such a memory is really a joke about a prevalent experience: fear bred by a visit to the dentist makes the pain vanish for a spell. All in all, are the duke's innovations genuine ideas, or just eccentric wheezes?

When he switches tracks to paintings, Des Esseintes eulogizes Gustave Moreau's *Salome*. In Buñuel's *Journal d'une femme de chambre*, an aged boot-fetishist, but a basically harmless dirty old man, M. Rabour, induces his sexy servant Célestine to read aloud to him the

passage about Gustave Moreau from *A rebours*. It expresses disdain for
common folk of whatever class. The severed head of John the Baptist
before which Salome dances leads Buñuel to make sex, violence, and
revolution interosculate. Rabour will die happy, chewing on a lady's
boot. Fetishism is, of course, also against nature. Des Esseintes proudly
confesses that such visualizations lend themselves to 'des éréthismes
de cervelle' (p. 87). What Rabour loved to picture when read to by
Célestine his brutal servant Joseph less aesthetically executes. Like the
fetishist, Des Esseintes is never truly inventive; all he can manage
is variations on the given. He spends much of his acreage of time
in reveries, a luxury occupation, centred as much on the past as on
imagined elsewheres or futures.

His sadistic imaginings of a friend's woes after marriage, that
ultimate cave-in, posit their sexual relations as attempting to fit a
square peg into a round hole. The dwelling with excitement on evil
thoughts is a far from morose delectation. Why the appeal of imaginary
transgressions? Is Des Esseintes's practice similar to the masturbator's
preference for envisionings over heterosex? Is it a lust for greater
control and immateriality, whereas physical sex is necessarily caught
up in two fleshes? In *A rebours*, the actual (that is: remembered) sexual
encounters all involve burlesque, misuse, fiasco, and joking. He is a
small-time Satan, even when he debauches a 16-year-old boy. Like
a big bad wolf, he instructs a brothel madame to mould the lad into
a murderer, a public enemy. Even if she could have succeeded, Des
Esseintes would still have acted vicariously.

One of his mistresses, Miss Urania (a strong whiff of pederasty
in this name, as in the old joke of Uranus/your anus) is a gorgeous hunk, a powerful American acrobat. Gradually she mutates
to a man, while Des Esseintes is feminized. Usually a control-
freak, he masochistically welcomes this domination, this rough
trade. Whatever Huysmans's own preponderant sexual proclivities,
he predictably gives his protagonist a homosexual dimension. As an
experimenter, Des Esseintes has to go against the grain, against nature, as homophobes would say. He is dead set against generation.
Small wonder, for he is, without anxiety, becoming increasingly
impotent. William Empson wrote: 'And I a twister love what I
abhor'.[8]

A ventriloquist, who also resembles a man, replaces the acrobat
when the latter is judged to be stupid in a stereotypically womanly

way. Her act is troubling. It practises voodoo on the inanimate, when she throws her voice into objects. Her affair with the duke is another fiasco. Fed up with women, Des Esseintes had then modulated to a young man of ambivalent appearance. This relationship lasted, unusually, several months; Huysmans eschews irony throughout his account of it.

Des Esseintes is a searcher, a hunter, but also a prey—a prey to memories of futility and to faces from the past, which haunt him like cheap songs or advertising jingles. The only drama in this novel resides in the succession and contrast of moods: a metronomic movement that all but makes him a Bergsonian automat, and by extension a laughing-stock to us headteacherly policemen. There seems to be little logic to his mood-swings. Religion is one such mood or fit, though his vainglory disqualifies him from prayer, and it is ecclesiastical paraphernalia and plainsong alone that enthral him. By a mechanical gear-change, 'une rapide volte' (p. 109), he swivels to sacrilege, and enjoys theological warfare more than steady creeds. Yet he cannot achieve blasphemy any more than prayer. Huysmans might have relished knowing that, in Péguy's wallet on his dying day, was found a cutting which detailed the chemical formula for the odour of sanctity.[9] In real time, Huysmans played obbligatos with oblature, while soft-pedalling the obligations of belief and practice. He cherry-picked. Whether in human or divine affairs, he forever tried to hijack and to personalize. He wanted to eat his wafer and have it. As Borie cuttingly puts it, Huysmans's 'tourisme religieux donne [à ses] ouvrages chrétiens l'aspect d'un Gault et Millau de la spiritualité: Chartres et Saint-Séverin, trois étoiles...'.[10] His undoubted sense of humour did not save him from conversion, but he was surely intelligent enough to realize that Pascal had got it right: it's a lottery. Perhaps the biggest joke or irony, the real hoot, about *A rebours*, though it is only just pulling itself together in the text, is that its author would go on to worship at various shrines of the established church, instead of, like Des Esseintes, officiating in his own idiosyncratic version.

Perversion is the natural activity of the existential malcontent, this more stationary Emma Bovary. 'Après les fleurs factices singeant les véritables fleurs, il voulait des fleurs naturelles imitant les fleurs fausses' (p. 118): a tongue twister as well as a mind-boggler. Whereas flowers are usually thought to comfort the sick, Des Esseintes favours sick-looking flowers, freaks. This is the humour of overdoing, of hobbies gone loco. In his research for monstrous hybrids he has a nightmare about syphilis. Before the ultimate failure, like Gide's immoralist, of his programme, he experiences many sporadic ones, as when his ambition for a hydrotherapy system is bathetically frustrated by the position of his house and the shortage of water in the village. Thus, though he enjoys some erections (exciting prospects), he suffers even more detumescences (let-downs). Like Gide's Michel again, who thinks he can break free from conventions but never learns to inhabit the state of freedom, Des Esseintes can never live in his new-found wonders; he has to keep replacing them, moving on, but on the spot.

Amid his fanciful illusions, he retains the capacity to play jokes or tricks on himself, as if an inbuilt sense of humour stopped him from ever succumbing totally to those chimeras. Listen to the way he talks about the language of smells. It is a *métaphore filée*, and thus to be regarded with scepticism and a smile, for any prolonged likenings get progressively less convincing. They become a thoroughly concerted excruciation: 'Il lui avait d'abord fallu travailler la grammaire, comprendre la syntaxe des odeurs, se bien pénétrer des règles qui les régissent, et, une fois familiarisé avec ce dialecte [...] Cet idiome des fluides' (p. 151). It is true that Des Esseintes treats everything, history or theology, and not just smells, as a language. In the section on exotic cocktails of fragrances, as sometimes elsewhere, he encounters a vicious circle: he ends up at square 1 with common-or-garden frangipani.

As for spatial as against imaginary travel exploiting the senses, Des Esseintes, like a good bourgeois consumer, mugs up England in a Baedeker before setting off, with excess baggage, for the country about which he has, anyway, very mixed feelings and to which he is hardly magnetized. (Huysmans himself never came here.) He had earlier substituted a bathhouse on a boat in the Seine, complete with rolling, for sea-voyaging. This ersatz brings to mind the eccentric eighteenth-century aristocrat, who used to take with him on his country strolls a set of screens painted with landscapes, thus providing insulation from the uncouth real.

The opinionated duke endorses the commonplaces: fog, rain, smoke. The English are haughty (*morgue* is a deadly term in French). Less chauvinistically, it might be thought that the succession of tableaux in *A rebours* has something in common with the English music hall (or, in French terms, the *café-concert*). Earlier in life, Huysmans had watched in Paris with appalled fascination the English duo, the

Hanlon Lees. He would second Baudelaire's reaction to English pantomime acts: 'C'était le vertige de l'hyperbole'.[11] Des Esseintes's list of stereotypes omits our gasbaggery, our love of rowdy, tasteless fun, and our slovenliness (the most 'Latin' of the Nordic peoples). He goes to an English restaurant in Paris, whose English customers repel him. He more or less enjoys a ponderous English meal. Usually for Huysmans, the world itself is a bad meal (as any seasoned traveller can verify, such meals can be had in that Mecca of gastronomy, France, just as easily as anywhere else). Food may stuff but never satisfy his heroes, who suffer from an alimentary Bovarysme. He gives up the cross-Channel excursion. Essentially, he is a 'voyageur immobile', and psychologically feels always 'tristis *ante* coitum'. 'A quoi bon bouger, quand on peut voyager si magnifiquement sur une chaise?' (p. 183). Perhaps he should have read the more optimistically Yankee Thoreau:

> Direct your eye inward, and you'll find
> A thousand regions in your mind
> Yet undiscovered. Travel then and be
> Expert in home-cosmography.[12]

Des Esseintes does not (half-heartedly) travel to broaden the mind: rather to narrow it. Gratefully, he sinks back into his bourgeois creature comforts.

   Much humour revolves around conformity to expectations (horrific mothers-in-law, argufying Jews). The would-be quintessential English clobber Des Esseintes dons is a comic hotchpotch, a bad copy. Like the circus clown trying to perform some intricate task and failing catastrophically, the effort is disproportionate to the result. At times, the hero all but disappears under the suffocating weight of catalogues. Des Esseintes's settling for physical stasis obviously smooths over the asperities, the nitty-grittiness, the resistance to our wishes, of real-time travel. The dandy control-freak wants everything impeccable, sinfully impeccable. Which half of Nietzsche's division of mankind fits Des Esseintes: 'A minority (minimality) who know how to make much of little, and a majority who make a little out of much'?[13] It is tempting to see resemblances between *A rebours* and Xavier de Maistre's *Voyage autour de ma chambre* (1794), which Nietzsche admired. But the earlier text is far less claustrophobic, much more openly humorous (de Maistre shares Sterne's love of digressions, theorizing and other ramblings, and sentiment liberally spread out).

Despite all the foregoing, we should not feel condescending to Des Esseintes's solution of artificial, effortless travelling, for what else do the rest of us do when we watch, from the couch potato-patch, travelogues, visit exhibitions of exotica, or indeed read books that do most of the work for us? Still, knowing how to find short cuts is a sign not only of sloth but also of intelligence. Des Esseintes goes through the motions. Even though phrased eloquently, his actions are dumb shows; he mimes real events, in creating for himself, and for any of us who stumble upon his private world, the illusion of spatial movement. Is it really armchair travelling? Does not the stress fall more on the ersatz, which like a fetishist he prefers. The ersatz is a limper form of that artifice which he worships. The use of stand-ins which saves the duke from having actually to set foot in England is not all that recherché, for all consumers buy a dream: the fetishized object grants access to what is beyond our physical reach.

His taste for perverseness takes a wilfully slummy turn when he gazes on a filthy urchin grasping a disgusting sandwich. To keep in harmony, he orders a duplicate, but in fact cannot down it. Like some pregnant women, he experiences 'une pica', a craving for inappropriate food: 'Cette immonde tartine lui fit venir l'eau à la bouche' (p. 222). In Malthusian terms, he wonders whether such wretched creatures as his cynosure should never have been born, though he salutes their survivability. This section is the nearest Des Esseintes gets to democratic sentiments, or at least level-ling ones.

Huysmans's humour lies so often in the antepositioning of adjec-tives (back-to-front again), which generates a bleak irony, e.g. the 'charitables réflexions' of the duke, which are all but genocidal. Style is paramount to his enterprise. He warms to the humour of certain writers, for instance Villiers de l'Isle Adam, for his 'bafouage d'un comique lugubre, tel qu'en ragea Swift [...] Un esprit de goguenardise singulièrement inventif et âcre' (p. 258). Though imprisoned in a lengthy, repetitive narrative himself, he yearns, like Nietzsche, for a highly quintessentialized, streamlined book, 'en quelques phrases, qui contiendraient le suc cohibé des centaines de pages toujours em-ployées à établir le milieu, à dessiner les caractères, à entasser à l'appui les observations et les menus faits' (p. 264).[14] He wants, in effect, a purified Zola, downsized to a set of haikus, and in addition reserved for a tiny elite.

Let down conclusively by his insides (that accursed Nature), Des Esseintes falls prey to multiple hallucinations (this time not of his own fabrication) and nightmares. In the mirror, he does not recognize himself, which shocks him even more than his 'dyspepsie nerveuse' (p. 267). A doctor (real hermits cannot summon them) prescribes a nutritious suppository (peptone). This is the final instance of his arseways-round philosophy of existence: eating via the fundament, from where the remains of eating more usually emerge. The duke makes a nicely judged or unconscious pun on his 'étrange palais' (p. 279), for lavatories are known as thrones. Everything is closing in: emaciated plainsong, miniaturized novels, food reduced to the bare minimum. He sees this as his last gesture against Nature, for to him orally swallowing a meal is vulgar. But he is defeated (his whole programme has been self-defeating): his doctor orders him back to something like normalcy in Paris. Society, and Nature, win. In retaliation, he utters anathemas on the bourgeoisie, the nobility, the clergy, and the United States. One of the richest, if unwitting, jokes in *A rebours* can be found in its hero's flight from his 'Americanized' times. For what is more stereotypically American than a (relatively) rich man's folly, an attempt to elaborate a one-seat utopia? The difference, of course, is that with precious little of an aristocratic tradition to exacerbate, an American writer wanting to withdraw from the materialistic hurly-burly of his day pens a *Walden* (back to nature), whereas *A rebours* kicks against Nature.

A decade after *A rebours*, the Lumière brothers filmed a gardener accidentally turning a water-hose on himself: 'L'Arroseur arrosé'. The biter bit, hoist by one's own petard, shooting oneself in the foot; the would-be captain of his fate becomes the architect of his own downfall. This is poetic justice, or in the more pompous French formulation, 'la justice immanente'. The ironical noble suffers the irony of backfiring. It is true, all the same, that, while his native neuroticism debilitates his physique, it energizes his psyche. He is a backward-turned neophiliac. Threshing about in his self-contradictions, Des Esseintes thinks, perhaps inevitably, of forcing himself into religious faith, but, finding mercantilism even in the sacraments—not all perversions are to his taste—he makes a joke about the substitution of potato-flour for wheat in the host: 'Dieu se [refuse] à descendre dans la fécule' (p. 289). He writes a wonderful, no-escape sentence where the first word kills the succeeding ones:

'L'impossible croyance en une vie future serait seule apaisante' (p. 293). His penultimate statement is diametrically opposed to Valéry's upbeat line in 'Le Cimetière marin' ('Le vent se lève [...] Il faut tenter de vivre'): 'Ah! Le courage me fait défaut et le cœur me lève!' (p. 294). His angst is admittedly well heeled, but no less acute for that. Huysmans has the saving grace of avoiding pathos, of refusing to bring out the sobbing violins.

A rebours, part narrative, part encyclopaedia, now lyrical, now mordant, is a hybrid text, like the concocted flowers it celebrates at one point. Often Des Esseintes seems akin to the crazy scientist, alchemist, or breeder unable to sort the geep from the shoats. He had planned to fabricate an artificial paradise, a rival to the Judaeo-Christian one, but the great drawback (or elephant's foreskin) of utopias is repetition and boredom. The constant search for newness is itself repetitive and finally unsatisfying. The preponderance of the imperfect tense keeps him running, or more aristocratically, sauntering on the spot. He is forever picky, without in any proper sense making a choice; he is the least existentialist of men, except as regards his undoubted stoicism. He is a big talker and a small doer. To that extent, he belongs to the ancient comic tradition of the *miles gloriosus*, the braggart non-combatant. For Borie, 'Des Esseintes sème à tous vents les graines du crime et ne récolte rien, sinon un comique d'une espèce étrange, douteuse, déconcertante—le comique du diable qui ne peut pas, du diable qui rate son coup'.[15] Does Des Esseintes show any signs of finding himself ridiculous? Or is the (unintended?) humour of *A rebours* dependent on his blissful ignorance of how risible he appears to others? At the same time, each of us feels he/she is different. From whom? From what?

Sac au dos, En ménage, and La Retraite de Monsieur Bougran

Sac au dos

And now for something nearly completely different. After the other-worldly, fancy-dressed *A rebours*, *Sac au dos* reveals Huysmans with his trousers round his ankles, down-to-earth (closet). This story proves how a sense of humour can preserve sanity, as well as breed mad inventiveness. It bares the underside or backside of the Franco-Prussian

War. *Sac au dos* is the only fictional text Huysmans wrote in the first person, mainly because he was already and invariably present in all the others he composed. The squaddy's name, Eugène Lejantel, is mentioned once only. Huysmans's own six weeks in uniform were farcical themselves, and so he had to invent little.

Sac au dos narrates a kind of non-event, not so much a phoney war as a SNAFU. Organizational mismanagement, and the common soldiers' instinctive skiving and malingering, give birth to an essentially privatized view of war. Not a historical view: there is no *revanchard* element, neither hatred of the enemy, nor an exalted hymning of defeated compatriots. Any talk of battles is only at second hand, as in classical French tragedy, where violence happens offstage. *Sac au dos* is a reportage of reports. The soldiers around the hero put up with the minor horrors. He and they stay sane, via their escape-routes—doing a bunk, sex, booze, and the occasional blow-out—amid the general lunacy of military life. They feel indignation, but little self-pity, as they revert to schoolboy japes and horseplay. *Sac au dos* is much jauntier in tone and outlook than any other text by Huysmans. Morale (which has precious little to do with morals, seen as respectability) is crucial to armies, and humour (that morale-booster) essential to the feat of surviving military service.

The narrator laughs at himself as much as at the army: he howls, like Flaubert shaving, when he looks in the mirror. He can see the farcical side of pain itself, when his suffering body undergoes a seesaw ride, strapped to one side of a mule, with a wounded soldier strapped to the other. He notes sardonically the military doctors robotically prescribing liquorice tisane for any illness or wound. It is a laxative, which is the last thing the hero needs, for colic plagues him throughout his brief service. He has an inner collapse (of the bowels) amid the national debacle. Thus, as Borie suggests, he does not need a 'good' wound to spare him active duty; his dysentery suffices.[16] Céline's *Mort à credit* provides its protagonist, similarly, with diarrhoea and vomiting as a bolt-hole when reality presses too hard. When Huysmans's hero eventually gets back to civilian life and bachelordom with its petty miseries but compensatory pleasures, he is immensely grateful for the privacy in which to crap, after the uncomfortable promiscuity of army camp.

There is strong irony in his regiment's name, the Garde Nationale Mobile, for all he sees of war is repeated and pointless peregrinations. These, however, are shunted mechanically; no individual will is engaged. The most active event, though hardly voluntaristic, is evacuation (of a position or of the bowels). In this respect, *Sac au dos* rejoins *A rebours*, as a text of mini-nauseas. And both terminate at the end of the body (strange that Des Esseintes does not relish Rabelais): dysentery and suppositories. Nature wins in the last resort, but far more rewardingly for the protagonist of *Sac au dos* than that of *A rebours*. *Sac au dos* appeared in *Les Soirées de Médan* (stories by Zola, Céard, Hennique, Maupassant, and Alexis), for which the group caressed the title *L'Invasion comique*, not finally taken up on allegedly patriotic grounds. Huysmans himself at one stage projected a collection of sardonic short stories entitled *Joyeusetés navrantes* (Distressing Delights), and was well known in company for his love of grimly humorous anecdotes. He is often pigeonholed as a dedicated pessimist, at home with Schopenhauer. Pessimists not uncommonly have a profound sense of humour, as Freud saluted in Lichtenberg.

En ménage

When the flaccid protagonist (or agonist) of *En ménage*, André, discovers, in a classic French-farce scenario, a man in bed with his wife, Huysmans directs the largely silent and non-violent scene with deadpan humour, or perhaps unconscious humour, which is equally poker-faced. Subsequently, André and his painter friend Cyprien pursue an aesthetic ethic of distaste for what life has to offer; they show a remarkable lack of fun or humour in their disquisitions. Huysmans appears to take them seriously, but must have intended that readers find their humourlessness amusing. He denies them his own gift of an unkillable and sustaining sense of humour. They need to be more Groucho and less grouchy; they are grumpy young men. *A rebours*, too, flourishes umpteen biliously purple passages. Purple connotes not only ecclesiastical finery, but also the apoplexy of fury. Ritual whining, like kneejerk optimism, is inherently comic.

En ménage, typical in this of the bulk of Huysmans's writings, is weak on transitions, except in the mechanical form of barely motivated mood-swings. The narrative is too clotted to be dynamic; it is more like a seesaw banging up and down between lethargy and rage. In Cyprien's case, the very idea of a wannabe rebel artist hankering for slipperdom is comic. Both he and André settle for a sedated life. As in *A rebours*, Huysmans operates largely by lists, seeking to conjugate a scene or atmosphere. Both heroes, too, love to classify, exactly like the pen-pushing clerks they mercilessly mock. There are elements of farce after the founding scene, for instance André contortedly smuggling his mistress Jeanne past his hawk-eyed concierge. As so often, Huysmans excels at strained scenes, friction, people rubbing each other up the wrong way ('à rebrousse-poil', a close relative of 'à rebours').

Borie speaks of 'cette politique du pire qui s'appelle l'humour'.[17] This worst-case scenario where Huysmans feels most at home calls Céline to mind. Vallès lampoons such *misérabilisme* when he has Jacques Vingtras kick himself vigorously up the arse for revelling in woe when writing a story. Jacques takes the piss out of the distended bladder of his self-absorption. The fact remains that Huysmans makes much literary capital out of his various characters' obsession with syphilization and its discontents. *Misérabilisme* can lead to nausea, a bellyful, about which the two friends of *En ménage* bellyache, like standard French concierges. Perhaps trying, unavailingly, to keep humour at bay in this novel derives from the laughable dread of allowing a ray of hope into the gloom, in case it should impair the narrative's demonstration of a mad, bad, sad world.

La Retraite de Monsieur Bougran

La Retraite de Monsieur Bougran features a simulated utopia, like *A rebours*, but on a much more prosaic level, though with even more room for thoroughgoing self-delusion.[18] It is perhaps the most bleakly comic take on bachelordom in Huysmans's *œuvre*. Bougran, a lifelong civil servant like Huysmans himself, has been so totally taken over by his bureaucratic scrivening that, when downloaded at age 50, he feels completely at sea as to what to do with himself. Eventually, he invents a solution by duplicating his old office in his flat, and employing a former colleague to act as his clerk. There, Bougran writes letters to himself, which he industriously works on and answers, on archetypal administrative conundrums. He also drafts a letter to the supreme instance, pleading his case for unfair dismissal. When he dies suddenly, this draft remains on his desk. In the guise of his superior, he has turned down his own request. This tale is a perfect example of professional deformation (one of Bergson's key comic categories), but it speaks eloquently to anyone unhappy in forced retirement.

This story stayed unpublished in Huysmans's lifetime, and was saved from the fire decreed by the author only by his secretary's unauthorized initiative. Perhaps Huysmans found it too near the knuckle. As so often, in it he keeps his face straight. As always, he marries the subject, but with probably considerable mental reservations. There is clearly nothing exemplary about the wretched protagonist, and so the inward slant on his suffering and his ultimate self-defeating choice are surely comic, while remaining touching in their controlled pathos. I think of Empson's line: 'And learn a style from a despair'.[19]

André Breton wrongly credited Huysmans, in his *Anthologie de l'humour noir*, with the inauguration of black humour, for somewhat earlier Homer had displayed the merrily sadistic gods cackling 'inextinguishably' at a cripple. Breton grants an ungrudging but typically constipated eulogy, when he cites the 'pincée d'humour noir', with which I launched this essay, as an indispensable condiment for Huysmans's mental appetite. Breton's view of *En ménage* is that Huysmans relies on us readers to locate and highlight what he as author leaves in a kind of limbo or holding position. Rarely capable of humour in his own writings, Breton manages to finger something important about Huysmans's comic strategy, which he describes as 'la manière atterrante-exaltante de l'écrivain'.[20] Huysmans energizes misery. Breton is again perceptive when discussing Huysmans's style:

Merveilleusement refondu en vue de la communicabilité nerveuse de ses sensations, [il] est le produit du détournement de plusieurs vocabulaires, dont la combinaison déchaîne à elle seule le rire spasmodique, alors même que les circonstances de l'intrigue le justifient le moins.[21]

To put it differently, Huysmans inveigles us to laugh, *against the grain* of his texture.

Going back-to-front easily entails exaggeration, for how else could Huysmans underscore the validity of his counter-creation? We will later see Vallès and Céline expertly practising hyperbole; in the field of distaste and way-out taste, Huysmans is a born escalater. The misery-guts can be the life and soul of the party. As Zola spotted, 'Il y a dans vos outrances un comique spécial que personne n'a'.[22] Even when lauding a painting or other product, he writes to outdo the original.

It is fortunate that Huysmans never perpetrated a theory of humour. Instead, he embodied his idiosyncratic humour in both his Naturalist and his Decadent texts. Black or sick humour is laughter against the grain. The whole idea of reversal is naturally comical. We can see Des Esseintes as mocking himself out of his own mouth, while remaining po-faced, in the proper, discreet, dandiacal tradition. This is the humour of misplaced solemnity. Perhaps the deepest humour of *A rebours* lies in its overall strategy of disconcerting the reader, wrongfooting us. We must set this possibility against the other one, that, like Rousseau, Des Esseintes does not realize often enough how funny he strikes others as being. What humour there is in Huysmans is of the delayed-action, slow-burn variety. And why not? We do not need, always, to consume humour on the spot, as Sartre said of books, like bananas.[23] On screen, slow-motion often excites laughter, so there is little explosive surprise there, as certain theories of humour insist is necessary. A whole text, or section of it, can be funnier *in toto*, *after all*, than any individual segment. There must be in all this some link with that 'esprit de l'escalier' which is most people's contribution to wit: thinking of a rejoinder or a joke when the moment has passed. Unlike Bergson, I do not believe that laughter is principally mocking or socially corrective. The best humour preserves the butt's humanity, while not sparing his/her comic defects.

I hope I have shown that a distinctive and variegated humour, easier to sniff out than to spell out, is more than that 'pinch of seasoning' in Huysmans's offered repast. It is an integral part of his largely lugubrious feast. Not 'une pincée': he is 'un pince-sans-rire'. Treating Des Esseintes, as I have done, humorously does not detract from his significance. He is not a cardboard cut-out figure, and he remains tough enough in his obstinacies to withstand rough handling. After all, he is each of us, writ large, or rather taken to extremes. We share his self-preference; we have our version of his idiosyncratic manias. But God help us (he won't) if we also experience his aloneness. *A rebours* was nearly entitled *Seul*. Des Esseintes is part of that splendid cliché, life's rich tapestry. As Montaigne said of a Siamese twin, 'there is nothing that is contrary to nature'[24]—even a dedicated opponent of it. Perhaps all of nature, and not just infant sexuality, is that 'polymorphous perverse' discovered by Freud.

In all his writings, Huysmans stuck to himself, like Velcro or certain envelopes; it was what he excelled at. Sartre's Roquentin does the equivalent. *A rebours* and *La Nausée* are monocular, monologic.

I am barely interested in the post-conversion Huysmans. All of us go to hell in our own way. With no regret, I am not cut out to accompany him towards or into monasteries, and have concentrated mainly on his imagined, lay, private place of retreat in *A rebours*. Always we have to offset his credulity about certain tenets of (generally wayward) Catholic faith against his undoubted love of mystification (cf. the non-believer Diderot), which of course plays on the credulity of others. A great admirer of the later Huysmans, Michel Tournier, salutes and would like to annex his 'naturalisme mystique', but warms even more to his humour: 'Il fait dans la noirceur, il broie du noir. Mais dans *Là-bas*, on rit. Il se rend compte qu'il écrit des énormités qui font rire, et j'espère que tous mes livres font rire'.[25]

On the other hand, the relentlessly witty Oscar Wilde, in his *Picture of Dorian Gray* (1891), though it is overburdened with brittle repartee, makes room for no humour. Wilde seems not to have responded to the active agency of humour in Huysmans's work. Dorian Gray scoops the pataphysical concept of 'anticipatory plagiarism' when he observes that 'the whole book [ostensibly *A rebours*] seemed to contain the story of his own life, written before he had lived it'.[26] Wilde, who said that he always sought a dose of poison in his imaginings, had read *A rebours* on his honeymoon. A major difference between the Huysmans and the Wilde texts is that Des Esseintes does not have a conscience to kill off, even though his exhaustive, experimental ordeal could be seen as a protracted if uncompleted suicide. A man so alienated from other humans has no motive for atonement. Wilde's only true perversity lies in his often formulaic upturning of propositions in dialogue, going against the grain, whereas very little of *A rebours* relies on dialogue. Des Esseintes talks almost entirely to himself. In Huysmans's novel, the supernatural is conspicuous by its absence till near the end, when it is not exactly invited in. It is active throughout the Gothic, melodramatic *Picture of Dorian Gray*, which is altogether a more ludicrous fiction than *A rebours*. It seems as if it is mainly Huysmans's style that bewitches Dorian Gray: 'That curious jewelled style, vivid and obscure at once, full of *argot* and of archaisms, of technical expressions and of elaborate paraphrases' (p. 125). Though bowled over by *A rebours*, Dorian Gray confesses to Lord Henry Wotton: 'I didn't say I liked it, Henry. I said it fascinated me. There is a great difference' (ibid.). How many readers of *A rebours* have felt the same? All in all, Dorian Gray is far more sociable, sinful, and criminal than Des Esseintes, who has little of the Faustian, for he gives up nothing in exchange for no bargain, whereas Dorian sells his soul. Perhaps the two writers meet most closely in Des Esseintes's and Wilde's wish to lead a life as a work of art, for that was where Wilde claimed to put his genius.[27]

4
A Little Bird Tells Us: Parrots in Flaubert, Queneau, Beckett (and *Tutti Quanti*)

Du temps que les bêtes parlaient
La Fontaine

This will be, there is no way of stopping it, a very talkative essay. It conducts a cross-talk act between an animal (noted for its cross talk, its tetchiness) and humans. The plagiaristic, incestuous nature of humour leads naturally to psittacism. In addition, I have always been struck by the cohabitation, the klang-effect, prevalent in French culture. Its strong consciousness of traditions, networks, schools of thought/writing, repetition, and reciprocal feeding leads to a kind of psittacism, sometimes knowing, sometimes semi-conscious.

Let's start with words and their peregrinations. According to Robert, *perroquet* derives from *paroquet* (1395). The word *papegai* (twelfth century) was borrowed from Provençal *papagai*, adapted from the Arabic *babaghâ*. On the English side, the *OED* says that *parrot* (the bird is of the genus *Psittaciformes*) comes probably from the obsolete or dialectal French *perrot*, diminutive of Pierre. The smaller *parakeet* (*perruche*) stems from the Old French *paroquet* (see above) (Italian *parrocchetto*, Spanish *periquito* or *perico*, which is the familiar form of Pedro (Pierre)).

The archetypal French parrot is christened Jacquot, which is also the name of a West African parrot, and either a diminutive of Jacques, or an onomatopoeic rendering of its natural cry. Thus the French bird likes reminding us of its own name. Historically, Jacques is either a peasant taking part in a *jacquerie* or uprising, or just anybody: Jacques

Bonhomme. 'Jouer à Jacques a dit' is to play Simon Says (follow the leader is what parrots do). In French slang, *jacques/jacquot* covers a motley bag of meanings: burglar's jemmy, penis, dildo, safe/peter (and *peter* is both penis and saltpetre), calf of leg, taximeter, clock. In other words, sexuality, explosive uproar, metronomic repetition. 'Faire le jacques' is to act the goat, and Maître Jacques is a jack-of-all-trades. A multivalent creature, this parrot.

In slang, *perroquet* houses: a flashily dressed person, or popinjay; a mast (by analogy with the perch); pastis with mint syrup (Flaubert reported a parrot getting high on spirits); a sniper; a sail; and bread-and-wine ('soupe au perroquet'). How all these words in the foregoing interrelate, interosculate, contaminate, and ape each other. A *poll* is a tame parrot (a *rara avis*), and a *poll parrot* is a user of clichéd phrases. 'Polly' is a conventional parrot name, altered from Moll, a familiar form of Mary. In Australian argot, a *pollie* is a politician, probably the greatest fount of parrot-talk or pap(egai). So altogether 'Pretty Polly' ('Bonjour Jacquot!') is a pretty kettle of fish.

Psitt (English *Psst*), a brief whistle to attract attention, reminds us that psittacosis is a catching disease. This chapter looks at our psittacism, a word which, according to the *OED*, Leibniz was the first to use, in its French form, *psittacisme*, in his *Nouveaux Essais sur l'entendement humain*. Why do parrots crop up so often, across cultures and epochs? Why do writers and owners promote this obstreperous creature, give it star billing, even if in a mere walk-on, or perch-on, part? Is it one of the multitudinous avatars of masochism, in which humans reveal resurfacing doubts about whether they are fully or actually human ('L'homme est à inventer chaque jour',[1] thought Sartre), and about the reliability of one of humankind's allegedly distinguishing features, namely the power of speech? The most articulate of us can on occasion 'talk like poor Poll', as David Garrick said in his epitaph for Oliver Goldsmith.

In real time, the common parrot remains an exotic bird. Not native to Europe, parrots are immigrants imported to fulfil functions we want to offload. They naturally depend on traders or seafarers to transport them and, on occasion, corrupt them. The parrot is never fully domesticated. Yet it seems so close. It sits up, like a person. It puts food in its beak with its 'hand'. 'Because manipulation looks so human, it always charms us, even if the animal is eating from its nose. This is what makes an elephant so attractive'.[2] It visibly suffers. It can mutilate itself by plucking out feathers when distressed, just as we tear our hair, or worse. Parrots notoriously echo some of what they hear. Owners strive to teach them by much rote learning, and thus egg them on to recidivism. As the naturalist Buffon noted, 'un de ces perroquets de Guinée, endoctriné en route par un vieux matelot, avait pris sa voix et sa toux, mais si parfaitement qu'on pouvait s'y méprendre'.[3] Parrots can lead us up the garden path.

The parrot is a cliché. We have stock responses to its conditioned reflexes. Like clichés, however, it can be ambivalent. Parrots are variously inane repeaters, gorgeous to behold, or inventive talkers. They are active and passive. Even if echoic, their speech can be satiric, as if they had mulled over what we say and remain unimpressed. In John Skelton's poem 'Speke parrot', the bird is the vehicle for mockery, but is itself prone to babble idiotically. Parrots can be used, like allegory, to wrongfoot censorship. They can show us up by linguistic virtuosity, pollyglottery, as well as being used as a model for the more mechanical varieties of language teaching and learning.[4] As it is exotic, the parrot can give us a telling slant, like eighteenth-century aliens, on our home affairs.

Why have several such creative/destructive, humorous, thought-full, critical minds as Flaubert, Queneau, Beckett (not forgetting *tutti quanti*) been magnetized to this multivalent bird? None of them, in their dramatic use of parrots, refers nakedly across to the others. Unlike people of my ilk, they do not merely parrot each other. In each case, the bird has occurred to and fascinated the writer. To that extent, it rules the roost; it hogs the limelight.

How central is psittacism to French culture (which is not unique in this respect, despite French umbilicism)? Consider dictation, oral recitation, rote learning in schools; the stress on tradition (however divided into groups) in all walks of life, so that, as though after eating radishes, history were ever repeating itself; the will at least to maintain family bonds at the price of making children chips off the old blockheads; the cult of cultural allusions and passwords; the rhetorical pomposity of public discourse. But then: the bolshiness (even parrots subscribe to the anarchist slogan 'Ni Dieu ni maître'). Poised on the jet of their (C)artesian wells, the French foist stupidity (*bêtise, bête*) on to hapless animals (whereas English favours stupor). This is animalism: piling on to innocent beasts the sins of humans, scapegoating them. 'Chacun a son chien', as Diderot observed in

Jacques le fataliste (note the hero's name).[5] Talking animals is a cliché, but a fantastic one.

Beyond the hiccoughing Hexagon and perfidious Albion, parrots perform frequently in universal jokelore. Jokes pitting humans and animals against each other follow a both-ways process, or, as some philosophers would say, a dialectic. In folk tales all over the world, parrots are commonly drafted in as stand-ins for subversives, especially children, who have comparable dirty habits. The birds talk coarsely but pointedly. As such, they recall ventriloquists' dummies, similarly unbridled and bent on getting away with murder. (Queneau expressed the wish to be a ventriloquist, but surely many novelists and playwrights share and practise this urge.) The context and the insinuation are often, though not invariably, sexual. In one folk tale, 'The Parrot pretends to be God'.[6] Versatile in all things, the parrot can be other-worldly, or human-all-too-human.

Flaubert and Loulou: *Un Cœur simple*

Much critical psittacism has spilled its seed, like Dorothy Parker's bird Onan (who like his anagraph Anon had his reasons for being secretive) on Flaubert's parrot. Indeed a whole book bears that title, in which Julian barnstorms his way subtly through Flaubert's work and life. Parrots and Flaubert, as many before and some since Julian Barnes have noted, like love and marriage go together like a horse and carriage. I will yomp on, unabashed.

Flaubert kept a newpaper cutting which reported a solitary man's obsessive love for his parrot. Its only talent, taught it by its owner, was to repeat a hundred times a day the name of his former beloved. Henri K. was shattered by its death, and gradually came to believe he was it: squawking, walking lopsidedly and perching in a tree. Unfairly, his family lured this harmless loon down with a large birdcage, then had him locked up in an asylum.[7]

Lest we robotically link parrots and inanity, remember Spinoza's (a favourite of Flaubert's) 'perseverance in being' (*Ethics*, Pt. III. prop. VII). Among other things, *Trois Contes* were for Flaubert a relief from his exhausting labours on *Bouvard et Pécuchet*, whose heroes, those excitable wet blankets, likewise persevere against all odds. Other black-sheep kin of Loulou are Rodolphe, Léon, and that shambling parrot,

Homais. And Emma herself on numerous occasions: she tries to repeat existentially what she has read on the printed page. Rodolphe is a rather more sophisticated parrot, who at least knows that he is reciting the predetermined script of love. Only Charles, young Justin, and the servant Catherine, in their dumbness, do not misuse or profiteer from language. At the Comices Agricoles, we are treated to a three-level psittacism: animal, oratorical, and the spiel of the seducer Rodolphe.

As regards *Un Cœur simple*, for his documentation and as a spur to creation, Flaubert obtained a stuffed parrot, which he installed on his writing-desk (a raven would not have done). 'Il y reste à poste fixe. Sa vue commence même à m'embêter. Mais je le garde, pour m'emplir la cervelle de l'idée perroquet.'[8] A bird packed with lifelessness gets on the wick of the writer trying to fill his head with parrothood: necrological bestialism hovers. He expects the dumb creature to be a spokesperson for its genus and, by ricochet, to comment on humankind.[9] Flaubert was having a rest from the Sisyphean exertions of *Bouvard et Pécuchet* and its fixation on *bêtise* when he wrote *Un Cœur simple*, in which a kind of inoffensive stupidity is elevated to poignant and heroinic status.

The principal artistic lesson of this tale is to intimate that, as appearances can be deceptive (Félicité *looks like* an automat), realism cannot be the be-all and end-all of literary representation. Appearances, of people as of things, are described economically and confidently, but there is a running suggestion, made overt by the end, that there is more to Félicité than meets the lazy eye. She has reserves of underused love, for her one man let her down brutally, and the children she adores move away. She remains a peasant: a tough bargainer who stands no nonsense in practical dealings. She knows how to deal with animals. Taking her employer's daughter Virginie to catechism-class, Félicité sees a stained-glass window on which the Holy Spirit hovers over the Virgin Mary. This is an artful plant, which will flourish at the finale. Similarly, the horses in the sky—in fact hoisted on cranes—that she witnesses at Honfleur. Later in the story, when Virginie dies, Félicité half-expects her corpse to open its eyes: 'Pour de pareilles âmes le surnaturel est tout simple' (p. 64). She brings religion into a close relation with her limited experience; she individualizes the collective and institutionalized. As it is too hard for her to imagine the complex Holy Spirit (bird, fire, breath), she pictures him everywhere, like Spinoza's pantheistic God. Dogmas escape her, and she them. Flaubert was well versed in the havoc engendered by theological disquisition, as he illustrates at great length in *La Tentation de Saint Antoine* and *Bouvard et Pécuchet*. Félicité, however, does pick up the catechism by heart (for she has one, like a live parrot) through frequent reiteration. Like Flaubert himself, she has the gift of projection, of imaginative transmigration: via Virginie, she gets the first communion she never had.

The parrot Loulou arrives, as a parting gift from a neighbour. Because of her nephew Victor's seafaring, Félicité has always associated this bird with the Americas, his regular run. This one has annoying, prototypically parrotish habits: scattering its crap, tearing out its feathers, spilling water. Its few refrains, taught it by its owner, show that it can only repeat, at second-hand. Loulou is a small-scale cliché expert. At least its name distinguishes it from the rest of its tribe, for the *doxa* holds that 'tous les perroquets s'appellent Jacquot' (p. 76). It is sulkily uncooperative, refusing to perform when looked at; it does not fancy turning it on for strangers, that is: it does not relish being laughed at, for Félicité takes it totally seriously. On the other hand, and presciently, it laughs mockingly at Bourais (later rightfully shamed by the local community), forcing him to slink past. Though the butcher's boy teaches it a few curse-words, Loulou is not the stereotypical foul-beaked bird (as, for example, in Beckett). With an unthreatening audience, and given the freedom of the house, Loulou waddles upstairs and downstairs, entertainingly. Once it flies off, then reappears from nowhere back to the anxiously hunting Félicité.

When she goes deaf, the sole sound she can still hear is that of Loulou. Not that the creature tells her anything spiritually heartening. It simply harps on the three phrases she has taught it, and further echoes the most common-or-garden noises it has picked up: 'Le tictac du tournebroche, l'appel aigu d'un vendeur de poisson, la scie du monsieur qui logeait en face' (p. 81). This last noise recalls Binet's lathe in *Madame Bovary*, which melds the shrill, the reassuring, and the maddening; it reinforces Emma's vertigo when she is feeling suicidal. A *scie* is also an infuriating catchphrase, at which parrots are past masters. In addition to her pet's cosily familiar sounds, Félicité can hear imaginary voices in her head, which prepare for her climactic vision. Meanwhile, despite Loulou's tiny clawful of phrases, the pair pursue a gibbering dialogue. Loulou is a doggedly loyal companion to the doggedly faithful servant. Loulou is in fact a child, or a lover.[10] It climbs all over her body. If Flaubert specializes in mismatched couples: Frédéric/Deslauriers, Emma/Charles, or Rodolphe or Léon, then, in *Un Cœur simple* as in *Bouvard et Pécuchet,* he pairs rightly. Each partner complements the other, as in the Platonic myth of the sundered halves of the original androgyne, who find each other to rediscover wholeness. Félicité is 'bestial', Loulou 'human'.

In a note on parrots, Flaubert wrote: 'Les mâles paraissent les femmes et les femelles les hommes'.[11] He was always much taken with the idea of the interchangeability of genders. Which sex is Loulou? The name could obviously be a pet form of Louis or Louise. Flaubert leaves the poser up in the air. Moreover, the very name 'Loulou' embodies repetition: another *scie*. When Loulou dies, it is still alive for her who has died to herself, like the modest, rough-and-ready saint she is. Though this has little to do with material possessiveness, she makes a fetish of the stuffed bird. How well Flaubert understands the compulsion to animate and venerate the ersatz. Her room, he says, is a cross between a reliquary and a bazaar; her emotional world (and ours?) is a pell-mell or *capharnaüm*. Always robotic to some degree, she now moves in 'une torpeur de somnambule' (p. 89).

At Mass, she overlays the Holy Ghost on the parrot. This naive and sentimental Catholicism/catholicity is backed up by an *image d'Épinal* (those unkillable clichés), where the Holy Ghost, normally depicted as a dove, looks to her the spitting image of Loulou. An interaction has taken place. The parrot is sanctified and the Holy Spirit made more user-friendly. As if on Judgement Day, the bird's enemy Bourais dies when his shady doings are made public; Loulou's earlier scoffing at him had been instinctively correct. Félicité prays on her knees before her moth-eaten idol. Her memento has become a memento mori, for Loulou has scooped her by dying first. Or is all this reverence debased Catholic worshipping of images? Flaubert has it both ways: the tale is absurd, and moving. In making a stuffed bird and the Holy Ghost (who also enjoys the gift of tongues) criss-crossable, Flaubert's structural spoonerism leaves open to doubt whether he is exalting nature or degrading the Paraclete. Though Loulou is worm-eaten, this does not matter any more to Félicité than the rotting corpses of saints to believers. As Flaubert strangely puts it, the extinct Loulou is not 'un cadavre' (p. 97). In the long line of Flaubert's misreaders, unlike Emma, Félicité is not spoiled but saved, possibly because her error is triggered by an image rather than a text. In this respect, the plastic arts are less corrupting than the written word.

The finale is a grand parade. The organ swells. The so often constipated Flaubert lets rip. At the apotheosis, he grants his blind, deaf, gammy peasant crone, like Emma Bovary, 'une sensualité mystique', and decks her dying in stirring similes: 'Comme une fontaine qui s'épuise, comme un écho disparaît' (p. 104). She associates the parrot always with the exotic (the tropics), and now with the supernatural (the Holy Ghost). As she is blind, she is left not with sight but a vision: 'Elle crut voir, dans les cieux entr'ouverts, un perroquet gigantesque, planant au-dessus de sa tête' (p. 104). It ascends no doubt to what has been called 'parrotdise'. Unusually for Flaubert, there are no puns in *Un Cœur simple*, except those I have smuggled in, but parakeet and Paraclete (in French, *Paraclet/perroquet* is also an *à peu-près*) hover in tandem over the text.[12] In its avatar as the Holy Spirit, the parrot transports the dying Félicité to heaven, as she deserves. In the cold light of day, the tamed, terminally stuffed, and flea-bitten Loulou no longer flies any more than its earth-bound owner. But the imagination, however commonplace in its appropriation of icons, and the power of love and faith, uplift both owner and pet. The oldest human dream has been that of flying.

An old debate is whether 'Félicité' is a 'significant name', a *Redende Name* or *arma cantantia*. If so, can she truly be called happy, or fortunate? She has led a preponderantly wretched life by our privileged standards. Is the name, then, an ironic misnomer? If so, what of her apotheosis, where, however deluded in her vision, she clearly feels she is on cloud lucky seven? To adopt Camus's version of the Sisyphus myth, 'il faut imaginer Félicité heureuse'.

Among his plans for *Un Cœur simple*, Flaubert jotted: 'Les perroquets sont des singes ailés'.[13] 'To take off' means to mimic as well as to leave the clogging ground. As a boy, Flaubert practised physical empathy, or self-projection into another's hide. Given his recurrent epilepsy, this was a dangerous game and, when it lampooned hapless people, a callous one:

Mon père, à la fin, m'avait défendu d'imiter certaines gens (persuadé que j'en devais beaucoup souffrir, ce qui était vrai quoique je le niasse), entre autres un mendiant épileptique que j'avais un jour rencontré au bord de la mer. [...] C'était superbe. Il est certain que quand je rendais ce drôle j'étais dans sa peau. On ne pouvait rien voir de plus hideux que moi à ce moment-là. Comprends-tu la satisfaction que j'en éprouvais? Je suis sûr que non.[14]

This black comedy predated his own epileptic fit; perhaps he would not have crowed so much later on. In a subsequent letter to Louise Colet, he exclaimed: 'Or nous sommes tous plus ou moins aigles ou serins, perroquets ou vautours', in which he sets up polarities between domesticated pets and free raptors.

Mimicry is reduplication. At a Trouville hotel, Flaubert reported this: 'Un perroquet répète du matin au soir: "As-tu déjeuné, Jako?" ou bien: "Cocu, mon petit coco." ' On top of all the other hostelry noises, 'et toujours le perroquet! Il siffle en ce moment: "J'ai du bon tabac!" '[15] (The American mockingbird, tellingly named *Mimus polyglottos*, joins the long list of Yankee and Southern humorists. They take off other birds, much to the bewilderment of ornithologists.) There is nothing intrinsically wrong with mimicry. It can be a powerful comic, and even political, weapon, in that impersonation can belittle the undeservedly great, by exaggerating their features, voice, tics, gait. 'Taking someone off', 'having someone off to a T' probably always have comic intent. As well as attack, mimicry can be self-protective colouring, as so often in the animal world with its multiple camouflages. But, as Robert Louis Stevenson put it, we are all 'sedulous apes'.[16] Mme Verdurin in Proust can only feign genuine emotions, and lives up to the misogynistic aside in *Les Plaisirs et les jours*: 'Les femmes, loin d'être les oracles des modes de l'esprit, en sont plutôt les perroquets attardés'.[17] It is true, however, that a male, Cottard, mistiming all his interventions in society *conversazioni*, is as intrusive as a squawking parrot.

Scientific or domestic attempts to teach monkeys or parrots to speak entail training them to ape people, rather like God creating Man in His own image. Thus mimicry can be voluntary or induced. As such, it has evident links with plagiarism, and indeed, in the metaphors we live by, such bandwagoning is commonly called parroting. (The aptly named Henry Parrot (*fl.* 1600–26) was much skitted for his echoing of other writers.) In defence of the birds, I might add that parrots have been defined as the only creatures with the power of speech that are content to repeat what they hear without exaggerating it.

In Jules Vallès's *L'Enfant*, the schoolboy hero Jacques (that name again), thoroughly drilled in the imitation of classical writers by the pedagogical practices of his day, composes under instruction a poem in

Latin on a dead parrot. (The pre-existent text which Jacques recycles for this mechanical exercise is probably Ovid's poem about Psittacus, Corinna's much-lamented pet.) In this way, pupils in nineteenth-century *lycées* were schooled into being performing parrots.

'Bien écrire le *médiocre*': thus Flaubert once expressed his ambition.[18] And so the downmarket shift from dove to parrot. Knowing her place, Félicité adheres to the static hierarchy, but, like anyone dwelt on in loving detail, she ends up exceptional if not exemplary. By his recourse to free indirect speech, Flaubert is able to have his cakes and scoff them. He seems to be sliding into his characters' innermost thoughts, yet retains an implicit irony, a mocking edge to such self-translation. There is indeed a good deal of slippage in Flaubert's prose, no doubt resulting from his trying to be detached or impersonal while seething with emotions of love or hate. A parrot plays a major part in his determination, in *Un Cœur simple*, that 'cette fois-ci, on ne dira plus que je suis inhumain'.[19]

Reverberating Chateaubriand's statement: 'Je sais fort bien que je ne suis qu'une machine à faire des livres',[20] Flaubert partly objectified and befeathered himself: 'Je suis un homme-plume. Je sens par elle, à cause d'elle, par rapport à elle et beaucoup plus avec elle'.[21] More honest sometimes than many a writer, Flaubert knew in his bones that emotion often lies in the writing-finger and its implement. Such knowledge enables him to empathize with the telegrapher on his high perch, and this is a different take on the parrot:

Quelle drôle de vie que celle de l'homme qui reste là, dans cette petite cabane à faire mouvoir ces deux perches et à tirer sur ces ficelles; rouage inintelligent d'une machine muette pour lui, il peut mourir sans connaître un seul des événements qu'il a appris, un seul mot de tous ceux qu'il aura dits [...] Un peu plus, un peu moins, ne sommes-nous pas tous comme ce brave homme, parlant des mots qu'on nous a appris et que nous apprenons sans les comprendre.[22]

Humans are mere uncomprehending transmitters, a very bleak slant on the standard view of language as communication. Transmitters, or repeaters. As Louis Guilloux notes, 'à partir d'un certain âge on radote, on rabâche, on se répète, on raconte pour la vingtième fois la même histoire, c'est l'âge qui veut ça'.[23] This sentence enacts what it expresses: it is meta-parroting.

The 'Copie' section of *Bouvard et Pécuchet* (where the pair act as graphic parrots, or psittacine copy-clerks) scooped Borges's Pierre Mesnard, who (re-)wrote *Don Quixote* verbatim but, Borges claims, differently. For Bouvard and Pécuchet would transcribe the idiocies and fallacies that they collected, but would remain superior to their scrivening, because their intention is quite other than that of the originators of such unoriginal material. And Flaubert's certainly was: he intended satire, a 'farcical encyclopaedia'. Of course, such shenanigans leave out of the frame that other distinct possibility: that too great a proximity to *bêtise* is very likely to infect you, whatever your intentions. Flaubert was very alive to this danger, as Queneau would later be, when knee-deep in his 'fous littéraires'. Flaubert's 'Dictionary of Clichés' aimed at causing all opinionating to self-destruct, in what he hoped would be the silencing of all psittacism.

As Philippe Bonnefis notes, 'le perroquet est l'oiseau fétiche de l'œuvre. A l'enseigne du perroquet, maison Flaubert'.[24] He further records that, three years after *Trois Contes* appeared, a Swiss doctor, J. Ritter, found a connexion between a pneumonia epidemic and the importing of diseased parrots: psittacosis was discovered.[25] It attacks the lungs, and, as in Félicité's case, produces mental confusion. Loulou, in the last resort, does not need to be visible or audible. It has taken up residence in Félicité's head, heart, and memory.

Queneau and Laverdure: *Zazie dans le Métro*

Mixing as so often the posh and the demotic, Queneau opined: 'La connerie, c'est parfois insondable.'[26] Flaubert had already said: 'Il y a des niaiseries qui me donnent presque le vertige.'[27] The temporal canyon across which Queneau and Flaubert converse is less gaping than the chasm separating the reciprocally yodelling Sartre and Camus. Queneau was obsessed with *Bouvard et Pécuchet*. In *Zazie dans le Métro*, Gabriel talks of 'le vulgue homme Pécusse' (*vulgum pecus*).[28] Though he read very widely and far more than most of us, Queneau is, however, less of a true encyclopaedist than a super-magpie.

What do idioms tell us about parrots? 'Etrangler un perroquet' (variants: *étouffer, asphyxier*) means to drink a cocktail of pastis and mint syrup, or absinthe (which notoriously makes the heart grow fonder). Several of the humans in *Zazie* would dearly love to take that figurative expression literally. In military parlance, *un perroquet* is a sniper (and Laverdure does take potshots at people). In legal argot, it denotes a barrister (Laverdure is something of a barrack-room lawyer). 'La soupe au perroquet' (and this bird is threatened with the stewpan) is bread soaked in wine: a sacramental coincidence that must have tickled the fancy of the anticlerical but spiritually inclined Queneau. For her part, Zazie is menaced by her would-be incestuous father with having to 'passer à la casserole' in another sense: to get raped.

The lugubrious and antisocial Laverdure's famous refrain is a *scie* (Vallès has a truly excruciating pun about mechanical humorists squatting on their *scies*. On 'le forçat du bon mot', he wrote: 'Je ne connais pas de métier plus fatigant [...] que celui de "causeur amusant", qui court après le calembour bizarre, [...] comme un nain à califourchon sur les dents d'une *scie*').[29] Although he/she/it (I will come back to that) says several things more than 'Tu causes, tu causes, c'est tout ce que tu sais faire', he/she/it could not be used to say a great deal, because (let's settle for 'it') it condemns human jabbering, and would thus be shooting itself in the claw. Its *scie* (jingle, catchphrase) is indeed a statement of fact, for Man is *homo loquens* (or *loquax*). Laverdure is irritated by incessant phone-calls in the café where it hangs out, another instance of the human propensity to rabbit on. Of course, 'causer' means also 'to cause'; talk is productive, if often only of nonsense or clichés. In the course of this novel, various people repeat the parrot's theme-song, as if by contagion.

Both Queneau and another of his culture-heroes, Rabelais (in the *Cinquième Livre*), were much taken with the language of birds. In *Les Fleurs bleues*, when a bystander claims that parrots (*papegays* in Rabelais) do not understand what they utter, Cidrolin retorts: 'Prouvez-le'.[30] In a taxi, en route for a gays' nightclub, the motley crew discuss this poser. 'Ces bêtes-là, dit Gridoux, on sait jamais ce qu'elles gambergent [ruminate] [...] Ils entravent plus qu'on croit généralement'. Madeleine gently supplies: 'D'ailleurs nous, est-ce qu'on entrave kouak ce soit à kouak ce soit?' 'Koua à koua, demanda Turandot' (p. 138). This squawking sound (*kouak*) renders humans themselves birdlike. On arrival at Les Nyctalopes (night-blindness, but also night-queers), the 'admiral' commissionaire asks the group if the parrot is 'one of them', too. He assumes they are homosexuals, and Laverdure is a female parrot, or he is using the frequent gay ploy of talking of males as 'she'. 'Laverdure' sounds feminine; there is a joke about 'le pays vert' (homosexual terrain). Like Flaubert, Queneau likes to flit between the sexes, be it of animals, or humans. The 'admiral' goes on to claim that such creatures give him complexes (today we might say 'do my head in'), which are often alluded to in *Zazie*, no doubt because of the American and thus French bastardization of Freudian psychology. In a heavily strained pun, Gridoux chips in with: 'Faut voir un psittaco-analyste' (p. 141). This portmanteau-word jibes at the less inspired kind of headshrinker. Laverdure's refrain might also hark back to the long-suffering analyst condemned to listen to months of patients' outpourings (Queneau himself underwent a lengthy *cure*, that *faux ami* which does not mean *guérison*).

Laverdure's first 'change of disk' is to say: 'Nous ne comprenons pas le hic de ce nunc, ni le quid de ce quod' (p. 141). Such pseudo-scholastic Latin foreshadows Beckett's would-be philosophical parrot. This is burlesque, in which characters are granted inappropriate (usually high-flown but also guttersnipe) dialogue. Even more so, when a parrot invents instead of merely echoing others, it is being comically out-of-line. Another employee, 'un Ecossaise' [*sic*] in a kilt, seems to imply that Laverdure too might be queer. On hearing the *scie*, he/she comments: 'Elle a de l'à-propos, cette bête' (p. 143). Towards the end of a very long night out, Laverdure dozes off, whereas Zazie fights her sleep. After all, she is less of a repeater than a questioner, though she does love her old jokes, and her own *scie* about what an 'hormosessuel' is. When it wakes up, Laverdure takes to flicking its crap out of its cage, like Loulou and countless unbookish parrots. Akin to industrious monks, parrots have famously dirty habits, as well as being prone to effing and blinding.

In the mayhem (possibly from the same root as 'maim') of the grand-slam finale, Laverdure is wounded in the perineum (a close relative to the anus, or *jacquot*) by a shrapnel of flying soup-tureen. 'Gisant au fond de sa cage, il murmurait en gémissant: charmante soirée, charmante soirée; traumatisé, il avait changé de disque' (p. 173). After taking the mickey out of humanity throughout, does Laverdure become human (i.e. parrot-like) in enunciating a phatic segment, a social cliché? Has it been shrunk to this, head-shrunk, or does changing the disk suggest that it has only ever been a jukebox *loquens*? Be that as it may, miraculously recovered from its trauma, like the indestructible cat in Tom and Jerry cartoons, it surrealistically swaps places with its owner Turandot, who then mouths the refrain, whereas the fleeing bird shouts 'Au revoir, les gars!', like everyone else in the grand dispersal. Queneau is mischievously suggesting that parrots and people are convertible, so why should not the pet carry its master's cage, as Loulou in effect transports Félicité to heaven?

In the murderous riot at the end of *Zazie*, we remember this novel's epigraph from Aristotle: 'Ho plasas ephanisen': the poet fabricated and destroyed it.[31] In other words, Queneau claims the writer's Śiva-like right to create and to demolish, to invent a fiction and then finally to smash it to pieces, rather like the auto-destruct objects of some modern sculptors, or Buñuel musing that he could envisage qualmlessly the burning of every centimetre of film he had ever shot. Of course, Queneau does not destroy; he fragments (the group scatters) what he has built up. We could translate the Aristotle quotation as 'Now you see it, now you don't': the archetypal patter of the prestidigitator (there is one in *Le Chiendent*). It also recalls the Surrealist blend-word (evoked in *Le Chiendent*) *littératurer*. Creation is self-deleting. Few writers have been so publicly self-effacing as Queneau. An alternative explanation for the mass punch-up, the dissolving into chaos, is that it is a convenient way of ending the book, which sways between characters operating on tramlines or suddenly scarpering (Zazie, who runs off 'droit devant elle en zigzag' (p. 52)). It could also be a homage to umpteen Westerns (the saloon-brawl), or to custard-pie battles in comedies silent or talkative. Finally, the violent finale is the natural culmination to all the lexical, logical (Carrollian), verbally pugilistic confrontations in the preceding pages. The characters have words, before they come to blows.

The parrot of *Zazie dans le Métro* joins Queneau's bestiary, which features also dogs (omnivorous gastronomically and sexually), and horses (talking). Even if intervening only intermittently in the text, Laverdure and its influence *inform* the whole. Like *Lolita*, *Zazie dans le Métro* is substantially about language: its mysteries, its daftness, its poetic potentialities, its conjoined aggressiveness and defensiveness; and the parrot is the language bird par excellence. Queneau's stated view of Laverdure's structural role is the 'dès que les gens commencent à envelopper ce qu'ils disent, à "mettre la sauce", c'est le rappel à l'ordre'.[32] It tells them to wrap up, like the bolshy Glasgow-student roomful when the new lecturer, Francis Scarfe, nervously announced his name. On occasion, as if by contamination (and psittacosis is communicable), some of the humans take up Laverdure's *scie*, and repeat each other mechanically. At one point, four men debate whether any of us can talk nonsense unless we have first contracted it from somebody else: a perfectly circular proposition. As the mini-controversy lurches along, the word *connerie* (Queneau's downmarket counterpart to Flaubert's preferred *bêtise*) acquires a sort of plus-value, as if talking rubbish were a social or artistic accomplishment (p. 67).

Laverdure mocks human discourse, or, in Gabriel's case, speechifying. Though he is often palpably a figure of fun, we are nevertheless not encouraged to feel superior or moralistic towards him. As Gridoux says pugnaciously of 'la bêtise humaine' rampant in Gabriel's night-club audiences: 'C'est un métier comme un autre, après tout, pas vrai?' (p. 75). And Gabriel, as well as nominally an archangel, is also 'un archiguide', conducting gullible tourists round the sights of Paris. These 'xénophones', speaking what Zazie calls 'langues forestières', add to the gaiety of nations. Gabriel declares grandiosely: 'Je ne parle jamais qu'en général. Je ne fais pas de demi-mesures' (p. 169). He is never really offstage, and dresses up language, envelops himself and his listeners in linguistic finery, just as he clothes his wardrobe-sized frame in a tutu in order to perform his nightclub act. Truly, 'il met la sauce'. Sauce, of course, is not indispensable, but many of us would miss it sorely if it were removed from our intake. Just so long as we do not kid ourselves for good that, with our dollops of sauce, we are chewing on the meat, the substantific marrow, of what is an always elusive meaning.

Though throughout *Zazie* language is shown in action as largely futile and ludicrous, it is also exploited therein for insult, seduction, browbeating, repartee, which is to say: power. Parrots, too, are preposterous, but they can have a tangible effect on us, as in that *other* Monty Python sketch, called 'News for Parrots', a satire on dumbed-down TV broadcasts, where three members of the team cock their heads on one side, and inanely repeat 'Pretty Polly' for what seems like hours. Besides, the characters of *Zazie* deliver speech that is now vacuous, now possibly full of hidden depths, or possibly profound emptiness. The grandmaster of the game, the author, does not spare himself from the ribbing. Under the umbrella of Macbeth's famous speech, Queneau intrudes to indicate that the whole tale, full of sound and fury, is maybe told by an idiot (p. 85).[33] Michel Tournier blithely recognizes that all authors are guilty of 'bavardage'.[34] Yet, for all its faults (and Queneau slips in deliberate mistakes, such as *œils*), language serves useful ends. Even if nearly all the characters hector each other, except 'la douce Marceline', finally revealed to be a no less gentle Marcel, and their conversations partake of duels or military exchanges, language is held to be serviceable for self-defence as well as assault: 'Se forger quelque bouclier verbal' (p. 10). Despite the final carnage, 'doucement' is a leitmotif.

Queneau's lifelong sharp ear for the parrot-talk of the human race leads him to dream up at times less voluble heroes, like the eponymous one of *Pierrot mon ami*, who 'thinks of nothing a great deal', where 'nothing' receives the strangely positive charge lent the word in *Alice in Wonderland* by that other wordplaying mathematician.[35] Though he extracts much urine from the inflated bladder of human speech, Queneau always knew how fundamental many human clichés and other linguistic automatisms are. (The 'observer' in *Le Chiendent* 'constate avec amertume que ces banalités correspondent parfaitement à la réalité' (p. 22).) Silence, naturally, is one sure way of sidestepping or minimizing the interminable chatter that so offends Laverdure. At several points in *Zazie*, rather than expatiate, Queneau simply inserts '(geste)', or '(détails)'. These indeterminate directions (*didascalies*) of course titillate the reader, just as various characters toy with each other, and keep each other on tenterhooks. Queneau knows how to script-tease his readers. (Around 1850, gestures were substituted on Paris stages for certain banned words, but then the gestures, too, were banned.)[36] Queneau's use of '(geste)' might well be a rueful recognition that words mislead, or are not enough or too much, and that only soundless motions are honest. It may equally be an acknowledgement that novelists cannot supply everything; they have to draw the line somewhere, at which point readers might be called upon to bestir themselves for a contribution. The French idiom for to silence someone, 'clouer le bec à quelqu'un', could refer to Laverdure and company.

Only sleep can silence the irrepressible Zazie herself. When awake, she takes everything personally (whereas her uncle Gabriel works hard to be 'compréhensif'). When the Métro turns out to be on strike and so not running to her order, she exclaims: 'Ah! Les vaches. Me faire ça à moi' (p. 10). Like Laverdure, she has her own refrains, such as the famous post-fix 'mon cul'. Turandot asks whether, when she mouths such indelicacies, 'elle joint le geste à la parole' (p. 18). Trying on her coveted jeans, she admires herself narcissistically ('Je suis formée' (p. 83)). Possibly on his own behalf, Queneau comments on the nymphet's charms: 'Il y a des amateurs' (p. 117). Above all, Zazie questions all things and everybody non-stop: 'Pourquoi qu'on dit des choses et pas d'autres?' (p. 92). This is unanswerable, but needs to be said. Gabriel allows that she 'a de la suite dans les idées' (p. 94), though he means mulishness rather than logical progression. Zazie is, like Laverdure, an insistent fact and, like it and Félicité, persists in her being.

'What I tell you three times is true', said Carroll's Bellman.[37] Repetition is variously, alternately if not indifferently, bad (or good). 'Gabriel est un tonton qui est une tata qui danse en tutu'.[38] Laverdure is a repeating pistol. Queneau described repetition as 'une des plus odoriférantes fleurs de la rhétorique',[39] and obsessively returned to Flaubert's reiterative tactics, especially in *Bouvard et Pécuchet*. The *fous littéraires* that kept Queneau in thrall for several years were just extreme cases of a common human propensity to say the same thing over and over and over again, repeatedly. Our *leit*motifs are often ponderous. Pushed too far, repetition collapses into the neurotic state known as echolalia. Though in language pathology this is 'the meaningless repetition of words and phrases', in educational psychology it is 'the repetition of words and phrases by a child that is learning to speak', and thus obviously not a meaningless activity.[40]

Like set phrases, *syntagmes figés* ('pick and choose'), language often hiccups. In zoological taxonomy, the laughing hyena is *crocuta crocuta*, and a rat *Rattus rattus*. Repetition is a superfluity we all find essential, rather as Voltaire deemed luxury a necessity. In conversation, a good deal of echoing of what has just been said takes place, and is a form of acquiescence, friendliness, or nervousness at being thought to be unconvinced. We shadow and duplicate each other. Poiret, in Balzac's *Le Père Goriot*. is called an 'idémiste' (dittoist) because he always repeats what he has just heard.[41] There is also, of course, preemptive repetition, when we anticipate what the other is about to, or is too slow to, say. In this way we are ventriloquists, putting words into other people's mouths. This scooping can naturally be performed sarcastically. It is often truncated, as with an echo in Nature. All in all, like lists, repetitions can become comic, as well as tedious, over time, as with sitcoms that have to earn their keep with their catchphrases and catch-situations. It is the humour of the stretched-out, elastic gelastics.

Camus nicely pinpointed Queneau's 'fantastique naturel' (matter-of-fact fantasy).[42] What was Queneau's own attitude towards humour? His onslaught on the very concept, in 'L'Humour et ses victimes', is very palpably an attack on *fin-de-siècle* humorists, and their baggage-train: Dadaists and Surrealists.[43] ('Humour' was of course to be later updated by postmodernists into 'irony', that is: a catch-all excuse and attempt to make oneself invulnerable to criticism.) For Queneau, 'l'humour à perpétuité est inévitablement une forme de la lâcheté intellectuelle' (p. 83) (cf. Vallès on automated *scies*). 'A perpétuité': life-imprisonment, or grave-concessions. It is relentless, destructive (deconstructionist) humour that he objects to. On the positive side, for Queneau, 'l'humour c'est "dire une chose pour en faire entendre une autre" sur le plan du comique (sur le plan tragique, ce serait le symbole). Et encore ce comique doit-il être discret, mesuré; l'humour est la sobriété du rire' (p. 87). 'Saying one thing to imply another' could embrace irony, and puns. 'Parmi les alcools de ma vie, il y aura eu l'érudition et le calembour'.[44] Now, some agelasts or misologists profoundly mistrust puns, and stereo-typically groan under the imagined *pun*ishment of this linguistic lash or club (the recidivist *Canard enchaîné* proliferates 'le calembour-massue'). But perhaps this is small wonder, when Queneau himself wrote: 'Ambition: élever le calembour à la hauteur d'un supplice'.[45] In *Zazie dans le Métro*, the ritualistic 'joyau de l'art gothique', fed to gaping tourists visiting the Sainte Chapelle, could be punningly adapted for the whole novel: 'Un joyau de l'argotique'. Like all true language-lovers or philologers, Queneau loves slang as much as pedantry, and enjoys making silk purses out of sows' ears. Yet his discretionary taste in humour, quoted above, ensures that he rations or doses astutely his verbal creations (neologisms, blends, Gallicized borrowings, etc.), and his twists on congealed expressions. Though he does not sniff at modelling his rewrites on actual speech or writing, his overall goal is less to mirror a linguistic reality than to shape his own discourse for his own seriously comic purposes.

Queneau had a jackdaw (a bird I am very familiar with) mind. He could not be fully aware of all that his texts signify or signal; no writer can. Readers can know better, more or other than he. Was it Henry James who said, hypocritically or not, that he wanted his readers to be more percipient than himself? Queneau was certainly given to the self-chastising process of de-learning, of living less, of evacuating or at least streamlining the overcrowded mind; this urge energizes more than one of his heroes. (The opposite of that near-homonym, 'kenosis', in Gnostic thought, is 'pleroma'. Kenosis is Christ's act of emptying himself of divine immunity so that, for instance, he could as a human feel pain.) Queneau's Gnostic forays and his personal eel-slipperiness would justify concocting the epithets *queneaustique* (and *quenaquatique*). It is in fact impossible to try to paste freezer-labels on Queneau: Surrealist, humorist, encyclopaedist, mandarin. He was ever the great escapologist, as in the drawing of a dog barking up an empty tree, while Queneau's disembodied head floats some distance off, wearing an inscrutable smile, like the Cheshire Cat.

Like Flaubert, Queneau transmogrifies the traditional dove/Holy Spirit/Paraclete into a parrot, who comments tartly on humanity's (supposed) gift of speech, or tongues. Like Beckett, to whom my perch finally swivels, Queneau was always taken with the idea of voidance, of lessness, indeed with the nothingness underlying all fullness of being, as in *Le Chiendent*: 'Ils ne se doutaient pas que l'assiette pleine cachait une assiette vide, comme l'être cache le néant'.[46] Laverdure mocks, and enacts, the human cover-up of emptiness, this existential act that suffices much of the time to make life curiously full and colourful.

Beckett and the Effable

'And perhaps also because what we know partakes in no small measure of what has so happily been called the unutterable or ineffable, so that any attempt to utter or eff it is doomed to fail, doomed, doomed to fail' (*Watt*, 61). In Beckett's *listing* and lugubrious work, parrots have their place and hold their own. 'I shall not finish this inventory either, a little bird tells me so, the paraclete perhaps, psittaceously named' (*Mal.*, 250). Apart from the phonic syzygy between 'paraclete' and 'parakeet', this learned joke could be a side-glance to *Un Cœur simple*, where Holy Ghost and parrot are melded by the simple-minded Félicité. Beckett is not simple-minded—Ay! there's the rub! Whether that criss-cross elevates parrots or downgrades the third person of the Trinity should best be left to theologians, who too often forget the Christian mantra about 'all God's creatures'.

Molloy claims to understand her parrot better than its owner, Lousse, perhaps because Molloy himself is 'peu causeur', and experiences his room as a cage, and the bird does not tell lies (*Moll.*, 48, 65, 67). This bad-mouthing bird

disait de temps en temps Putain de conasse de merde de chiaison. Il avait dû appartenir à une personne française avant d'appartenir à Lousse [...] Il ne disait pas grand'chose d'autre. Si, il disait aussi Fuck! [...] Peut-être qu'il l'avait trouvé tout seul, ça ne m'étonnerait pas. (p. 48)[47]

Thus, the limited freedom donated to humans in Beckett's world can be extended to animals. Robert Louis Stevenson's she-parrot, Captain Flint (named after an illustrious pirate), 'swears passing belief for wickedness'. The mutilated sea-cook Long John Silver's explanation is that 'you can't touch pitch and not be mucked, lad. Here's this poor old innocent bird o' mine swearing blue fire, and none the wiser, you may lay to that.'[48] In 1883, no printable samples were possible. We explicitly hear only the world-famous 'Pieces of eight! Pieces of eight!', and the nautical command: 'Stand by to go about' (pp. 54–5). Yet it is Captain Flint who, acting as self-appointed watchdog, wakes the sleeping Silver and his gang of cutthroats when Jim Hawkins stumbles into their lair. She repeats 'Pieces of eight', 'like the clacking of a tiny mill' (pp. 147–8). Although the narrator calls it her 'wearisome refrain', the bird has the last word, for its *scie* haunts Jim's recurrent dream (p. 191).

'No doubt the parrot once belonged to Robinson Crusoe', hinted Stevenson, whom we have heard earlier playing the sedulous ape.[49] Robinson is thrilled when his parrot speaks for the first time, after he has schooled it. It picks up still more from his monologues about his insular isolation. Robinson calls it 'the sociable creature'.[50] It is clear, however, that the bird is a mere part of the process of Robinson's establishment of sovereignty over this desert realm, and that it is indeed, as Boehrer comments, 'Robinson's first lackey, a Man Friday with feathers'.[51]

Back to Lousse's parrot. When she tries to brainwash it with the stereotypical 'Pretty Polly', Beckett writes, 'je crois que c'était trop tard. Il écoutait, la tête de côté, réfléchissait, puis disait Putain de

connasse de merde de chiaison. On voyait qu'il faisait un effort'
(p. 48). Despite its best intentions, the same beakful. In *Malone meurt*,
Jackson's only 'mute companion' is another parrot,

gris et rouge, auquel il apprenait à dire *Nihil in intellectu* etc. Ces trois premiers
mots, l'oiseau les prononçait bien, mais la célèbre restriction ne passait pas, on
n'entendait que couah, couah, couah, couah. Et lorsque Jackson, s'énervant,
s'acharnait à la lui faire reprendre, Polly se fâchait tout rouge et se retirait
dans un coin de sa cage […] Moi je m'y serais senti à l'étroit.[52]

Thus the bird manages to parrot the Latin axiom as to the first three
words, but baulks at the following ones. The net effect is to install
nothingness at the heart of the human mind.

In *Mercier and Camier*, Beckett features a soundless bird, a cockatoo
which, understandably, 'caught the eye':

It clung shakily to its perch hung from a corner of the ceiling and dizzily
rocked by conflicting swing and spin […] feebly and fitfully, its breast rose
and fell, faint quiverings ruffled up the down at every expiration. Every now
and then the beak would gape and for what seemed like whole seconds
fishlike remain agape. Then the black spindle of the tongue was seen to stir.
The eyes, averted from the light, filled with unspeakable bewilderment and
distress, seemed all ears. Shivers of anguish rippled the plumage, blazing an
ironic splendour.[53]

This is closely observed and beautifully, almost too beautifully, written;
it unclosets a heart nearer to the sleeve than Beckett often allows
himself. In *Film*, a parrot in a cage remains largely covered over,
except for a close-up of its eye. This bird must be an integral part
of the theme of this text: *percipi* (being perceived). I think Beckett
would have relished Pliny's description, in his *Natural History*, of the
ring-tailed parakeet from India, which

greets its masters, and repeats words given to it, being particularly sportive
over the wine. Its head is as hard as its beak; and when it is being taught to
speak it is beaten on the head with an iron rod—otherwise it does not feel
blows. When it alights from flight it lands on its beak, and it leans on this and
so reduces its weight for the weakness of its feet.[54]

This fanciful account irresistibly evokes an animated cartoon, with
its mixture of violence, physical impossibility, and a world turned
upside-down (the head-first landing). In *Molloy*, near the start, the
narrator rhythmically strikes his decrepit mother on the head in order
to communicate with her.

In Chapter 8, I write on bad jokes in Beckett: jokes that fall flat or, in Beckett's residually mobile scheme of things, crawl flat. Since failure provides a great deal of the material of comedy and humour, it is unsurprising that the failed joke can also be laughable. The same gap between pretension or intention and achievement or performance yawns in both areas. Besides, most of us have probably a more intimate experience of failures than of successes (male members of the club will nod limp assent). The root-meaning of 'gag' is 'strangle', so that the good joke gets us by the throat and makes us choke with laughter, the bad one with boredom or fury. Strangle is no doubt what certain of Beckett's protagonists, or more strictly agonists, would like to do to uncooperative pets. 'What a blessing I'm not talking to myself, enough vile parrot I'll kill you'.[55] Here bird and human seem to have coalesced.

Finale

Pour l'autocritique je suis doué, à la condition qu'on ne prétende pas me l'imposer.

Sartre

According to Long John Silver, Captain Flint is 'may be, two hundred years old, Hawkins—they lives for ever mostly'.[56] The famous dead-parrot sketch in *Monty Python*, featuring an unlikely 'Norwegian Blue', offers an aggressive (and therefore parrotlike) take on the more asininely euphemistic and clichéic properties of the English tongue, which can be used nonetheless to protest in trading terms, and indeed to rescript reality. *Pace* the Pythons, parrots have not yet perished. They go on nagging at us, like consciences. Immoral, slovenly, derisively impersonating us and revelling in its own brand of laughter, the parrot is the comedian of the animal world. Until we have, as with other species, bumped them all off, there seems, like instincts, to be something unkillable about parrots.

If there is (and who could seriously doubt it?) an inherent comedy in words, then parrots bring home to us this fact of life forcefully, mutinously, and with deadpan faces. The reputedly sagacious Solomon talked to the animals, like Dr Dolittle and most people at some moment

or period of their lives. In some writers, the animals talk back. Unlike
in everyday life, where a passion for animals often appears to betoken
an aversion from human beings, the treatment of communicative
animals, in literature, jokes, or on the screen, is humanistic. It is
an alternative slant on tackling the intricacies of the human comedy
in general, in all its ludicrous seriousness. By periodically making
parrots more talented than they can be, human rewriters of course
reduce people below the level they lay claim to. It is a punitive
exercise (though never forget that the avian chastiser is often a good
companion, too). Some of us want these not so little birds to tell us
home truths, but it is self-evidently humans who put the words into
their beaks, by a kind of ventriloquism which is a variant form of
rhetoric. Talking animals are thus, and can only be, a medium, an
angle of observation, or a surprise element in the general drone or
hubbub of human discourse. Though anthropomorfictitious, they are
still capable of 'crittercism'.[57] We know (don't we?) that parrots do
not know what they are saying, but we want them to say something
recognizably meaningful, to mean what they say, or even to say what
they mean. Instinctively, we listen and read for meaning, and are loath
to acknowledge impenetrable nonsense. Writers exploit parrots to say
what the writer is thinking.

Like children, parrots learn to talk and, similarly, on repeated
encouragement echo a selection, often a mishmash, of what they
hear. Do we adults remember our own stage in this evolution when
we fix on parrots? (Zazie, of course, is far from an infant, but she
is still, actively, expanding her vocabulary.) Is the parrot a living,
externalized embodiment of all human beings' tendency towards
imitation? In its shortcomings, its limited repertoire as a copyist, it
is a parody of us unfeathered ones, who are so frequently already
parodies of ourselves. As the whole globe suffers today from language
loss, we can ill afford to spurn that supplementary lingo which
human speakers the world over, from time nearly immemorial, have
implanted in the beasts of the field, air, sea, and cage.[58] Their voice is
less a superfluous echo than a sybilline pronouncement in the comic
mode. It is clearly a comic device to have a parrot talk above its
station (as happens in Queneau and Beckett, if not in Flaubert, where
Loulou hovers 'gigantically' above its). Technically wrong at times,
but poetically and dramatically dead right overall, all three novelists
(and the *tutti quanti*) wanted their parrot to be and to mean more

than a mere echo-board pet. Besides, 'why the fear of the derisive parrot, when it may be precisely parroting that makes our hearts strong?'[59]

It could all be worse. Thomas Sheridan recommended slitting a starling's tongue in two, so that it would *doubly* chatter.[60] But the parrot remains, when all is said and done, the language-bird. From the smallest of the genus, the budgerigar, to the biggest, macaws, they remind us that we are, so very often, them. They make us twitchers uneasy. Parrots are our oppos (from 'opposite numbers'), in French: *homologues*. Every lecturer, student, politician, schoolteacher, or priest, indeed simply all of us, has to spare parrots a thought. Cynics, like ironists, presume that they are in a class apart. We are never that self-sufficient. I cannot, in all conscience, use parrots to beat my fellow humans over the head, without placing myself foursquare on that selfsame perch, from which they and I will one day fall.

In this essay, in which Flaubert has had the biggest say, Queneau the next, and Beckett (inevitably) the least, parrots have had *their* say, had their way, with me (with us?). They have led us a dance, merry or leaden-footed. What this little bird has told us touches on language itself; mimicry, mockery, imitation; creativity; cliché, stupidity; religion; obscenity; repetition; comedy, humour, folklore, and jokelore; the parrot qua watchdog and as truth-teller; and the parrot in functional roles in texts. Have I, to gaily mix metaphors and genera, milked the parrot for all it/he/she is worth? Some readers, and they may not be mistaken, will find my disquisition on psittacism pedantic and, for that very reason, comic; that is, unintentionally comic. As I myself have always liked side effects and other windfalls, it is possible that so do others. Should I accept this American verdict on a different project? 'The psittacine linguistic and cultural activity with which this argument begins is a very dead duck at the argument's conclusion'?[61] My hope is that the overall shape (or misshapenness) of my essay possesses something of the intuitive, loose association of ideas that informs the acts of certain stand-up comedians of some standing, or lying.

Time to put the cover over my cage.

I cannot, however, like a parrot, resist a last word, borrowed from Valéry. He compared 'parrot-words', all those vocables that do not stand close inspection, to observing a specimen under a microscope with the wrong magnification. The result is nebulosity.[62]

5

Blague Hard! Vallès

W̲e Anglo-Saxons borrowed *blague* from the French. Strange how loanwords are the only area where we can borrow without having to pay back. (But what of plagiarism?) The French etymology (and snuffling among roots is not confined to truffle-pigs) appears to come from military life. In all French dictionaries, *blague* bears the basic meaning of 'bag' (from Dutch *balg*, a sack), and secondarily a joke. There is a probably apocryphal story that the original soldiers' tobacco-pouch was a pig's bladder. Veterans would offer conscripts their pouch in exchange for having their bellies rubbed. Farts were released. By association, *blague* came to signify windbag, joker.[1] For his part, Vallès wrote: 'J'écris à la diable et en toute franchise; la blague pourra paraître parfois trop forte, elle ne sera que l'expression de la vérité, grossie par le rire. Quand on rit, les joues gonflent'.[2] Inflation is thus at the heart. In olden days, *inflatio* meant fart or burp. With time, *la blague* was commonly held to be quintessentially Parisian, though such an annexation may be due merely to metropolitan umbilicism, navel-reviews, in this respect rather like New York Jewish humour.

The *blague* is polysemous, jack-of-all-trades. First, I want to treat the oblique mode. Vallès began on the slant with his provocative text *L'Argent*, probably his most sustained *blague*. With contorted and jovial irony, he was already talking of his life-chances as a stock-market commodity, which he would later phrase in *Le Bachelier* as 'le Vingtras est en hausse' (*Bach.*, 612). Such twisted irony, such a shotgun marriage between satire and eulogy, says what it only partly means, in order to raise a laugh, always easier than raising a loan. In ostensibly worshipping at the capitalist shrine, he is not, however, turning his rebel's coat but rather his *cache-misère*, that is, barely respectable outer clothes concealing a shabby interior. The laughter feigns a moral suicide.

I would christen this 'amplificatio ad absurdum'. The ironist, here, is a con-artist, not unlike P. T. Barnum's use of 'humbug' to describe his illusion-spreading publicity. ('Humbug' possibly derives from 'deceitful devil'.)[3] This overlap of irony and humbug mixes the hard sell and soft soap. Such risky tactics can, of course, result in the ironist, by ricochet, shooting himself in the foot, by a kind of self-contained friendly fire or collateral damage. Despite its indirectness, irony still aims at frankness. As Vladimir Jankélévitch notes: 'Il ne faut pas croire l'ironiste, il faut le comprendre; il faut savoir ce que parler veut dire'.[4] Don't be stupid: *verb sap.*

In the badlands of a largely brutalized childhood, Jacques Vingtras, Vallès's stand-in in the trilogy of *L'Enfant*, *Le Bachelier*, and *L'Insurgé*, claims to value being beaten unmercifully by his parents, for it will toughen his hide for the sailor's life he longs to run away to. This stance is richly ambiguous. Is it overloaded irony, or a defence-tactic (put on a brave face and rump), or hyperbolic blarney (a safety-valve): all aspects of the *blague*? Freud inscribed the id in 'kid', though no doubt caveman parents, if less articulately, scooped him. 'To kid' (hoodwink or josh) might stem from 'kid'. Jacques's attitude towards his genitors is complex. He always labours to find some good, or a less gratuitous evil, in these apparently denatured people. Besides, putting himself in the enemy's boots by appearing to espouse their viewpoint (namely that beatings are good for him) is an adroit strategy which allows him to resist them and to undermine their tyranny from the inside—useful training for his future oppositional militancy in political life. I am reminded of the 'whisper-jokes' of dissident citizens in Nazi Germany.

As well as a general attitude, *blague* also connotes one-offs, concentrated humour:

Petit-fils d'ouvriers, qui avaient la parole grasse, j'avais la gueule bien fendue, le rire large, un fonds de gaieté que n'avait pu assassiner la gravité de parvenus à laquelle se condamnaient mon père et ma mère, qui avaient passé à la bourgeoisie, et dans le mauvais coin! Il fallait que mon besoin de rigoler se satisfît—en sourdine. Quelquefois je devais me contenter de bien peu. (*SEP*, 84)

His revolt could not, as a child, be blatant: his parents, in effect, made him into an ironical *blagueur*. The tolerance of the son seems as gratuitous as the cruelty of the parents. He acts as a buffer-state between 'le discours de ma mère et l'effroi de mon père' (*Enf.*, 198).

'J'aime toutes les formes de l'ironie, adoucies, violentes, polies, barbares. Elle ne fait peur qu'aux faibles, et elle est la leçon et l'honneur des forts'.[5] Romantic irony is another variant on *la blague*. It erects a serious edifice which is then sabotaged by second thoughts which were really first thoughts all along. You can *blague* yourself, as when Vallès boasts of his 'réputation de gaieté et d'entrain à quelques mètres à la ronde' (*CP*, 353). He knew also how easy it is to strike a joking pose; he calls this 'crocodile irony' (*Bach.*, 567). The blackest dramatic irony in his life was that others were mistakenly killed for him during the chaos of the Paris Commune, in which he played a leading role: an atrocious quid pro quo, by which others copped it in his place; whipping-boys stood in for the previously whipped boy. Disguised as a doctor, in an ambulance picking up corpses, he escaped the carnage. Death saved his life (*Ins.*, 1083).

In many ways an upfront man and writer, part of Vallès revelled also in mystification, like Diderot. He did live in an age of oppressive censorship not far short of a police state, and so contraband writing was perhaps unavoidable. Even so, in Vallès restraint (irony, litotes, more rarely euphemism) alternates with expansiveness (anger, lyricism, exuberance).[6] If rhetoric is the art of persuasion, Vallès's variety is seldom hidden persuasion. Even when ironizing, he spills the beans.

To bridge, perhaps shakily, the gap between oblique and straight-up modes of the *blague*, I pass to sentimentality, which is both head-on (it assails our emotions), and devious (it has designs on us). It is the other side of the would-be hard-faced *blague*. Now, sentimentality is one of those terms redolent of a French peasant's sock: into it can be stuffed gold coins, or just smelly feet. Some of Vallès's fiction is miserabilist. It piles on the agony, attempts to browbeat the reader into predetermined responses, putting us on our honour as sentient moral beings. For all its aggressiveness, such sentimentality is clearly lacking in self-trust, or it would not overstate so much. Melodrama relies on over-the-top sentimental reactions. Luckily, Vallès handles it badly, as in an episode from *La Dompteuse*, where a kind of schizophrenia sets in: 'Il s'en voulut de ce mouvement, et s'empoignant par l'habit, comme si c'était un autre: "Ah! ça, Franju", dit-il, faisant mine de se brutaliser'.[7] Just as the mother beats out a tattoo of blows on her son's body, so Vallès rings (or wrings) the changes on his central obsessive theme: a misloved child. As a result, his humour is often hectoring. The dross of his vivacity is a sporadic sentimentality, yet even in this area he can write some truly shocking pages on a little girl being systematically battered to death over a period by her supposedly 'rationalist' father. You start with cerebration, and you end up braining your child. This lethal outcome had been preceded by her father and Jacques's assigning noble roles to each other. The girl's father 'dit en grinçant des dents, comme s'il écrasait un dilemme et en mâchait les cornes' (*Enf.*, 313). Vallès here extracts new life from a hoary expression (horns of a dilemma): the man's imminent brutality excites itself as if by an aphrodisiac (rhinoceros horn).

Also flagrant is gallows humour. Describing a guillotining, Vallès notes that the executioner wears a scarf to *protect his throat* in the early morning. He watches smoke-rings *die* away; all present wonder how to *kill* time. Such black humour does not detract or distract from the true blackness of the legal murder, which it underlines. A sideshow freak, legless, gives birth to two sons that she proudly shows off as fit and '*conformés comme vous et* MOI'.[8] Jacques Vingtras pens a yarn about a hydrocephalous child, which he hopes will bring in much-needed money, and make him 'une grosse tête' or big-wig on the magazine (*Bach.*, 636–8). The pun underscores the hero's exploitativeness.

Caricature, that visual *blague*, usually isolates a part of a whole and amplifies it, not always with cruel intent. Children's drawings, after all, overemphasize the head to the detriment of the rest of the body. Vallès frequently highlights the abused arse of his child-hero, and makes of it a star. Or he latches on to the febrile, loquacious hands of a dumb aunt, and turns them into an eye-catching silent film, featuring this gesticulatory chatterbox. Vallès once sincerely praised André Gill's caricature of himself attached to a mongrel: 'Chargez: allez-y, forcez la dose!'[9] When we bang our funny bone (situated near the *humerus*), our grimace is a weeping laugh. Jewish humour milks such wry suffering, and, as Beckett's Nell in *Endgame* says (and she is an expert): 'Nothing is funnier than unhappiness'.[10] For some, indeed, the *blague* can slump towards cynicism, nay nihilism, in its urge to cut pretensions down to size, to level experiences out.

Vallès was much drawn to marginals, *réfractaires*: dropouts who all the same wanted desperately to drop in, parasitic independents. Some of those he selected for his journalistic essays were living, or barely existing, *blagues*: they too were insolent, practised passive resistance to all authorities, and were wilfully anti-exemplary. Their very lifestyle is over-the-top while they remain lodged at the bottom of the pile. By their chosen eccentricity, these *lumpenbourgeois* stand out from the common herd. They stress their own ridiculousness, thereby compounding their problems of survival. More organized marginals were the showpeople also dear to Vallès. The *parade* of these *saltimbanques* is, taken literally, seismic: 'La nouvelle parade, où défilent déjà les filles en maillot, les musiciens, le sorcier, l'hercule, *tout le tremblement!*'[11] This *parade*—the procession and the spiel outside their booths—also means 'parry' in fencing. Just so: they defend their interests by their presentational attack. Their performance is naturally hyperbolic, hits hard to grab attention (like Barnum), and is the very antithesis of classical, or bourgeois, decorum. The spiel, 'les bagatelles de la porte', refers both to barkers' patter and to sexual foreplay. Six of one and half a dozen of the other, then: barker and love-maker both seek to stimulate, to seduce, in order to lubricate entrance. Unlike the political hucksters of middle-of-the-road nineteenth-century French republicanism that Vallès so enjoyed lampooning, these travelling mountebanks practise entertaining ham-acting, not ideological playing to the gallery. As that canine cartoon showed, Vallès was a great barker himself, and a willing sucker for the charms of show business. When he orated on political platforms, he tried to remember not to 'faire ronfler la toupie des grandes phrases' (*Ins.*, 941). Sometimes, nevertheless, like a spinning-top, his rhetorical tact, and his humour, run out, flop on one side. Not that his democratic fervour was ever blandly ecumenical. He always saw human exchanges as contestatory, diamond-cut-diamond. In his eyes, gatherings even of supposedly like minds were governed, to use a nice neologism from the Canadian novelist Réjean Ducharme, by 'unanimosité'.[12] Cross-talk acts were his bread-and-butter.

Vallès's political commitment was never humourless, and he consistently felt that, if being a militant meant being bored witless, he would sling his hook (see *Bach.*, 482). He was viscerally incapable of abstract thought or theorizing, in many ways a refreshing handicap in a French writer. In his survey of committed French literature, Sartre failed to include Vallès as a rampaging forebear, one with real claws, even though Vallès himself disbelieved in the possibility of uncommitted writing. Those who think they are exempt resemble 'platonic' customers in a brothel.[13] In his jumpy account of the Paris Commune, *blague* becomes reprisal, or at least riposte and protest, and the very opposite of blasé, even though in many other hands the *blague* often borrows the tone of world-weariness. The stereotypical *blagueur* wants to appear permanently undeceived, whereas Vallès was ready to be the dupe of his own most rooted beliefs concerning justice. The whole business is a two-way traffic. If political commitment needs humour, humour never precludes militancy. 'Le calembour n'empêche pas les convictions' (*Bach.*, 503). His laughter was inextinguishable, and in that curiously akin to that trademark of the Homeric gods that he loved to deflate. Still, he knew that agelasts abound: 'Il paraît que quand on pète de rire, c'est mauvais signe. On me dit, chaque fois que ça m'arrive, que je mourrai sur l'échafaud'.[14] He should be shot for his intemperate laughing. He remained buoyant, to reassign the motto of Paris, even in desperate circumstances: 'Fluctuat nec mergitur'. In *L'Insurgé*, he hijacks the dismissive image of himself as an organ-grinder's monkey performing on the Parisian thoroughfare: that is, often pathetic, cavorting but tethered by his chain, rattling a bowl for handouts, but capable of both entertaining and biting deep.

He refused to be taken by the French reverence for formal education. All the Latin dinned into him at school was, he maintained, like a poultice on a wooden ... head (*Bach.*, 538). Like many a *blague*, this claim is both lying and truthful. He had in fact an excellent scholastic record, but a fat lot of good it did him when job-hunting. In the school context, the teacher is a *blagueur* in a pejorative sense: pulling the academic wool over the eyes of pupils; and rebellious school children are *blagueurs* in a meliorative sense: resistance-workers, fighting back against brainwashing. Schools stuff, but incite to disgorgement in response. On his countryside holidays, Jacques learns to unlearn. Even in school, he counter-attacks by going over the top. In *L'Enfant*, he imitates an existing pastiche of a poem about a dead parrot: psittacism squared, plagiarism exploited to make a telling point about enforced pedagogic copying, modelling your modern self on the Ancients. The emotion he simulates in his poem is patently fake, for he has lost nothing or nobody. He wins the master's approval for his exercise in stylistic larceny, though not quite enough to come first in the class, only second—a suitable position for a plagiarist, a cobbler dealing in 'le retapage et le ressemelage' (*Enf.*, 321). Vallés was fully aware as a writer that *signer* (authenticate) and *singer* (fabricate) are both a source of typos and graphic kissing cousins. Recalling school exercises in imitating the classics, he makes a pointed comparison with the new technique in his day of *rhinoplastie* (nose-jobs), a term which

underlines the connexion between the human hooter and the horn
of a rhinoceros: 'Dangereux et terrible pour l'humanité, cette école
de rhinoplastie qui veut qu'on couse à la page neuve des lambeaux
de peau morte'.[15] One of his heroes boasts that, at the age of 17, he
could write as decrepitly as an Academician (*SEP*, 97). Such knowing-
ness ensures that indoctrinated plagiarism becomes learned take-off.
'Wheeze' is a trite saying (and 'wheezy' suggests last legs), but also
means a scheme ('a jolly wheeze'). As voodoo knows, the dead can
be reanimated.

Jacques's schoolboy psittacism, rewarded in the copycat ethos of his
educational era; his father's sedulous aping of the Roman paterfamilias;
the political follow-my-leader that Vallès scorned on Left or Right:
the cult of the past and the dead (necropolitics) that he attacked even
in the otherwise admired Blanqui: all of this energetic but deadly
imitation, this dependence, is studied in 'Les Victimes du livre', where
Vallès puts his unwavering finger on a key feature of French, and no
doubt many another, culture. 'Ai-je lu cela ou l'ai-je pensé?': Camus's
Clamence asks for once a 64-dollar question for any consumer.[16] The
groupie mentality Vallès captures perfectly in his yarn about a whole
family, hopelessly enamoured of Walter Scott, who ups sticks and
settles in Scotland.[17]

The *blague* is the locus of tension, a confrontation between opposing
choices (e.g. passive ventriloquism, or finding your own voice). As a
teacher's assistant, *un pion*, landed with menial chores, Jacques is ab-
surdly proud of his flick of the wrist when he wipes the snotty noses of
his little charges. In this fashion, the *blague* can help to make virtue out
of necessity. The insistent nineteenth-century topos of the foundling
would suggest that, while some writers regretted that they were,
others wished they could have been, parentless. The hero's mother
in *L'Enfant* often fails to recognize her offspring in her disappointemt
over how he has turned out, and exclaims 'You're not my son'.
This could be traumatic, but Jacques turns it into a metajoke about
abandoned children and aristocratic bastards.[18] She always manages to
place him eventually for, after all, with her constant whippings, she has
marked him for life. She herself is a composite rhetorical figure: a living
oxymoron (her maternal solicitude is brutal); a mixed metaphor (she is
a peasant petty bourgeoise); a chiasmus (she has the ambition to jump
from one class to another); and a pun (she is grating, often atrocious).
These tropes are all frictions housing stacked or conflicting urges.

As well as the mind, the body can secrete resistance-movements. Jacques's limbs are anarchistic, accident-prone. Yet his very gaucheness has a saving grace(lessness). He is a bullock in the china-shop of social life. The ironies of fiasco, however, confront this would-be ironist. So often does he find his projects frustrated that, in perplexity, he wonders: 'Contre quoi se cogner la tête?' (Bach., 566). The *blague* is always outré. As Jacques says of a rare windfall of candies, 'je les aime quand j'en ai trop' (Enf., 183). It is possible that the ubiquitous humour of Vallès's fictional trilogy, which he started writing during his eight-year exile in England after the Commune, was inflected by his experiences of *rosbif* life. He accused us English, whom he found in the main sombrely life-denying, of never laughing except in a sickly fashion. He found the English Christmas pantomime too over-ripe for his residual Gallic taste: gross hamming of gestures, rampant cross-dressing, sentimentality galore. Yet the freedom of speech and of assembly that he witnessed at Hyde Park Corner must have loosened up his native comic sense. It certainly encouraged him to have the courage of his convictions, and to freely paste *blagues* on his English hosts: 'Par esprit de patriotisme, parce qu'ils ont le Derby et la mer, ils ont tous des têtes de cheval ou de poisson'.[19] Many of us, no doubt, but all? His *blague* often engenders such freakish pictures. Just as he often caricatured ordinary people, he worked hard to naturalize freaks, those sports of nature. A legless but sexy fairground freak announces her warmingly monstrous vision of a school for deformed children, where each one could come to find the partner to supplement or offset his or her lack or excess: perfection arising out of deformity.[20]

In Vallès's work, corporeality largely replaces mentation. The pun, similarly, often takes figurative expressions literally. In her strategy of dominating her 'clan', so does Proust's Mme Verdurin, but in her case we see the ignorant obverse of the coin of literalization much tossed by comic writers like Vallès. 'On taille un jambonneau, et une bavette [...] Puisqu'on est sûr de la défaite, on peut bien boire le coup de l'étrier, avant de recevoir le coup du lapin' (Ins., 1067). After a perfectly judged zeugma, a play on the multipurpose *coup*. From stirrup cup to rabbit punch: departure and liquidation are tightly conjoined. Sometimes, Vallès twists a saying towards a meaning that is still metaphorical, but different: 'Ah! tant pis, je prendrai la vache enragée par les cornes' (Bach., 653), which condenses the ideas of grappling and of hunger. On Voltaire's profit-making at the Prussian court he makes a punning paradox: 'Il ne travaillait pas pour le roi de Prusse, le vieux malin!'[21] His street-cry might well be '*Cent calembours pour un sou—demandez*' (*Bach.*, 652). His *réfractaire* 's'en va battant la campagne le long des ruisseaux de Paris'.[22] True: he forages, and he's not all there. The two senses cross-breed, for lack of food can nourish hallucinations. The 'sapin' conveying the two friends to their potentially lethal duel in *Le Bachelier* bears two meanings: cab/coffin (*Bach.*, 693). When Jacques flees his pedantic family to play with a cobbler's children, he notices that these phonetically slaphappy kids 'parlaient avec des velours et des cuirs;—c'est le métier qui veut ça' (*Enf.*, 201–2). As Jacques is repeatedly drawn to improper liaisons, this remark is totally unsnobbish. Jacques Vingtras is himself an existential pun, shuttling between concrete and abstract, astride different senses, grimacing and grinning. He is often sacked from jobs; his mother dresses him when a child like a sack of potatoes; he can rarely feel that anything is in the bag.[23] His *blague* is organic. In *L'Insurgé*, the reactionary politician Thiers is described as 'vautour à tête de perroquet, taupe à lunettes, polichinelle tricolore' (*Ins.*, 9). The reader here needs to do a rapid series of double takes, have double vision, as in any punchy pun.

It is not too much to say that life for Vallès was a long series of puns: often excruciating, toothless, or pointed, full of coexisting but not necessarily reconciled tensions. Both the pun and life can make you laugh, on the other side of your face. Vallès, this existential punner, sometimes ran, but more often punned, for his dear life. Punning lies at the heart of his experiencing and his rendering of reality. The very availability of puns in language can remind any of us that, while we are inescapably subject to the 'system' or to multiple subsystems, there remains play in the system, some elbow-room for the jostling pun. It is a kind of aside, a glancing blow, uttered out of the corner of the mouth or the mind.

For Philippe Hamon, one of the distinguishing features and locales of *la blague* was the artist's atelier, with its heterogeneous clutter (unfinished paintings, in different styles, dressed people mingling with nudes). In this view, the *blague* is 'une énonciation disparate'.[24] In this mini-tumult, much histrionic big talk, the puffing of images, hype. Hamon's view indicates that the *blague* is indeed a moving target that necessitates the use of a critical scatter-gun.

To widen the enquiry, I want to look at Baudelaire, Flaubert, and the Goncourts on *la blague*. For Baudelaire, laughter was a direct outcome

of the Fall, which begat internally divided humankind. The only
fall Vallès stooped to consider was the pratfall. Baudelaire occupies
the pseudo-metaphysical end of the *blague* spectrum. His out-on-
a-limb jotting: 'Belle conspiration à organiser pour l'extermination
de la race juive' lends weight to Walter Benjamin's claim that the
cult of the *blague* later became an integral part of fascist propaganda (e.g. Céline's murderously anti-Semitic *Bagatelles pour un
massacre*).[25] Baudelaire's jotting recalls the illiberal Flaubert's dream
of making his readers unsure whether he was taking the piss out of
them or not. When Vallès met Baudelaire, he unsurprisingly detected
a poseur. Vallès's own version of the *blague* is never refrigerating in
the Baudelairian way, but bracing. He never sinks into the armchair
comfort of facile despair: 'Je sais que la lutte est inutile, je m'avoue
vaincu d'avance mais je vais me blaguer moi-même, blaguer les autres,
hurler mon mépris pour les vivants et pour les morts' (*Ins.*, 917).
Joshing and jibing to the bitter end.

   In Flaubert's usage, *blague* possesses umpteen connotations. On the
one hand, Flaubert wanted to contemplate this world 'au point de
vue d'une blague supérieure, c'est-à-dire comme Dieu le voit d'en
haut'.[26] Such a would-be Olympian posture was totally alien to the
ground-level Vallès, who even hated trapeze-work in gym lessons, as
it left this earth behind, and who loathed the space-flights of Victor
Hugo. For Flaubert, *blaguer* was to pose, to be a charlatan. On the
other hand, Flaubert advised a melancholy friend to 'resteep himself'
in *blague*, evidently seen here as a pick-me-up.[27] He himself expressed
his intention to achieve 'le comique arrivé à l'extrême, le comique
qui ne fait pas rire, le lyrisme dans la blague'.[28] This sounds somewhat
despairing, but Flaubert did see that a superior *blague* could out-*blague*
an inferior, trivial kind, and thus counteract the more futile varieties of
hyperbole. His 'Garçon' was a serial *blagueur*, a personified, ritualized
blague.

   Concurrently with Flaubert, the Goncourt brothers, influential
cultural commentators if no great shakes at creative writing, wanted
to blackball the *blague*, which panicked them, by its proliferation in
their day, into belittling it as 'cette grande démolisseuse, cette grande
révolutionnaire, l'empoisonneuse de foi [a pun on *foie*?], la tueuse de
respect'. The *blague* was clearly for the bachelor boys a devouring
woman who held nothing sacred: honour, family, motherland. They
tended to equate it with progressive opinions, which they did not

share, and refused to allow that jokes are often the only resource the
have-nots have.[29]

As for Bergson, or Bergçon as *Le Canard enchaîné* might have spelt
him, surely the most overrated and least persuasive theoretician of
humour ever, Vallès knew instinctively far more than this world
authority who, as if he were an industrialist, sought and of course
found the blueprint for 'the manufacturing process of comedy', or
'a pharmaceutical formula for witticisms'.[30] Humour for Bergson
was a cop on the prowl, blowing the whistle on disorderly play,
and bullying people to toe the line (p. 151). He dreaded eccentric
steps, different drummers. Tournier flatly contradicts him by calling
laughter 'un appel au désordre qui est vie' (*VP*, 196). For Bergson, an uptight proponent of the dynamic flux of life, in theory
the comic should be the triumph of the elastic over the inflexi-
ble, but he reverses this pattern. Why should society be thought
flexible and eccentrics unbending? It is far more likely to be the
other way round: anarchist comedians in conservative communities.
Like a racist (and Bergson thought blacks and hunchbacks per se
risible), his tactic splits humankind into the initiated and the expelled. The Jew Bergson strangely favoured ghettos. His most-quoted
definition of comedy, 'du mécanique plaqué sur du vivant' (p. 29),
drew from Arthur Koestler, a much subtler theorist of humour,
this cutting gloss: 'If "we laugh each time a person gives us the
impression of being a thing", there is nothing more funny than a
corpse'.[31]

In contra-distinction, Vallès knew in his bones and elsewhere that
only one part of the male body has a duty to be rigid, and then only
on the right occasion. When his hero Jacques sets off for a crucial job-
interview, in an over-tight, begged-and-borrowed suit held together
by so many pins that he has to jump down the stairs feet together,
he still succeeds in mouthing a joke about 'la raideur anglaise',
which Vallès attributes elsewhere to our having swallowed whole
the flagpole of the Union Jack (*Bach.*, 601–3).[32] He is duplicating
what he is mocking, not just the stiff upper lip that some Englishmen
glory in possessing, but the stiff-jointed whole body and the inelastic
attitudes. Even so, a humorist/comedian can get trapped in a role
(or be willingly confined to entrapment and exploit it). We want
him/her to live up to our expectations (basically: 'Épate-nous', as
Cocteau urged Diaghilev); they give us what we clamour for. Jacques

descending the stairs like a demented robot is offering kinetic *blague*,
a sight gag. Above all, Bergson is humourless. 'Laughing at someone'
exempts himself. 'Nous ne sommes risibles que par le côté de notre
personne qui se dérobe à notre conscience' (p. 129). The humourless
man does not realize how funny he sounds. Bergson's idea of fun is all
about correction: pedagogic, normative, punitive, like a headteacher.
The sections on professional deformation ring truest, and apply, in the
first instance, to the author himself.

Tournier, an opponent of Bergson, as Vallès was *avant la lettre*, speaks of 'le sérieux meurtrier de l'adulte [qui] a pris la place
de la gravité ludique de l'enfant dont il est le singe, c'est-à-
dire l'image renversée' (*RA*, 125). Patently very drawn to Vallès's
novels, Tournier finds that they 'valent surtout parce qu'ils font
retentir à nos oreilles une voix dont l'accent ne ressemble à au-
cun autre' (*VV*, 190). The verb 'retentir' suggests reverberations
(Veuillot spoke of vibrations): echoes, anything but a one-way
relationship.[33] Louis Guilloux, whose Cripure in *Le Sang noir* favours
la blague, also responded to Vallès's singular voice. He relates how
he discovered Vallès, when himself an impoverished *pion*, very
appropriately on a second-hand bookstall at a fairground: 'Nous
étions livrés aux professeurs, c'est-à-dire à la mort sous toutes ses
formes [...] Vallès m'introduisait à un monde dont j'avais soif,
un monde de santé, d'audace, de fierté, d'ironie, d'insolence, de
liberté, vrai monde de la jeunesse.'[34] Youth is not a talent, nor
even an age; it is a state of mind. Vallès is all of a piece and,
like every man Jacques of us, a mishmash. I would coin: chop sui
generis.

Vallès's constant recourse to all the moods of *la blague* does not rule
out other uses of the sensibility. There are many vivacious scenes in the
Trilogy: sound-bites, eye-bites, nose-bites. It embraces an unsneaky
juvenile eroticism, as violent and all-absorbing as that of any age. Sex,
sensory rapture, and humour, each in league with the other, fight a
running battle with the forbidding parents, the carceral school and the
repressive society, all of which are contrasted with the rumbustious
local pub, all noise, laughing, and horse-trading. Sexual arousal can
be made palpable without being totally explicit, as when Jacques grips
his curvaceous cousin Polonie when riding behind her on her horse.
The *blague*, Vallès proves, can arise from sheer *joie de vivre*: this lifelong
kid loves to act the goat. His colloquial vim scrubs encrusted language

clean, and democratizes Mallarmé's mandarin programme: 'Donner un sens plus pur aux mots de la tribu'.[35] Tribal words suit Vallès fine.

A French Vallésian, Pierre Pillu, once gently chided me for pulling Vallès over to the Anglo-Saxon side of the communal bed. Despite his critique of us in *La Rue à Londres*, surely we can borrow him, like the term *blague*. While incontrovertibly as French as Montaigne or Diderot, Vallès does strike me as 'Anglo-Saxon' in several ways: his love of sport, physical expenditure, and fresh country air; his fondness for eccentrics; his empirical bent which made him suspect all systems—Jacobin, Proudhonist, or Marx; his alertness to overlap and contamination between all compartments of thought or behaviour; his passion for exploiting, by wordplay or coinage, the often underused potential of his native tongue; and his support of and identification with the underdog, the plucky loser, the moral victor. He was too French for the English, and too English for the French. Always *à cheval*: in mid-Channel, straddling, like the pun.

I have blatantly been speaking of the *blague* not strictly, but loosely and broadly. After all, it has been called a 'microsystème', 'un terme à facettes'.[36] I have tried to suggest how Vallès illustrates and embodies one of the most intriguing things about humour: its shifting, shifty relationship with seriousness ('La blague ayant toujours sa cible sérieuse' (*Ins.*, 918)). As the French humorist Alphonse Allais is widely alleged to have said: 'Les gens qui ne rient jamais ne sont pas des gens sérieux'. Vallès rarely goes in for one-liners. His humour is always *in situ*, dramatic, organic, existential. It is very likely true, as the incomparable Gershon Legman has it, that 'your favourite joke is your psychological signature. The "only" joke you know how to tell, is you'.[37]

The lexicographer Pierre Larousse opined that Rabelais should have invented the word *blague*.[38] Vallès did not invent it, either, but he did better. He exemplified more than most this wonderful, honourable, dishonourable blackguard, *la blague*.

Riff on Black Humour

Black (or sick, gallows, calamity, graveyard, doomsday) humour is thumbscrew humour (cf. Sartre's thumbscrew theatre).[1] According to Jankélévitch, 'le cynique croit à la fécondité de la catastrophe; [...] il fait éclater l'injustice, dans l'espoir que l'injustice s'annulera elle-même par l'homéopathie de la surenchère et de l'esclandre'.[2] The grass-roots doctor Céline would not have had much time for homeopathic remedies. That elegant statement sounds much more like the strategy of the gallows-humorist than the cynic, who is hardly in the business of amelioration, preferring to rub our noses in the horror, full-stop. Disaster jokes utter the unspeakable, and for that reason are preferable to euphemism. As Elliott Oring argues, 'black humour might be an instinctive refusal by ordinary people to kowtow to the reverential tone imposed by the media'.[3] They say: 'Don't tell me what I ought to feel or say'.

'Sardonic', in the medical sense, refers to a death-grimace, a rictus. Gallows humour is strictly the last laugh, and it cannot be a long one, except that mortality means that we are on the gallows from birth. Of course, such last-ditch humour makes us laugh against the grain, which, like forced tickling, is not pleasurable. Very often, black humour is protean: we know not where to have this neither-fish-nor-flesh. A rather gentler form, 'le rire mélancolique' receives this joky tutorial from Lautréamont, and it is a distinct improvement on Pagliacci: 'Riez, mais pleurez en même temps. Si vous ne pouvez pas pleurer par les yeux, pleurez par la bouche. Est-ce encore impossible, urinez'.[4] More soberly, black humour must have some kinship with the 'black bile' (melancholy) of the traditional humours. Of the four, black bile is the sole imaginary, yet the richest in meaning, for it is closely allied to creativity, as in the Dürer engraving which partly inspired Sartre's *La Nausée*. Black humour gainsays the horrors of reality, which is one way of not denying their existence. Of course, jokes at any time can also act as tranquillizers, taken before any discomfort can kick in. John Irving said of the 'collegiate' humour prevalent in some TV news-rooms: 'Life was a joke; death was the final gag'.[5] A gag is not only a joke but also a silencer.

Tournier privileges what he calls 'white humour' over the black variety, presumably because his basically anti-tragic stance and his love of inverting conventionality demand this switch. As a colour and as a humour, white is more anodyne than black. And, despite being the colour of mourning in certain cultures, it is generally celebratory. In Tournier's 'La Jeune Fille et la mort', what could have been a blackly comic tale of despairing and suicidal youth is whitened. The heroine dies laughing.

Black humour is the last resort of those who will not stand the idea that life's miseries may win in the final reckoning, ensuring that the joking, like the kissing, would have to stop.

More so than its English counterpart, *dérision* plays it both ways: provocation and retaliation. The defence offered by derisive writers is that they are merely matching the absurdity out there and all around. For them, we can deride anything and everyone: death, the late God; we can deride (the regretted) Derrida. *Dérision* can take the form of inflating, belittling, or distorting. It has close links with parody, carica-ture, *la blague*, and the grotesque. The pun is a linguistic agent, like the grotesque, of seeing double troublingly, and of bloating resemblances.

The grotesque, for Hugo in his preface to *Cromwell*, springs inevit-ably from the Christian stress on duality. As the reverse of the sublime, it is inseparable from it, and indeed often its senior partner. Flaubert exploits the grotesque as a means of active derision of the *dérision* or risibility of human effort, including that of the derider himself.

In mythology, Momus is the proponent of sarcasm and ridicule. In Kafka's *The Castle*, he is the functionary stupidly infatuated with himself. Momus mocked even the Olympian gods, a feat not equalled by Kafka's lickspittle scrivener. Kafka, who had better, more fruitful nightmares than most of us, frequently and loudly laughed in company, especially when his own writings were read out. Black humour can house both arrogance and a strong sense of the futility of your endeavours.

All of my authors except Tournier are dead, and white males, into the bargain.

6

Upping the Anti/e: Exaggeration in Céline and Vallès

There is a literature of understatement: Racine, Voltaire, Laclos, Gide, and one of overstatement: Hugo, Huysmans, Vallès, and Céline. The 'juste milieu' or happy medium hardly gets a look-in in high literature (cf. bland jokes or toothless puns).

In the small world, it is by way of a critical commonplace (and the common place is where, by definition, most of us live) to say that Céline's *Mort à crédit* takes off in various ways from Vallès's *L'Enfant*. At the very least, they are validly comparable. For his part, Céline remains today an outsize bone of contention in French culture, because of his alleged, and real, collaboration during the Second World War. I am principally drawn to his comic practice. The latter does not justify the former; neither does it need to be excused, only analysed. I do not claim that Céline's humour saves him. Humour is a salvager, not a saviour. Did he have, in the normal sense, a sense of humour? Could he see the frequent ridiculousness of his own hyperbole? He certainly had a talent for vituperation, but so do many disbelievers in the value of humour.

Sartre once wrote that a communist could not write a novel proper, because, believing in the inevitability of the historical process, he could only underplay the freedom, both of character and of narrative, essential to the novel (that is, of course, the novel bourgeoisly conceived).[1] Along comparable lines, it has often been assumed that fascism and humour make unhappy bedfellows. Dictators do indeed appear to lack a sense of humour (a sense of proportion)—except of the most gloatingly sadistic variety.

The title *Mort à crédit* picks up on the old *image d'Épinal* (popular edifying print) entitled 'Crédit est mort' (No Credit), a motto very current among small shopkeepers. The title, especially in its American translation, *Death on the Instalment Plan*, also introduces the chief theme: dragged-out decay and demise. On publication, *Mort à crédit* was almost universally panned, on both Right and Left, first for doing the dirty on humankind (the would-be humanist reaction), and secondly for its gutter-level language. The family at its chaotic heart—the father who never rises above the rank of subsidiary clerk in an insurance firm, and the mother who struggles endlessly to sell laceware—are excluded, or sidelined, from the French economic system of their day, based upon credit and the gold standard. (Céline's actual family-life was considerably more comfortable than and different from that depicted in *Mort à crédit*.) In a vain effort to keep up with the times, the father, Auguste, buys a typewriter which with black irony will later be the very weapon with which his verbally brutalized son half-kills him. The name Auguste refers both to the autocratic emperor Augustus, but also to the archetypal French circus-clown 'l'Auguste'. The father is indeed dictatorial, comic, and manic. *Mort à crédit* as a whole imposes a spasmic view of life as inherently conflictual, violent and unstable. Bodies, projects alike decay and fail. The desperate parents will put up with anything for the sake of a sale. For instance, dogs foul the pavement in the passage where the parents and their pathetic business just about live. Passers-by take the hint and ape the canines. There is no point in complaining: 'Souvent ça devenait des clients, les pisseurs, avec ou sans chien'.[2] This circumscribed home territory is the old central Paris of covered passages, but it is far from the bullfight phenomenon, *la querencia*, the place in the arena where the targeted bull feels safe. In *Mort à crédit*, nobody feels safe.

The son, Ferdinand, is sickly, loose-bowelled, and given to frenzied, superlative onanism. He lives as if everybody and everything were out to get him, and maintains a vigilant distrust of all. He lives the programme of *Voyage au bout de la nuit*: 'Noircir et se noircir'. The racist Céline blackens all. Throughout, Céline keeps his finger firmly placed upon the panic-button; he favours all worst-case scenarios. He is on 'hyperbolic steroids'.[3] The father, like the teacher/parent in Vallès's *L'Enfant*, is pitifully proud of his classical schooling, his *humanités*: he often resorts to Latin quotes when declaiming anti-son anathemas, which are presented as virtuoso performances. In everyday experience, anger can lead us to and be fuelled by overblown repetition that is largely self-igniting. Anger overstates the case. Auguste is too big for the claustrophobically tiny family flat. His mainly one-way discourse is, however, constantly let down by physical fiascos, as when he drops a bar of soap, and all three hurl themselves to the floor, poking with a broom-handle under the piano, and hitting each other about the head in the cack-handed process. It is funny how the rough remedy proposed by common sense—'Their heads should be banged together to make them see sense'—when translated into an accidental collision, produces the opposite effect. In all this mayhem, the victimized offspring does not try to understand, forgive, justify his genitors, as does Vallès's young hero Jacques Vingtras. As narrator, Ferdinand certainly gives them their head and, overall, is himself embroiled undetachably in the seething family mess. He comments: 'Je lui demandais pardon d'avoir été insolent. Pour la comédie, puisque c'était pas vrai du tout' (p. 560). This contrasts with Jacques Vingtras's more complex efforts to take on board his mother's brutal 'logic', the harsh 'système' of her child-rearing. Both authors, nevertheless, exploit the difference between what is expressed and what is communicated, but it is a difference that depends on the recipient having eyes to see. Ferdinand's crippled mother, somewhat kindlier than her spouse, receives this Beckettian testimonial from her son: 'Elle a tout fait pour que je vive, c'est naître qu'il aurait pas fallu!' (p. 552). That first noble sentiment is strangled by the disabused tack-on (a common dodge also in Vallès). Despite his attempt to murder his father, any talk of Oedipal triangles, although Céline did have wind of Freudian theory, seems reductive in this context.

The mother and father fatalistically regard Ferdinand as incorrigible, whereas the Vingtras couple always strive to reshape their lad. Ferdinand's parents are supported by a Parisian Greek chorus of neighbours who chime in to indict the boy. After a particularly vicious verbal onslaught from Auguste, Ferdinand, maddened uncontrollably, knocks him down with his precious typewriter, and then tries to throttle him (pp. 823–4). He has to be hauled away by neighbours, who proceed to beat him up. As happens repeatedly in other scenes, Ferdinand collapses into diarrhoea and vomiting. Later, after voicing some pity for the multiple woes of his crumbling parents, he switches to moaning about their lack of compassion for him: 'Martyrs! Il fallait pas comparer!' (p. 989). Céline's reiterative tactics remind me of Nathanael West:

All the materials of life are rubbing in such a way as not to satisfy the itch or convert irritation into active pain, but so as to increase the size of the irritation, magnify it and make it seem to cover everything—hysteria, despair.[4]

For a long spell, *Mort à crédit* moves cross-Channel to Kent. The boy longs to get to England alone, so as to disappear, to stop being the dead centre of adult critical attention, indeed to blot out talk altogether. To this end, at the sardonically named Meanwell College, he becomes a kind of elective mute, refusing to learn English, while acquiring a Martian perspective on its phonology: 'Je détestais pas l'intonation anglaise. C'est agréable, c'est élégant, c'est flexible. C'est une espèce de musique, ça vient comme d'une autre planète' (p. 738). As with Jacques Vingtras, Ferdinand's obsession with the sea, with 'partir!', shows how ready he is to 'se dépayser', to go foreign if not to go native. In practice, however, he resembles the literal-minded homing pigeons late in the novel, who only ever embark on short, sad flights (pp. 858–9). On his arrival, he had lost himself in a Saturday-night crowd in Chatham, where he achieves the anonymity he pines for, as he moves across a social spectrum going from the Salvation Army to the Kentucky Minstrels. At the college, after establishing himself as king rat, he befriends a mentally subnormal boy, who drinks from drainpipes, tries to eat doorknobs and the headmaster's false teeth. Do we always know for sure what *is* exaggeration, over-egging the pudding? Aren't we too often small-minded? Adynaton, since way back, has denoted impossibility, which has thus always been conceivable. Céline, this starveling-looking man, made a meal (often a dog's dinner) of everything. It is fitting that he should coin 'circonlocutasserie', which mimes as it mocks long-windedness, beating about the bush.[5]

Back in Paris, Ferdinand spends more time and energy avoiding work than finding or doing it. He is stretching his credit. Eventually, he teams up with the would-be encyclopaedist and inveterate inventor Courtial des Pereires, reminiscent of some *fous littéraires* or literary cranks of the nineteenth century, who is one of nature's hyperbolists: 'Il magnifiait, écrasait, imprévisiblement d'ailleurs, par la parole, la plume, le manifeste' (p. 836). He is even capable of reverse aggrandizement: miniaturization, without ever shifting from loud to soft pedal. Courtial's greatest work is 'l'œuvre complète d'Auguste Comte, ramenée au strict format d'une

"prière positive" en vingt-deux versets acrostiches' (p. 840). Trying to give this prayer 'un petit goût entraînant bien français, il
l'avait déduite en "rébus", retournée comme une camisole … rendue
revancharde … cornélienne … agressive et puis péteuse' (ibid.). He
varnishes his detachable collar, then wears it for two years.

What purpose does exaggeration serve? It seizes on one, or a minor,
aspect of an idea, a spectacle, a phrasing, and underlines it, divorces
it from its context, and inflates it. As with caricature: all head and
little body, so as to make the viewer concentrate on the head in
near-isolation; and also, naturally, so as to convey an element of
big-headedness, pretension. We can, of course, via distorting mirrors,
sit for our own caricature, create our personal grotesque monster. Our
temporary, and writers' more permanent, fabrication of the grotesque
is no doubt an apotropaic tactic, in other words, a magic attempt to
conjure away deeper fears about our defective and risible humanity.

Courtial is a creature of violent seesaws: larger than life, then petty
in the extreme. His inventions range from balloons (inflation) to
submarines (blowing tanks), from the empyrean to Hades. Fleeing
the city, he takes up agriculture, and runs a 'Phalanstery of the
New Race', which sounds like a Nazi eugenics programme, though
on the ground the young pupils in fact gain a counter-education,
for they are allowed to run wild criminally and to ransack the
neighbourhood. This programme turns out to be another of the many
business failures of *Mort à crédit*. Finally, Courtial blows himself to
pieces. A trowel and a wheelbarrow are drafted in to scoop up and
transport his *disjecta membra* (pp. 1043–4). A mad cleric plunges his
hands ecstatically into these gory remains. Even in death, Courtial
goes over the top.

Exaggeration can also reduce the value of something, be*little* it.
So, not 'intelligenti pauca' (a word to the wise), but 'intelligenti
multa' (a plethora to the percipient). Céline not only makes the big
bigger, he makes the small loom larger. When Ferdinand contemplates
running away from Meanwell College, he immediately thinks that
this desertion would sink the failing establishment for good; it would
no longer have enough pupils for a football team (p. 737).

Céline is highly conscious of his own extravaganzas:

Je les surpassais tous de beaucoup question virulence par l'intensité de
ma révolte, l'enthousiasme destructeur! La Transe … l'Hyperbole … le gig-
otage anathématique … c'était vraiment pas concevable à quel prodigieux

paroxysme je parvenais à me hausser dans la colère absolue … je tenais tout ça de mon papa. (p. 875)

In a different context, I am reminded of Jacques Vingtras saying when he gets a windfall of sweets: 'Je les aime quand j'en ai trop' (*Enf.*, 183). Nobody sounds prouder than Céline about the sheer pleasure of verbally swollen wrath, exorbitance. The constant bellyaching is at times dithyrambic, as with the archetypal French concierge. As Barthes said of Léon Bloy: 'Le bonheur de l'invective n'est qu'une variété de ce bonheur d'expression, que Maurice Blanchot a justement retourné en expression du bonheur'.[6] No wonder that the French place Bloy in their long tradition of 'les grands exaspérés'. It is not a case of William Blake's piously hopeful 'the road of excess leads to the palace of wisdom'.[7] Céline would second Bloy's 'On ne voit le mal de ce monde qu'à la condition de l'exagérer'.[8] It is Thoreau who puts the case most persuasively for justified hyperbolism:

I fear chiefly lest my expression may not be *extravagant* enough, may not wander far enough beyond the narrow limits of my daily experience, so as to be adequate to the truth of which I have been convinced. Extra vagance! it depends on how you are yarded. I desire to speed somewhere *without* bounds […] for I am convinced that I cannot exaggerate enough even to lay the foundation of a true expression.[9]

In other words, exaggeration, traditionally associated with falsity, can in fact be redeployed so as to serve the cause of truth. But extravagance also implies wastefulness. Fontanier makes the same point as Thoreau more abstractly and soberly:

L'hyperbole augmente ou diminue les choses avec excès, et les présente bien au-dessus ou bien au-dessous de ce qu'elles sont, dans la vue, non de tromper, mais d'amener à la vérité même, et de fixer, par ce qu'elle dit d'incroyable, ce qu'il faut réellement croire.[10]

By definition, an author (*auctor*) is an augmenter (Latin *augere*). 'To improve upon' also means to increase. Making mountains out of molehills is a variant on the artistic ability to make something out of nothing.

In *Mort à credit*, a cross-Channel ferry in rough seas begets an epic mass vomiting, in which virtually the entire boat-load literally feeds the fishes, shoots cats, barfs, upchucks, spews, and exhibits a technicolour yawn (pp. 622−5). In Céline, heaving with laughter and eructating because of high waves, excess intake, or traumatic anxiety, are coterminous. His comedy, and this is a richly comic scene, is never a relief but an exacerbation. There are fevered sections (literal or metaphorical), and the narrative is consistently febrile in structure and tone. Even if much of the narrative is static, it is frenetically so. This stasis is varied by the hero's instinct for vagrancy—the picaresque as permanent digression. The notorious three full stops separating phrases or sentences embody fragmentation, hiccupping, anger, laughter, retching. Such syncopation is of the Jazz Age. Yet, despite everything, the atomizing Céline stays very attached to linkages. In a letter he spoke of his ambition to 'tenir cette espèce de délire en élan'.[11] Of the climactic duel scene in Vallès's *Le Bachelier*, he wrote: 'L'une des rares scènes de délire que l'on trouve dans la littérature française [...] Cela n'a jamais été égalé ni chez les Russes ni chez les Américains—La littérature française ne délire presque jamais'.[12] Can exaggeration be controlled, like a skid by an expert driver? It is a key element in advertising and humour. Many jokes are wilfully excessive, highlighting inordinately stupid ideas or behaviour, or exceptional finesse. (Cf. also the southern French *galéjade* or the American-frontier 'tall tale', which strain likelihood, without exceeding it altogether.)

The effect of much of Céline's dialogue (or more accurately monologue) is that of reading aloud a French version of Roget's *Thesaurus*: variations on themes, proliferating synonyms (e.g. 'Tu t'en balances! ... Tu restes hermétique n'est-ce pas? Calfaté ... Bien sanglé au fond de ta substance ... Tu ne communiques avec rien' (p. 865). Comparably, in Vallès, the physical variations on beating the child anticipate the maddening rhythms of Ravel's *Bolero*. Virtually the only relief for Céline's agonist from verbal diarrhoea, diarrhetoric, is elective mutism. Discourse here *is* exchange, but only in the military sense of broadsides, sniping, parting shots, and not in the sense of dialogue. The frequent *engueulades* (slanging-matches, bawlings-out) are largely inconclusive; nobody persuades anybody. The total impact of such full-frontal attack on the reader is very often, of course, punch-drunkenness. Céline labours his points by belabouring his audience. He is such a natural and curiously democratic escalater that he grants virtuoso powers of vituperation even to the enemies of his protagonist.

Céline raises the poser: can laughter ever be totally nihilistic, iconoclastic? Surely, however tenuously, it still keeps some kind of faith with what we can agree to call life. Laughter, in Céline, is always *le rire jaune*, laughing on the other side of your face. Julia

Kristeva describes him as 'libérateur d'un rire sans complaisance mais néanmoins complice'. This formula captures both the ruthlessness and the appeal of Céline. In general, Kristeva sees in him 'un rire horrifié: le comique de l'abjection [...] Devant l'apocalypse, il s'exclame d'une horreur voisine de l'extase'. She likens this laughter to that of the Hebrew prophets (Céline himself counted St John in Revelation as a master).[13] In his corner of existence, like a trapped rat, Céline's hero, despite his creator's entrenched anti-Semitism, takes refuge in Jewish humour: the wailing-wall of lamentations, putting God on trial, and sharply querying the point and the equity of creation. Often Céline brandishes powerless Spanish figs, two-finger exercises, at the whole caboodle.

If not overtly fascist, except in some of the father's outbursts, *Mort à crédit* constructs a fictional world ripe for a fascist takeover: economic crisis, class hatred, dirt and decay and disorder everywhere, and a largely irrelevant republican government. Céline's humour is anti-humanist. It is anti-*bonhomie*, anti-charm. He makes few efforts, à la Gide, to *disarm* readers, but many to browbeat and suffocate us.

For Jules Vallès, the *blague* was an existential strategy, an artifice of self-preservation.[14] Though in his writings he milks suffering for all it is worth, he shows discretion over real-life experiences, whereas Céline is decidedly indiscreet about mainly invented ones. Vallès's *L'Enfant* is no joke, and richly, complexly funny. Its hero Jacques Vingtras *gags* (i.e. jokes and retches) against parental *gags* (vetoes). In a typical example of pointed hyperbole, he finds the local jail gayer in atmosphere than his grim home or authoritarian school. Frequently, Vallès exploits Romantic irony, in which the second part of a sentence militates against the spirit of the first part, and thereby hints that second thoughts were first ones all along. Here is the mother lining up the child for a beating; 'Elle me battait pour mon bien, voyez-vous. Sa main hésita plus d'une fois; elle dut prendre son pied' (*Enf.*, 202). The mother hesitates, but only to make the swing of her arms more accurate. If we readers fail to see this special irony, we are as stupid as she who cannot manage irony, but only sarcasm. She is a one-woman band and her son the drum: 'Elle m'a travaillé dans tous les sens, pincé, balafré, tamponné, bourré, souffleté, frotté, cardé et tanné' (*Enf.*, 258). Like his mother in her own sweet way, Jacques is governed by a perverse but dogged logic. How is he to find good, or a less gratuitous evil, in parents to all appearances monstrous? This child, wanting to be loved or at least to lead a less denatured life, assumes the thought-processes of his intra-family foes, while retaining an instinctive sense that theirs is not the way that people should live together. Against the proverb, he knows that to understand is not to forgive, but to mitigate resentment and to try to fellow-feel. Thus Vallès makes the boy seemingly internalize his mother's force-feeding (of onion hash, precepts, or leatherings). He allows for the well-documented fact that battered children often do blame themselves for their suffering, and protect their abusive parents by all manner of subterfuges. Besides, the mother's tyranny proves that her son is indeed a rebel, which is in fact his choice of being. In all this, he is striving to understand the motivation of the enemy, an invaluable lesson that he will go on extending in militant adult life. As a child already, he instinctively loosens or breaks corsets, in order to go over the top. His verbal stagflation calls to mind Cocteau's witticism: 'Le tact dans l'audace c'est de savoir jusqu'où on peut aller trop loin'.[15]

Mother and son fight a running battle: his desire to be expansive versus her private ideology of constipation. There remain, all the same, as in Ferdinand's family, ineradicable bonds. At school, too, Jacques fights a rearguard action against the pedagogical rhetoric of his day. His superaddition ('en rajouter' is a French term for exaggeration) takes the mickey out of the officially prescribed *amplificatio* in school essays. As a well-drilled rhetorician, Jacques knows how to subvert enemy discourse. To the rhetorical question: 'What could take a mother's place?' Jacques replies: 'A shillelagh' (*Enf.*, 212). *L'Enfant* is propelled, via its insistent graphic present, between rapidly shifting moods and tones. This family drama is shown to have wider social implications. Citizens, too, are in the position of children: spoken for, talked down to, kept violently in their place, which is to be seen and not heard. But to legislate for all polymorphous and often perverse children is a mug's game, especially as children are, according to Santayana, natural mythologizers.[16]

As in *Mort à credit*, exaggeration is rife. A rare kiss from the mother projects Jacques against the wall, where his head knocks in a protruding nail (*Enf.*, 273). Overall, the mother piles it on thick in her treatment of her offspring. For his part, the father harps on the need to suck up to superiors. And Jacques competes with this pair of inflaters by upping the ante in his narration. In his own right, clumsy in all things except jumping over gates, Jacques has a saving gracelessness, which I would call 'maladroiture'. *L'Enfant* houses much knockabout farce, silent comedy, as when Jacques's jagged shoe eviscerates his headmaster's carpet while he tries to advance in reverential fashion. The multiple fiascos are both hilarious and troubling. No wonder that Jacques feels he is the stooge or fall guy for his parents' pitiless needs. They are a trampoline from which he yearns to take off, but to which he inevitably has to keep returning. Mother and son are natural, habitual, reciprocal overreachers. It is a kind of Yiddish mother-and-son cross-talk act, though we should keep in mind the Jewish proverb: 'Crooked parents can produce straight children'. The already treated plagiaristic poem on a dead parrot reminds me of Bardamu, in *Voyage au bout de la nuit*, who pens a synthetically patriotic poem in order to protest the lie of war: falsehood squared.

In Vallès, as against Céline, laughter is a sign of life, a style of commitment, a dampener of stereotypical exclamation (that recurrent vice of French literature and life). *L'Enfant* rings with defiant laughter from the boy in the teeth of his joykilling genitors.

Why compare Céline and Vallès? In both, the context is petty bourgeois; the hero is an only child. Both sets of parents struggle unavailingly to hoist themselves above the lower echelons. The two fathers are inordinately proud of their formal education, yet essentially failures in their professional lives. Both sons want to do violence to the paterfamilias (Céline's succeeds), and work to reject their schooling. Sex is natural and healthy in Vallès, and unhealthy in Céline (voyeurism, much misogyny, as well as a capacity for adoration of selected women—Ferdinand desires to literally eat the headteacher's ravishing wife (p. 742)). Both authors love freaks, *fêtes foraines*, especially their shooting-galleries.[17] Throughout, we see Jacques simultaneously or by turns as a sideshow freak and a perfectly normal child. Céline several times declared a strong affinity with Vallès, who also knew bitter and protracted exile: 'Je me vois plutôt très Vallès'.[18] In many ways, they were enemy brothers, terrible twins. In both, childhood is portrayed as crucial, and excruciated. As George Darien, in several ways a bridge between Vallès and Céline, says in *Le Voleur*: 'L'enfant qui souffre a [...] des yeux qui grossissent les gens qu'il déteste'.[19] In *Bas les cœurs!*, good advice is offered to the juvenile narrator: 'Voir les choses, plus tard, avec tes yeux

d'aujourd'hui'—that is, remain faithful to your young perception of
adult ignobility.[20]

In Céline, the body is disgusting but veracious; in Vallès clumsy
but truth-telling, and the source of our intensest pleasures. Unusually
in the French tradition, both are very corporeal writers. In political
terms, Céline is obviously far more negatively apocalyptic, and he does
not in any way share Vallès's vaguish faith in 'le peuple'. Above all,
Céline warms to the iconoclastic verve of Vallès's prose. Melodrama,
to which both are prone, is the site of hypersignificant signs, and thus
the natural stamping ground for these two early semiologists, Vallès
and Céline.

Exaggeration can have links with the absurd. Céline may often be
ideologically, but not semantically, crazy (he believed the admittedly
all-pervasive British Intelligence Service was controlled by Marks and
Spencer). Vallès remains sane even in his hyperbole. Neither segues
into Nonsense.

These two magnifiers help us to see more clearly, or at least
more interestingly and intricately. They were both rebels, in their
nonconformist ideas, in their destabilized structures, and in their
humour. What Barthes in his more firebrand youth said, pretty
pompously, about revolutionary rhetoric goes very well towards
describing the breath of fresh, or in Céline's case often stinking, air
that the pair let into French literature: 'L'écriture révolutionnaire
fut ce geste emphatique [...] Ce qui paraît aujourd'hui de l'enflure,
n'était alors que la taille de la réalité [...] Jamais langage ne fut plus
invraisemblable et moins imposteur'.[21]

Apart from this instance, we all exaggerate non-stop. Where Tacitus
wrote 'Omne ignotum pro magnifico' (we all enlarge what we do not
understand), the rest of us could even more laconically say: 'Omne
pro magnifico'. Zola, who had an edgy opinion of Vallès, and who
broke a great deal of ground for Céline, once boasted to his acolyte
Henry Céard: 'J'ai l'hypertrophie du detail vrai, le saut dans les étoiles
sur le tremplin de l'observation exacte. La vérité monte d'un coup
d'aile jusqu'au symbole.'[22]

As certain blockbuster films periodically remind us, for as long
as human beings go on exaggerating and valuing escalation, giants
will never become an extinct species; nothing can sink the titanic.
The phenomenon of escalation, whether of terrorism, nuclear capacity, nonentity celebrities, or political slanging matches, is, no doubt,

over-familiar. The opposite of hyperbole (overkill) is litotes or euphemism (underkill). But isn't litotes a form of overstatement: small
means large? Darien pulls the two ends together by recommending 'la
plus extrême modération'.[23] The danger of inflation, however, is that
it can lead to devaluation and redundancy.

An anonymous novelist once said of fiction: 'You just take reality
and water it down', which establishes some sort of balance.

Exaggeration, we have seen, can aggrandize or minimize. It can
generate comedy. Laughter, in turn, can reinforce rebelliousness.
Archaically, 'to enlarge' meant to set free. Hyperbole is a serious joke.

Riff on Politics

Humour needs targets, enemies. You don't laugh in utopias. Politics involves the choice of opponents. The hard-won success of Jewish humour, and (in the twentieth century) the upsurge of black, gay, or female comedians, all testify to the power of humour: not necessarily the power to change anything concrete, but the power to keep the maligned or neglected group in the public eye, and to remind other comparable groups of their vigorous presence. Humour is assertiveness. It can empower, or disempower, by rendering us helpless with mirth, or breaching the defences of our sense of propriety. It can, of course, be just a substitute for action, a makeshift. In a less polarized way, humour can be a vital adjunct to militancy, as we have seen in the works of Jules Vallès. Vallès once boasted that he could 'faire de la politique par ricochet'.[1] He blithely discounts the risks involved with ricochets, 'dont le trajectoire sémantique est si difficile à contrôler [...]; l'on peut rater ceux qu'on vise et blesser les siens'.[2] Your own might include shooting yourself in the foot.

This is the risk taken by all ironists, who work obliquely and not always recognizably. Here, however, is Proudhon offering a splendid salute to irony:

Ironie: vraie liberté—c'est toi qui me délivres de l'ambition du pouvoir, de la servitude des partis, du respect de la routine, du pédantisme de la science, de l'admiration des grands personnages, des mystifications de la politique, et du fanatisme des réformateurs, de la superstition de ce grand univers et de l'adoration de moi-même.[3]

This is the pure programme of anarchism, and it shows how irony, a sense of humour, is consubstantial with political choices. Anti-authority political jokes bear the same, crucial message: I may go through the motions of acquiescence, even toe the party line in words, but I refuse to be brainwashed. Nobody jokes in the dystopian *Nineteen Eighty-Four*, except for the acidulous sarcasms of the power-holders. The programme of Ingsoc, 'doublethink', a perverted form of the pun, 'is also a grim joke'.[4] Its outcome is a meaningless babble, 'duckspeak'.[5] In Koestler's *Darkness at Noon*, like *Nineteen Eighty-Four* a nightmare—that is, unreal but terrifying—the show-trial accused, Rubashov, is troubled by his own contestatory dreams as he labours to see the logic of the repressive Soviet regime. Gletkin, his persecutor/prosecutor, has more than one objective in depriving Rubashov of sleep. More proactively, his and his fellow-prisoners' system of inter-cell communication (tapping on pipes) makes room for rhythmic laughter, which anybody knows is a source to be tapped.[6]

In less definitively nightmarish situations, enough thoughts of bravado may graduate into bravery. The cumulative effect of polit-ical jokes might be a scattered and disorganized, but still potent, resistance-movement. All political humour is, to reclaim Freud's term, tendentious. It takes liberties. Censorship wants to take away our freedom to laugh; it imprisons. In sleep and dreams, at least, we are free. No wonder that many sleepers have an insolent smile on their face. As Ramón Gómez de la Serna pointed out in one of his *greguerías*: 'Durante la noche, el gobierno está en crisis total'.[7]

Much politics is destructive, whether it operates top-down or bottom-up. Can language destroy? One of Georg Lichtenberg's 'im-possible objects' is a bladeless knife lacking a handle. After this disappearing act, only the name remains. Of course, the idea of a knife pre-existed Lichtenberg's vanishing-trick. We have to know what a knife looks like before consenting to its abolition. Usually, objects are only too insistently there (like authorities). Etymologi-cally, an 'object' is thrown towards us, a thing thrust at our mind. A 'subject' is a thing thrown from a lower position, and so, in the etymological scenario, objects come out on top of subjects. Words can evoke things. Can they make them dematerialize?[8] Ad-mittedly, Lichtenberg's disembodied knife is a *faux ami*, a source of confusion.

Ethnic jokes involve power-relationships, and are thus political, in that they involve superiority, domination, submission, or of course rebellion: striking back. A major indictment of racist jokes would be that they refer, unlike a good many other kinds of jokes, to real

behaviour and situations, e.g. torturing and killing that has actually
happened and could recur. Even so, we should not stop our ears or
eyes against them, for we need to discover and be regularly reminded
how the enemy thinks. If a good liberal agrees to read *Mein Kampf*
or *The Protocols of the Elders of Zion*, why flinch from jokes expressing
similar sentiments? Ethnic jokes are multifunctional. Who tells them?
In what context? With what intent? With what kind of reception?
Some regard them as a left-handed, i.e. ambiguous, compliment.
Mocking some group at least shows that they have got under your
skin. From the other side, self-mocking racist jokes, whether on
an individual, regional, or national level, proclaim: 'I am still in
charge of my image. I control even what attacks me and wishes me
ill'. This hypothesis, however, if pushed to the limit, would rule
out the possibility of genuine self-criticism. Surely, without being
masochistic or getting tangled up in defence-mechanisms, we can
honestly acknowledge our mistakes and our faults, and await whatever
social sanctions may ensue. Reviewing Christie Davies's *The Mirth
of Nations*, the sociologist Laurie Taylor objects to his 'sleight of
hand'—the fact that Davies is so keen to counter the politically
correct view that ethnic jokes betray real hostility, that he does not
allow for other, reasonable objections to such humour. For instance,
'the wholly admirable moral sense that there is something profoundly
disturbing—even obscene—about so gratuitously adding insult to
injury'.[9] This is the decent response, but it runs up against very
strongly entrenched practices. Like rumours or urban myths, joke-
cycles spread like epidemics. Very many jokes rely on stereotypes
(mothers-in-law, Jews, blacks, women). To that extent, humour
simplifies, often grotesquely so. The best kinds complicate.

I want to consider an individual case of political humour, not from
'high' literature but from journalism: *Le Canard enchaîné*. 'Canard'
is a popular, disrespectful term for a newspaper: a rag, and also a
hoax, a misleading rumour. Clemenceau had, before *Le Canard*'s
origins in 1915, retitled in 1914 his oppositional *Homme libre* to
L'Homme enchaîné, in order to point up wartime censorship of the
press. To escape this censorship, Clemenceau sometimes addressed his
suppressed articles in discreet envelopes to subscribers and sympathetic
political notables. When, however, he became *président du Conseil* in
1917, he changed his tune and defended censorship. 'The title,

Le Canard enchaîné thus bears a double semantic load, its name signifying both falsehood and subservience. What better way, in a climate of patriotic bombast, to stake a claim to independence and veracity?'[10] This antiphrasis was an excellent means of striking back; irony has always been an indirect weapon of subversion. Douglas salutes the *Canard*'s 'uncanny ability to play both sides of any issue at the same time, to exploit stereotypes while undermining them' (p. 183). This is the strategy of the pun. Douglas adduces the Cretan Liar paradox: 'Saying the opposite of what one meant stood side by side, in the columns of the *Canard*, with its opposite—that is, saying exactly what one meant' (p. 247). A combination, then, of the oblique and the full-frontal, as in the best kind of irony. To pictorialize its objective, it printed a cartoon of a tethered, squawking duck, quacking: 'Tu auras mes plumes. Tu n'auras pas ma peau' (p. 24), a spot-on pun.

Le Canard enchaîné has, in its long history, generally enjoyed a charmed life. It has never been seized. One prime minister, urged to ban a particularly outspoken issue, retorted that he had no wish to become a national laughing-stock. Similarly, General de Gaulle refused to send Sartre to prison for lending his name to an underground paper, explaining that 'On n'arrête pas Voltaire', conveniently forgetting that in more openly brutal days Voltaire was flung into jail for his polemical pains. *Le Canard* works hard to justify its self-appointed pedagogical role, the training or encouraging of alertness in reading the press or consuming official handouts. It aims to have the same relationship to the daily press (it is a weekly) as satirical puppet-shows have to the straight theatre. It ridicules its trade-partners for their readiness to censor themselves.

Its principal ambition is to give an articulate voice to what many French people like to think of as typical Frenchness: *débrouillardise*, *bon sens*, occasional *engueulades*. *Private Eye* is a very rough counterpart in the English context, with its scoops based on leaks from insiders and whistle-blowers, and its often schoolboyish thumbing of the nose at authority, although the *Canard*'s writers are mainly middle-aged or older, and their dissidence is less flashily contemporary; they are very rude about any form of modishness. Its close contact with its readers (it receives a heavy postbag) lends to the *Canard* the air of a (non-exclusive) club.

It is a club, too, in another sense. Its comic tactics range from winking and nudging innuendoes to loaded spoonerisms and thumping puns: 'le calembour-massue'. Founded to combat Great War *bourrage de crâne*, its counter-offensive takes the form of a relentless 'calembourrage de crâne'. Many readers complain of the mass-production of generally dispensable puns in the headlines and elsewhere of the world's press. *Le Canard* is a different kettle of fish. Its puns are pointed, targeted, aimed to hurt, jolt, and remind the guilty parties and the suffering citizenry of what's what: 'Ne disiez-vous pas, Monsieur de Gaulle, que les Français étaient des veaux? Ils ont veauté pour vous'. In the age of jetting popes, it reminded His Holiness to take with him on his global journeys his Holy ejector-See. It maintains its 'fliconoclaste' tradition of police-bashing. Among its many productive neologisms, it coined the very useful 'bla-bla-bla' in order to nail hollow speechifying.

Its policy of accepting no advertising, either open or concealed, makes it unique in the French press. The result, however, is a rather grubby, old-fashioned appearance, which perhaps reinforces its image as a rebellious old warhorse. Its standpoint is that of the *frondeur*, the defender of individual and minority rights. The tone is often that of an embittered but still virulent idealism. In many ways, *Le Canard enchaîné* is outdated and sentimental (one of its heroes is Victor Hugo), but it undoubtedly reflects a native, widespread distrust of politicians. Its peculiar kind of immunity goes with its status as a licensed fool, and an institution. Do licensed fools lose some of their bite? Governments can point to the *Canard*'s largely untroubled existence as proof of their own liberalism, though this myth was punctured when the paper's offices were found to be bugged.

Like its cousins, the geese on the Capitol in ancient Rome, it sounds an appealing alarm at every encroachment on home territory and personal freedoms. Financially, it has the last laugh. The *Canard* is the least lame duck of the French press.

But, like all satirical agencies in the world of today, 'que peut faire Don Quichotte contre des moulins à vent mous comme des montres de Dalí?'[11]

In March 1992, I read in a newspaper that in India 10,000 peasants had resolved to transform all their activism against the regional government into collective laughter directed at every official pronouncement.

After all, in democracy we find *mock*. This venture would be mass-exaggeration in action, and it proves, if this were really necessary, that hyperbole can be a political act and, at its best, is not to be sniffed at, to put it mildly. The grass roots can grow into a threatening forest.

7

Drôle de philosophie: Sartre

In *Images d'une vie*, there is a photo of Sartre and Nizan at the École normale supérieure (ENS). What with their linked arms and their natty togs, they look ready to break into a soft-shoe shuffle. Indeed even after the ENS, for a good many years, they kept up a more distanced double-act, in which Sartre, that fairly late developer, was the straight man and Nizan had all the best lines. At the ENS, an absent-minded professor rebaptized them Nitre et Sarzan. Daniel Lagache, who was later to inject Sartre with mescaline in an experiment, recalls the student cabarets: 'Sartre et Nizan écrivaient le texte de la revue, un texte plein de contrepèteries, de jeux de mots, de couplets amusants. Sartre avait une prodigieuse facilité pour ce genre d'exercice'.[1]

During the 1930s, Sartre progressively became himself. By the time (1943) of *L'Être et le Néant*, he was making 'l'esprit de sérieux' as big a bogey in his system as 'bad faith', to which it is obviously affianced:

> Le résultat principal de la psychanalyse existentielle doit être de nous faire renoncer à l'esprit de sérieux. L'esprit de sérieux a pour double caractéristique, en effet, de considérer les valeurs comme des données transcendantales, indépendantes de la subjectivité humaine, et de transférer le caractère 'désirable' de la structure ontologique des choses à leur simple constitution matérielle.[2]

This blind belief in certainty, one's own or that of your social class or a process, is what *La Nausée* sets out to shatter, in its lampooning of 'les salauds' of Bouville, to whose habits of mind the hero Roquentin is sometimes uncomfortably close. If Sartre's philosophical essays are, in their ponderousness, rarely funny, his fictional and dramatic protagonists, and the fine messes they are in, are able (spasmodically) to cease taking themselves so almightily seriously: Roquentin, Inès, Frantz, the self-ironizing author of *Les Mots*, and the judging/conniving author of *Le Mur*.

Is the opposite of 'bad faith' and 'l'esprit de sérieux' irony, ludism? 'La mauvaise foi est un certain art de former des idées contradictoires'.[3] So is the pun. Is over-seriouness funny in itself? In the same period as he was writing *L'Être et le Néant*, Sartre stated in his *Carnets de la drôle de guerre*, from his base in the army:

S'il est quelque unité dans ma vie, c'est que je n'ai jamais voulu vivre sérieusement. J'ai pu jouer la comédie, connaître le pathétique et l'angoisse et la joie. Mais jamais, jamais je n'ai connu le sérieux. Toute ma vie n'a été qu'un jeu.[4]

Possibly even Sartre himself did not know how serious he was in rejecting seriousness. Certainly, it is hard to deny the importance of game, *comédie*, playing with words in the total phenomenon of Jean-Paul Sartre. A sense of humour is clearly operative repeatedly in *La Nausée*, *Les Mots*, *Le Mur*, and various plays; it is dramatically crucial. It boxes its weight.

La Nausée

Sartre is unafraid of sounding grotesque. Often he approaches what are essentially comic issues with pedantic gravity. It may be that 'absurdity' as a philosophical theme cannot altogether evade its everyday associations with ridiculousness. Roquentin gets highly worked up about the colour of the barman Adolphe's braces. They are mauve. This harmless fact strangely irritates Roquentin, who insists to himself that mauve is an in-between colour, that it is not really trying, but should let it rip and become violet. It is the indecisiveness of mauve that appals him. He scolds it as if it were a weak-kneed acquaintance. Similar finickiness is involved in his attempt to distinguish himself from a table, because in a kind of reverse solipsism the table seems to have more reality than he does. Even with the near-sanctified jazz-music, Sartre (unwittingly) courts mockery by choosing as his antidote to the philosophical blues a not very distinguished piece of vocal ragtime.

In *La Nausée*, he everywhere rejects images of digestion (complacency), and substitutes emetic images (shock). It is a highly deflationary text, with an inflationary ending. Sartre engineers the visitation of nausea into Roquentin's life every bit as craftily as Mauriac does that of God's grace.[5] The first onset was in Roquentin's past. Faced with accompanying an archaeological mission *à la* Malraux to the Orient, he feels the opposite from, but also the mainspring for, his later cult of hardness: 'J'étais rempli de lymphe et de lait tiède'.[6] Actual nausea, in its special Sartrian sense, takes a couple of hundred pages to come up, surely the slowest onset in a novel or a life on record. In *Les Mots*, Sartre accurately compares *La Nausée* to a microscope. What Roquentin unearths in front of the chestnut-tree root in the public park is the swirling mass of matter that presents itself to any eye gazing at a sample down a microscope. The previously familiar or anodyne is defamiliarized. We can feel we are seeing into the true messy core of things. Of course, obsessive concentration on objects can betoken a variety of madness, or just the extreme care of the scientist or craftsman. Roquentin is in grave danger of thinking himself into inexistence, in his efforts to escape the greedy maw of existence. He overloads the material world, thus giving himself and his putative readers a real bellyful of it. Nausea is an excellent symbol for this strategy. Hence the increasingly berserk meditation on the Cartesian *cogito* (p. 142), by the end of which both he and we have almost had enough of thinking itself. Despite the self-injunction on the opening page: 'Il ne faut pas mettre de l'étrange où il n'y a rien' (p. 11), throughout Roquentin exploits the inherently comic device of defamiliarization or estrangement. The aim is to justify and to find virtue in *not* living 'bien bourgeoisement dans le monde' (ibid.).

The opposite of the honest microscope is the bourgeois—all those who erect façades and try to impose shapes on their largely amorphous existences. Most such live dozily, switched off; even their eyes stop focusing. Roquentin's sardonic humour will act as correcting lenses in their place. Is the bourgeois Everyman? 'Tout existant naît sans raison, se prolonge par faiblesse et meurt par rencontre' (p. 189).[7] It is perhaps only Roquentin's aggressiveness, topped by his fiery red hair, that keeps any sort of interaction between this solitary and the herd of Bouvillois going, for hatreds, like love, can bind. His very gaze on the town's denizens is that of the stranger, indeed the alien, who finds a sinister comedy in all the myriad bourgeois pretensions that he witnesses. He indulges himself in heavy satire of the mass Sunday promenade. In another piece of sarcastic bravura, his visit to the municipal art-gallery climaxes the extended mockery of the town elite, the worthies of Bouville. This section is pure iconoclasm: he shatters the public image of the notables. He thinks hard and unforgivingly against the good people of the town and their iconic representatives, though the citizenry is blissfully unaware of the would-be machine-gun spraying them with contempt that would like to be bullets. In general, Roquentin's disgust and his satirical urge freeze the Bouvillois, so that it is difficult to imagine them exercising the freedom of choice supposedly available to them. That his gaze would love to be lethal is made clear by the intellectual inverted snobbery that makes him rejoice to find, in the middle of the town's classiest district, a squalid little shop selling insecticide and rat-poison. There is schoolboy humour in his dream of spanking Maurice Barrès, a great literary father figure and the prime exponent of patriotism on the French cultural scene in the early twentieth century. Though unmistakably French, Roquentin is, wilfully, a lackland.

When he writes that 'rien de ce qui existe ne peut être comique' (p. 181), presumably he is talking of the non-human as being indescribable even in comic terms, and implicitly comparing its unceasing self-transformation with the social unchangingness of humans: this kind of (false) essence *is* comic. Roquentin, however, refuses to laugh at Dr Rogé's joke: 'Je ne ris pas, je ne réponds pas à ses avances' (p. 98). Nor does he laugh much on his own: 'Il est rare qu'un homme seul ait envie de rire' (p. 18). Laughter, no doubt, is largely a collective phenomenon (even if we laugh while reading alone, there are two participating agencies). Sternly puritan as he often is, Sartre denies any genuine group-feeling in company: we laugh alone, together.[8] More terrestrially for once, Valéry asked: 'A-t-on jamais expliqué la contagion du rire, du bâillement ou de la nausée?'[9] Roquentin tries to insulate himself against any contagion from his fellows; he would loathe to see *his* nausea spread to others.

Comic exaggeration recurs in *La Nausée*. Sartre would later astutely analyse, in his massive *L'Idiot de la famille*, its importance in Flaubert's life and work. He says of the youthful Flaubert's attempt to turn the peer spectators of his 'Garçon' performance into a proper audience: 'Il est amené à pousser à l'extrême sa comédie comme si son hyperbolisme, par un passage à l'infini, parvenait à compenser l'inconsistance du geste, lui conférait la réalité d'un acte et finissait par emporter l'adhésion du spectateur'.[10] This is Sartre's frequent pun on the two crucial meanings of acting: make-believe and authentic deeds. Though he is talking of the young Flaubert, for Sartre (cf. *Les Mots*) the child is father to the man. *Dérision*, too, plays between active scorn and the sorry human comedy itself. The first responds in kind, giff-gaff, to the second. For all the voluntarist Sartre's critique of Flaubert's fatalism, he could but admire the thoroughness of Gustave's artistic and philosophical globalization, his levelling of all playing-fields in a kind of democratic nihilism best typified by *Bouvard et Pécuchet*. There Flaubert goes over the same basic ground umpteen times like a manic mower. I think of Cyril Connolly's nifty coinage 'futilitarianism', which tightly melds a key nineteenth-century concept and utter pointlessness.[11] On the same page, Connolly maintains that 'behind the concept of futility is a passionate belief in art, coupled with a contempt for the subjects about which art is made'. We find a comparable schizophrenia in Roquentin's dubious artistic solution to his disillusionment with the world and its people.

You cheat if you impose shape on naturally amorphous experience, by telling concocted anecdotes, or laying claim to 'Experience'. So, if Roquentin ends by aiming to modulate his messy life into the verbal equivalent of a piece of music, to make his life a song, it is because he longs to escape the material and social worlds, where the only alternative to fake solidity *à la* Balzac is chaos and absurdity. The longed-for hardness would have to be somehow impalpable: musical notes, words on a page. And not the hated bourgeois version: a bronze statue, which in its way also seeks some kind of eternity. The target of 'dureté' is an intangible hardness, and also implacability. Is this hypothetical, virtual book Roquentin's counterpart to bourgeois 'mauvaise foi', i.e. an attempt to cling to an essence, however immaterial? He does have the decency to doubt his own solution, for 'il n'y a que les salauds qui croient gagner' (p. 221). Like an honorary Brit, Roquentin wills himself to be a gallant loser. On numerous occasions in *La Nausée*, Sartre seeks to make impalpable things physical, for example when Roquentin likens Rollebon's presence in him, which he is about to liquidate, to 'une chaleur légère au creux de l'estomac' (p. 136). With his own Nausea, however, he seems to aim for the opposite: fleeing the physical (vomiting), and seeking to convey an abstract experience, a philosophical illumination. He is trying, like the pun, to have it both ways. The opposite of an analysis (a breakdown) is a construct, a fabrication. An analysis resembles an autopsy. A construct is more like the invention of a new life. 'L'homme est à inventer chaque jour'.[12]

In *La Nausée*, we see comic exaggeration in descriptions, for instance of the café card-player: 'Ce type à moustaches possède d'énormes

narines, qui pourraient pomper de l'air pour toute une famille' (p. 36).
Or the Autodidact, compared successively to a dog, a chicken and
a donkey (ibid.). Roquentin can even ridicule himself as a Baked
Alaska, 'un bloc de glace enveloppé de feu, une omelette-surprise'
(p. 163). More widely, his scorn for the middle class, his annoyance
at Adolphe's mauve braces, and, above all, his strategy of attacking
anthropomorphism (the attempt to make anarchic nature cosier) by
injecting an overdose of it into himself, all widely share Flaubert's
'hyperbolisme'. In the process of losing any semblance of control
over the endlessly proliferating chestnut-tree, for Roquentin the phenomenon of growth is switched from the Tree of Knowledge (which
empowered and then damned humankind) to the Tree of Nescience.
Old habits of animism die hard. In his constipated if dyspeptic view,
the tree's sap circulates reluctantly (p. 189). He might have felt, but
for his programmatic aversion from anthropomorphism, some kinship,
for both it and he are 'de trop': superfluous (p. 180). Yet, at the end of
his epiphany in the park, he suddenly exclaims, surprisingly: 'Le jardin
m'a souri' (p. 191). A kind of complicity? Do things talk to him as to
nobody else? Are they and he sharing a joke, an in-joke that nobody
else knows about or could twig? Is this the elision between comic and
cosmic that we will find haunting Michel Tournier?

Roquentin certainly shares little with anyone else. He does consent
to a painfully hilarious meal with the Autodidact, the milksop humanist, where this earnest pain-in-the-neck displays indignant dignity,
whereas his guest can manage only surly humour: 'J'avais envie de
déjeuner avec lui comme de me pendre' (p. 110). Despite the comparisons with assorted animals, the host is barely real to him: 'Avec
l'Autodidacte on n'est jamais deux qu'en apparence' (p. 109). The
clerk shoots himself in the foot when he says of a banal idea he might
just have been capable of conceiving: 'Si c'était vrai, quelqu'un l'aurait
déjà pensé' (p. 156). This is self-deprecation carried to the point of
self-deletion. Yet part of the implicit or unconscious joke about the
contrast between the two men is that Roquentin also, inasmuch as
we are uninformed about his formal education, is a self-taught man.

What about his other pseudo-relationship, with Anny? At their
final meeting, she laughs twice, rather enigmatically (pp. 192–3).
She laughs at a private joke, which cannot be shared. No wonder
that the nonplussed Roquentin has 'un sourire très faux' on his lips
(p. 194). There is something funny about a man who believes he has

just cracked the riddle of the universe being discountenanced by a histrionic actress. She seems to him different from the cross-section of humanity that he has learned to detest, but, while he feels different from them, too, he does not altogether like it in her. As for her, she now sees him not as a rock of reliability, a constant lover, but as a mere milestone, a mark she has passed (p. 202). Altogether, she is a 'Méduse', and so he feels in the wrong and the object of her petrifying judgement (p. 203). The one amusing memory she retains is of their first kiss, when she was sitting on nettles (p. 210). The distance between them is made complete when, like a voyeur, he watches a man help her up on to a train at the gare St Lazare (p. 218). The whole affair has been strained, 'unnatural', and it has bred only false, dutiful laughter.

Roquentin comes more alive in solitary sex, as when he riffles through booksellers' displays on the Paris *quais*, 'et tout particulièrement les publications obscènes, parce que, malgré tout, ça occupe l'esprit' (p. 218). In this respect at least, Antoine is a stereotypical normal man. More revelatory is his apocalyptic vision of a world running sexually amok (p. 224). 'Alors, j'éclaterai de rire' (p. 225): a sadistic, triumphant laugh. He enjoys thinking that he is a mute Cassandra (ibid.).

It is the more neurotic moments of Sartre's existentialism that are the most risible. You don't have to be a woman to mock the section in *L'Être et le Néant* on 'le visqueux': 'C'est une activité molle, baveuse, et féminine d'aspiration, il vit obscurément sous mes doigts et je sens comme un vertige, il m'attire en lui comme le fond d'un précipice pourrait m'attirer'. He goes on: 'Le visqueux apparaît comme un liquide vu dans un cauchemar et dont les propriétés s'animeraient d'une sorte de vie et se retourneraient contre moi' (pp. 700–1). Sartre's horrified version of the classic 'vagina dentata', though toothless, is just as devouring. In terms of imagery, male (macho) is hard, female squidgy. To such a mind and body as his, the viscous is especially fearsome, as it is neither truly solid nor truly liquid: you know not where to have it/her. It is gooey, like what Roquentin comically calls that 'ignoble marmalade' (p. 190).

Wittgenstein talked of a 'serious and good philosophical work' that could be written, and 'that would consist entirely of jokes (without being facetious)'.[13] More casually, Robert Escarpit has ventured that 'Jean-Paul Sartre affirmant que l'existentialisme est un human-isme aurait pu aussi bien (et peut-être plus efficacement) dire que l'existentialisme est un humour'.[14] For W. J. Harvey, '*La Nausée* is an entirely serious novel but it is also a huge joke'.[15] Mary McCarthy spoke of those books ruled by 'arcane laughter'—a kind of in-house humour shared by the author, the hero, and any unusually alert reader.[16] Rewriting, as in this novel Sartre does to Descartes, is usually a humorous activity, involving comic chutzpah. In-jokes, like jargon or slang, are the secret language of a coterie, though of course, as all language is mobile, all these lingos filter up, down, and gradually be-come common currency, or at least achieve wider spread, by hearsay. Bookishness, and *La Nausée* is haunted by foregoing writing, can open up possibilities, rather than narrow them down.

Of my chosen authors, it is Diderot, Huysmans, and Tournier whose works seem the most comparable or contrastable with *La Nausée*. Diderot's Jacques is an anti-Roquentin. He derives his life's meaning from the contingent (and he was earlier a soldier). Sartre makes a show of avoiding conventional plot by using the discrete discourse of the diary form. For Roquentin, anecdotes falsify reality, by congealing lived experience into sound-bites. For Jacques, they are the very stuff of life itself, mini-novels or biographies. The reactions of the listeners to the Mme de la Pommeraye story interact with the narrative itself. Thus anecdotes are a community venture: all muck in. You can't imagine Roquentin telling jokes or anecdotes, or listening to them with any pleasure. His natural bent goes towards satire, that is: distancing. In humorological terms, he is a Berg-sonian. Though he hates 'l'esprit de système', he is serious-minded. Without anecdotes, jokes, or other shaped narratives, life would be just one damned thing after another. *Jacques le fataliste* is social, *La Nausée* alienated.

As for Huysmans, Jean Borie calls *La Nausée* 'ce livre huysmanien'.[17] *A rebours* and *La Nausée* are alike elitist, with solitary heroes much fixated on proliferation, and in response striving to catalogue and shape what threatens to overwhelm them. Above all, in both books we witness the erection of artifice against sprawling nature and detested fellow humans.

Tournier's early worship of Sartre (both of them Germanophiles) turned to bitter disillusion, when the idol vulgarized his austere philosophy into the mould of humanistic existentialism. Yet Mélanie, in 'La Jeune Fille et la mort', experiences a Sartrian nausea, which ultimately she laughs at with her dying breath. In *Les Mots*, when Poulou's mother sings to the child Goethe's 'Le Roi des aulnes', he stops up his ears, because the child in the verses is snatched away from his parent by Death. For his own part, of course, Tournier relishes contemplating such abductions.

A possibly acceptable antidote to the philosophical blues is therapeutic mirth, or in Roquentin's uptight case, a sardonic wryness and a grim gaiety. How seriously does Sartre take Roquentin? The 'editor's note' about the notebooks that we are about to read says they were found among the papers of Antoine Roquentin. This ploy has been a literary joke since the eighteenth century, in order to explain the provenance of manuscripts. Is a dead man speaking in *La Nausée*? Has Sartre killed off his protagonist offstage, like a Cornelian hero, at the summit of his wannabe decisiveness (he may write a book)? Did he? Well, at least he wrote the story of a man who wanted to turn his life up to that point into a novel. Is Roquentin the sub-human in this quote: 'Le rire provoqué par le comique prétend nous révéler que tout homme est un sous-homme qui se prend au sérieux'?[18] Sartre started out on what would become *La Nausée* in 1931, calling it his 'factum [lampoon] sur la contingence'. Despite his acidic comments on it in *Les Mots*, ten years later Sartre freely admitted that *La Nausée* was in all likelihood his major work, presumably because, as he aged, he refound his initial anarchism of spirit.[19]

Humour in *Le Mur*

Sartre's concept of 'la contre-finalité', which he uses mainly in an economic context—self-destruct capitalism—can be converted to the more familiar Sod's Law: that backfiring, gang-agley feature of all human life. In the title story of *Le Mur*, despite its place in the literature of extreme situations, Sartre exploits the gallows humour of a fundamentally absurd situation, illustrated in *L'Être et le Néant* by an aristocrat quipping, like Sir Thomas More, on his way to the scaffold (p. 617). In preparation for his final and lethal joke, Pablo Ibbieta feels amused by his eye-battle with his interrogators. His cult of being 'un dur' makes his mulishness comic even to himself: 'Une drôle de gaieté m'envahit'.[20] This hilarity lubricates his playing a practical joke on his captors ('leur faire une farce' (p. 33)), to send them on what he imagines will be a wild-goose chase. In so doing, he believes he is reinventing himself: 'Je me représentais la situation comme si j'avais été un autre' (ibid.). He remains, however, part of the comic conjuncture: 'Ce prisonnier obstiné à faire le héros, ces graves phalangistes avec leurs moustaches et ces hommes en uniforme qui couraient entre les tombes; c'était d'un comique irrésistible' (ibid.). He cannot visualize death, his own or another's, but he can enjoy in fancy this fool's errand. In earlier life, Pablo had played at politics, so his endgame is in keeping. Besides, as an anarchist, he acts solo, in aleatory fashion. His random naming of a location for the fugitive Ramón Gris becomes blackly, and doubly, a shot in the dark. He has not achieved praxis, but only parapraxis; his ludic gesture produces murderous consequences. At the finale, all that remains for Pablo is to laugh, bitterly, on the other side of his face, in this variant instance of *Galgenhumor*.

Pablo is nevertheless nearer the angels than the other sorry agonists of *Le Mur*, but he too is riddled and undermined by disabling ambiguities. I am reminded of Empson's

> Waiting for the end, boys, waiting for the end.
> What is there to be or do?
>
> .   .   .   .
>
> Each of us enisled, boys, waiting for the end.[21]

In 'La Chambre', the schizophrenic Paul, by a comic turnaround, finds 'normal' people funny, instead of meekly accepting himself as a candidate for the funny farm. In 'Erostrate', Sartre inserts a joke against himself for dragging in a classical allusion (Eratostratus), for the reference is made by an office colleague, Massé, 'qui avait des lettres' (p. 88). Erostrate's failed, seriously defective humanity and his piously hoped-for antihumanism ironically make him more human, though still a miserable specimen. Sartre is having it both ways with a vengeance: he ridicules Paul Hilbert while satirizing stereotypical humanists. Sartre's anti-exemplary hero in fact voices his own prejudices against the professional humanist, which of course Sartre would himself later become. Like Roquentin's archetypal bourgeois bugbears in *La Nausée*, Hilbert depicts these loathed humanists as appropriators of exclusive rights. All told, Erostrate is heroicomic, seriocomic. As with circus clowns, the spectacle of a struggling wretch engaged in pedantically meticulous preparations for what results in fiasco is unavoidably comic. The Lobster Quadrille of siding with/deserting, of magnetism and repulsion, so palpable in this story, is a shifty constant in Sartre's work (e.g. the studies of Baudelaire, Flaubert, or Genet). The demarcation-line between the empathetic, the vicarious, and the judgemental is never steadily applied.

Much of the undeniable comedy of 'L'Enfance d'un chef' resides in the blindfolded behaviour of the hero's parents, who do not notice the psychic disarray of their young child, which is more thoroughly anguished than his later Barrésian angst, borrowed and not self-generated. After beheading some weeds in the family garden, Lucien Fleurier tries to lay down the law to a chestnut-tree, a foretaste of his climactic bossing of employees. Naturally, he lacks the sophistication of Roquentin in face of his obdurate tree: the fact of life that names are only labels; things in themselves are strictly unnameable. Humans can in their heads organize nature, but not order it about in the open air. Before the mutism of the tree, unbiddable, bloody-minded, Lucien concludes that it must be 'de bois': stony-hearted, unresponsive. A perfect truism and pun. Lucien is beating his head against a ligneous wall. The result is that nature is denatured, for having refused to lick the budding boss's boots. Finally, Lucien unleashes a kick at this object guilty of lèse majesté. He is, however, also learning violence, and the trick of derealizing your inferior opponents at will. As his story progresses, or rather runs away with him, Lucien will speak more and more a 'langue de bois', made up of clichés and slogans.

The frequent comedy of this novella keeps Lucien recognizably human: he undergoes the pains and embarrassments of many an adolescent. He thus discovers his gawkiness: 'Quoi qu'il entreprît, il avait toujours l'impression que ce corps était en train d'exister de tous les côtés à la fois, sans lui demander son avis' (p. 171). His own sporadic and often less than wilful jokes act as a sufficient, if not a saving, grace. Besides, most of the rest of the cast in this story are much more unredeemably laughable than Lucien. His test for whether he is a pederast is wonderfully comic. He gazes intently at the nape of a cop to see if the sight troubles him. It would be difficult to imagine a less erotic sexual object. When he discovers girls and kissing-competitions,

Sartre grants him a mouth which seizes up after hours of statutory smiling. At school, Lucien had stumbled upon the power of mockery, directed at his gangly frame, in the approximately spelt graffito: 'Lucien est une grande asperche' (p. 169): beanpole/prick. When later he joins a protofascist gang, he experiences laughter as 'l'affirmation d'un droit' (p. 228). He injects himself with anti-Semitic jokes (tellingly borrowed as a family inheritance from his factory-owning father), and revels in his image as a Jew-baiter. Sartre sums up wittily: 'Lucien n'avait pas son pareil pour reconnaître un Juif *à vue de nez*' (p. 230, my italics). Despite touches of humour, Lucien cannot see how ludicrous his posture is. Flaubert and his fellow *collégiens* were more brutal: 'La dérision [...] est un lynchage mineur. Chacun s'entraîne ici à se lyncher pour pouvoir lyncher les autres'.[22] When Lucien finally and joylessly loses his virginity, Sartre refers back to that school graffito by describing Lucien as 'une grande asperge souillée' (p. 235).

The search for authority, chiefhood, subjacent *per absurdum* throughout, is not for the fainthearted. Hence Lucien's decision at the end to grow a moustache. The movement of the story goes from the fog of uncertainty to apparent clarity of purpose, but this is a false *clarté* in which we can detect a veiled satire of the Cartesian tradition and the enormous French myth stemming from it. The irony, everywhere present, is that this nascent chieftain has let himself be led from his birth: he is a social fabrication. This is parody of the *Bildungsroman* where the hero does not construct himself in any truly wilful sense. The collection *Le Mur* relates four stories of failure and one of undesirable success. The humour of 'L'Enfance d'un chef' throws a bridge, however shaky in the wind, between Sartre and Lucien. Parody written *con amore*, for there is complicity as well as duplicity, as well as judgement.

The Theatre

In its demystifying (more strictly, counter-mystificatory) passion, Sartre's theatre is wilfully iconoclastic:

Je crois, moi, profondément que toute démystification doit être en un sens mystifiante. Ou plutôt que, devant une foule en partie mystifiée, on ne peut se fier aux seules réactions critiques de cette foule. Il faut lui fournir une contre-mystification, et pour cela le théâtre ne doit se priver d'aucune des sorcelleries du théâtre.[23]

This is no doubt true, but high-handed. 'Hypocrite' means stage-actor. 'Mauvaise foi' relies heavily on 'comédie', in both senses; posing, and affording a comic spectacle. Sartre never believed that anything could simply be laughed away, but he did believe that any writer worth his salt should try to dissolve (or at least pit) resistant enemies in a bath of critical acid.[24]

Huis clos is black comedy, and the gallows humour comes *after* the drop through the trapdoor. Of the three people hounding each other in hell, Inès is the most adept at this excruciation. 'Eh bien, ils ont réalisé des économies de personnel. Voilà tout. Ce sont les clients qui font le service eux-mêmes, comme dans les restaurants coopératifs'.[25] In this self-service Hades, each of the three laughs at some point, mockingly, dryly, in order to accentuate their reciprocal torture.

Their situation is absurd. They protest innocence when no new verdict is possible. They are no longer able to be dead serious about anything. They are the dead unserious, the stalled earnest ones, hence their strained hilarity. In the last lines, however, the laughter has a dying fall, as they fully register the ineluctable merry-go-round of their fate.

In the body of the play, the attempted murder of Inès by Estelle is inherently comic: you cannot stab to death a corpse or ghost. More efficiently than the one in the play, the bell, of course, tolls also for us. What have we got to hide? How do we try to justify ourselves?

In *Les Mains sales*, counter-finality, unintended result, Murphy's Law reign supreme. Hoederer's dying words are 'Ah! C'est trop con!'[26] The fantasies of Hugo and Jessica—of passing from a life of *comédie* to ballasted living—come true, but not in the way that either of them expected. Like the rootless Oreste in *Les Mouches*, Hugo had hoped to attach his crime of political murder round his neck like a millstone, so that gravity would take over from levity. 'L'esprit de sérieux' includes party-mindedness, blind faith, exhibited by Louis in this play, to which even Hugo's *comédie* seems preferable. Like Hugo, Roquentin had wanted to keep his hands clean, as evidenced by his distaste for the slimy pebble. He wants in effect to live in an ivory tower, and to possess for himself the clear-cut edges of glazed earthenware.

Black comedy excruciates and is thus a variant torture in both *Huis clos* and *Les Séquestrés d'Altona*, which have much in common.[27] The German term *Galgenhumor* seems peculiarly apt for the tone of much of the dialogue in *Les Séquestrés d'Altona*. Think of the manic giggling that comes over some people in desperate situations. Sartre's hostility to 'l'esprit de sérieux' has a countervailing ludism, but always a pointed and loaded playfulness. Early in the play, the industrialist von Gerlach refers to his terminal cancer as 'une mort industrielle'.[28] He and his son will die from a different industrial death, in a self-chosen sports-car crash.

Puns are a notorious branch of excruciation. The stock reaction to them is to wince or grimace at the collision of meanings they engineer. The crippled woman crouching by the wall in Frantz's 'dream' moves from the literal 'Je suis au pied du mur' to the punning literalization: 'J'ai mis au pied du mur un soldat de chez nous' (p. 289). Back to the wall is moreover the favoured stance (or *querencia*) of the defensive/aggressive punner. The crucial pun on 'cancer' refers also to the zodiac sign, the Crab. Frantz's neuroses about these crustaceans have gone to lodge in his father's throat. Obsession with his son helps to kill him just as his son's fixation on him leaves neither of them with anywhere to fly to except joint suicide.

Leni says, offering another tape to her recording demon of a brother: 'Qu'est-ce que tu veux, maître chanteur?' A Meistersinger perfectly suits the apocalyptic, Wagnerian tonality of the play. And Frantz, like all the family players in turn, is the other kind of 'maître chanteur': an expert emotional blackmailer.

The image of the 'tourniquet', much exploited by Sartre in his massive study of Flaubert's 'neurosis', and which centres on excruciation of attitudes and language, resurfaces in this play. A tourniquet is a painful antidote to pain from a wound. In military slang, it means a court-martial, which Frantz escaped but for which he substitutes his tribunal of crabs.

Sartre's honesty makes him see the funny side of everything. Johanna says to von Gerlach: 'Tout est comique, au rez-de-chaussée, même vous qui allez mourir' (p. 217). The other kind of *comédie*, theatrical, develops upstairs, too, between Frantz and this former actress. Frantz says to her: 'La chambre a reçu le vide en coup de faux' (p. 166). This could mean either that her essential vacuity scythed into the room, like Death; or that something counterfeit has derealized the room. Neither interpretation flatters this glamorous lady.

As a would-be absolutist, Frantz necessarily exaggerates. He lifts up to hyperbolic levels what Sartre consistently sees as a universal human disability: we are all, always, in danger of not acting but play-acting. As

Christina Howells says: 'Sartre uses the inherent insubstantiality of the theatrical medium both to embody and to denounce play-acting'.[29] In other words, he uses self-referentiality (as in Frantz's in-jokes with the audience), not to break the scenic spell, which he valued highly, but to underline the inescapable link for him of living and *comédie*.

On the charge of hyperbole often laid against him, Sartre's response comes indirectly via his defence of Jean Genet: 'Il enfle nos sophismes jusqu'à les faire éclater [...] il exagère notre mauvaise foi jusqu'à nous la rendre intolérable'.[30] Maybe this does not answer the charge; it dismisses it, and counter-attacks. A variant exaggeration, exacerbation, rules *Les Séquestrés d'Altona*. Far more acutely than in Anouilh's 'pièces grinçantes', people here grate on each other's nerve-ends. In addition, Frantz grinds his oyster-shells implacably together. The audience gnashes its teeth.

At times, we are subjected to that *marivaudage* which Marivaux himself generally avoided: verbal conceits, excessively clever points-scoring, but never so cripplingly as in the elephantine *Nekrassov*. Frantz has the courage of his excruciating convictions. He debonairly converts Henry of Navarre's historic 'Paris vaut bien une messe' to: 'L'Allemagne vaut bien un crime, hein, quoi?' (p. 311).

Piège and *pièce* are graphic cousins. All Sartre's plays are mousetraps of a kind undreamt of by Agatha Christie. In *Les Séquestrés d'Altona*, the whole dysfunctional but mutually magnetized family act out their 'ample comédie aux cent sketches divers'.[31] They all put on a non-stop show ('We never closed') for each other, each of them spotlit from his/her particular advantage-point. If it often seems a shrill, histrionic play, it is so, inevitably. Its family has derealized itself, has become (like the family thespians of *Les Mots*) a repertory company. Beneath all the bandages of sophistication raw wounds leak. Sartre applies the tourniquet to his characters and his audience. His category of 'contre-finalité' is at heart a blackly comic concept, like any kind of ironical backfiring. It stresses our ultimate lack of a say, over things, other people, or even ourselves.

Sartre and Punning

'La passion des calembours—comme on voit chez Flaubert—n'est pas une mauvaise préparation à la littérature': cuckoo-like, Sartre is forever offloading his own scions on to his enemy brother.[32] Unsure scions, they embody and breed ambivalence. The child at the chilly heart of *Les Mots* confesses as much: 'Je fabriquai des mots à double sens que je lâchais en public'.[33] A thoroughly programmed bourgeois, he capitalizes on the oracular wisdom (for oracles often speak in puns and conundrums) with which he is accustomed to being credited: his ill-gotten gains. He supplies to his captivated consumers all that, and even more than, they demand.

The boy-actor, like his senior fellows, operates on two planes: in his case, the little old man and the discountable child. Small wonder that he avenges his perverted state and his humiliation by all manner of duplicities, verbal twists as well as gestural grimaces. Even novice readers are struck by the ambiguities, the inconclusiveness, of *Les Mots*. Some commentators have remarked incidentally on odd puns at work there, but have not seen them globally as central agents of the text's ambivalence.

Portmanteau words are often verbal plays, as in Lewis Carroll. The composite name or blend encapsulating the grandparents, 'Karlémami', is the first occurrence of the phenomenon which gives the book its title: the power of words to dictate, to forge, reality. Linked phonically by their telescoped names, the grandparents seem to be linked intrinsically, and so to form an indissoluble couple or essence. Punning takes words for things or relationships, sounds for substances. A true unity is absent from the actual marriage, as so often in puns. As well as falsity, the pun can accommodate authentic ambiguity. *Esprit* straddles both spirit and mind, and thus encourages grandfather Charles's belief that the cultivation of the mind is a spiritual exercise (an implicit joking reference to Jesuit practice; indeed Poulou, that premature stiff, could adopt for his motto 'Perinde ac cadaver'). The mind is seen, conveniently in the short term but disastrously in the long, as bodiless. Sartre lays claim to a fundamental *légèreté*: lightness, freedom from gravity, frivolity—the result of lacking a ponderous father. Another paternal gap, the superego, is evoked with punning cunning ('sur moi'/Surmoi): 'Eût-il vécu, mon père se fût couché sur moi de tout son long. [...] ces géniteurs invisibles à cheval sur leurs fils' (p. 11). The absent rider is treated in cavalier fashion. Riderless (but surely the stand-in jockey Charles is worth his weight in lead?), the boy could pursue his lifelong *fuite en avant* (Sartre's private hymn would be 'Onward, unChristian soldiers!').

This double bind suggests not only forward motion, the semblance
of progress, but also the urge to escape. Was he running towards
or away? Either way, the future, like the past, overdetermines his
present.

If we modulate from movement to position, we meet the running
joke about 'elevation', already current in *Le Rouge et le Noir*, twisted
round his little finger by Clamence in *La Chute*,[34] and here centred
both on the altitude of Sartre's successive apartments above street-
level, and his psychic sense, not of a superiority-complex so much
as an elsewhere-complex—difference, uniqueness—in relation to his
fellows. To contrast his alternation between idealist ascension and
realist plunging, Sartre chooses the curiously close images of the
Cartesian diver (*le ludion*) and the deep-sea diver (*le scaphandrier*); the
bottle-imp rises in a water-filled container, and the heavyweight sinks
to the ocean bottom. The compass of the contrast is not wide: five
of one and half a dozen of the other. But perhaps that is the very
point. By the end of *Les Mots*, Sartre will opt out of this shadow-play
between up and down, and will settle for being level with the rest
of us.

Even there, of course, he will still be immodestly common-or-
garden, just as earlier he had been an unassuming maniac (the
'anonymous saviour'). Beneath all this chiasmic and oxymoronic
patterning lies the fundamental vacuity: the young Sartre, a Lackland, had no concrete base. In English, 'the Good'/'goods' offers too
small-scale a doubling. *Le Bien/les biens* affords the most telling of the
numerous lacks which helped to constitute and define the juvenile
hero. The entirely natural and potentially healthy generation-divide
was not operating; it was in fact a *missing gap*. As a result, the child
felt superfluous, that is: filling no gap. He therefore creates a cavity
he can fill—that of the indispensable, mandated, providential writer.
Usually, just as Sartre championed the bastard, he would value the
negative state of owning nothing as a bonus. If, in this context, he
seems to hanker for that bourgeois foundation, it can be only as a
starting block to kick off against. Lacking which, he ran for years on
the spot. He was a *spoilt* child: cosseted, overripe, all but ruined.

Another set of puns focuses necessarily on *la répétition*: reiteration, and rehearsal. This is an important hinge-pun, for it alludes
both backwards (re-enacting the past) and forwards (anticipating the
future). The child is caught between restaging Charles in his own

theatre (pastiche resembles the approximate pun, for it too overlays the original with a near-likeness; Charles pastiches Victor Hugo, who was already a self-parodist), or imagining in advance a self-generated future. In his first writings, however, he rehashes what he has read, but in the hope of bringing the future, via this literature of wish-fulfilment, to irrigate his desolate present. The grandson's misfortune is to take for his role model a man whose life was already done with, and who is merely repeating himself. In addition, the boy-writer locks himself in as vicious a circle as that *tourniquet* which Sartre identifies in Flaubert's existential position, for his stories endlessly replay Good defeating an ever-resurgent Evil. At his apparently most dynamic, he is still marking time. *L'enchaînement*, another polysemous motif, implies both logic and enslavement, and much of *Les Mots* indeed sways between these two possibilities. Is Sartre, despite his resolve, still being constrained by verbal logic into pattern-making out of contact with the facts of life? Are we condemned to be free, or do we freely damn ourselves? Sartre relishes, or cannot evade, such ambiguous words, because the situations he is dealing in are ambivalent, fishy, Catch-22. A book so bedevilled by words quite expectably delves regularly into wordplay as a means of exorcism.

Aping the cuckoo myself, I would say that there is another continuous play on *grandes personnes*, the term generally preferred by Sartre to *adultes*. No doubt this is partly due to the child's-eye view, but it also connotes the boy's excessive respect for authority (*personnages*). Yet the boy learns to pierce such façades: *personne* is also nobody. Lastly, Sartre eschews *adultes*, for the older generation in *Les Mots* is not grown up in any proper sense. Charles is in his second childhood; Anne-Marie, Poulou's mother, suffers arrested development (this widowed mother and her fatherless son are taken in by her parents, in more ways than one); the sceptical grandmother acts as enfant terrible. The *comédie familiale* is the most naked of the puns; the Schweitzers' histrionic imposture is a long-run comedy, though the laughs engendered by *Les Mots* tickle the meninx more than the thorax.

The actor leads a double life, 'toutes deux mensongères' (p. 109), but is always conscious of his illusion-making. This involves a divided consciousness, a form of schizophrenia, though Sartre in fact never uses this catch-all term in *Les Mots*. Poulou's alienation is psychic as well as social. For Freud, an entire neurosis could take the shape, as in the 'Rat-Man' case (*Rate, Ratte, Spielratte, hieraten*), of an elaborated pun. In his study of Genet, Sartre discusses the artifice of self-preservation embodied in Genet's strategy of self-surveillance, by reaction against and in exacerbation of the fact of being spied on by all and sundry: 'Prendre vis-à-vis du langage l'atttude du paranoïaque vis-à-vis du monde, y chercher tous les symboles, tous les signes, toutes les allusions, pour pouvoir, le cas échéant, les reprendre à son compte et les faire passer pour l'effet de sa volonté'.[35] Sartre terms his own extended delusion about his mission in life a neurosis. Like Genet, he fights back with an acute sense of the double-edgedness of words. The notion of the doubled-up self, besides, permeates everyday language: 'to be out of one's mind', 'to be beside oneself', 'to come to one's senses'. Throughout *Les Mots*, the mature Sartre is the chastising doppelgänger of the child Sartre. He plays Mine Own Executioner, in order to preempt our strike.

He applies the tourniquet. He squeezes, he milks language for maximum yield. Like Flaubert, he piles it on thick, in an act of *hyperbolisme*.[36] When the boy, with only rhetorical veracity, answers the public questionnaire during the First World War by claiming that his dearest wish is to become a soldier and to avenge the French dead, we see that it is only in words that he goes over the top. Throughout he exaggerates his grandfather's conditioning, and thus upstages the old ham. Excruciation is the Flaubertian mode par excellence, and in it mingle pedagogic urges (to teach a lesson) and *Schadenfreude*. Queneau spoke of his neo-Flaubertian ambition, 'élever le calembour à la hauteur d'un supplice'.[37] In Flaubert, playing with words and agonizing over them shared a bed. Not long before his death, recalls Sartre, Flaubert wrote to his niece: 'Suppose que je m'appelle Druche. Tu me dirais: tu es beau, Druche'.[38] This lumbering set-up for a knock-kneed gag (*baudruche*: windbag) underscores a lifelong taste for making others squirm but also, in this instance, a pathetic plea for camaraderie, for the warmest insults are the ones we direct against or receive from those closest to us. Hence the desperate gaiety of Flaubert's cult (an antisocial in-game) of *farces et attrapes*. The pun was known of old as a 'catch'. A trap, a trapdoor for the unwary listener (or the incompetent punster). Sartre's pervasive irony and other double-dealing in *Les Mots* set many snares for the reader. The mirror before which Poulou is often reduced to pulling faces is a *miroir aux alouettes*: the joke is on us as often as on him.

Puns, including the best, are more often approximations than perfect matches. Dissecting the 'Hôtel des Farces' episode in the epic of 'Le Garçon', Sartre moves from 'la fête de la Merde, lors de la vidange, où l'on entendait résonner dans les couloirs les commandes suivantes: "trois seaux de merde au 14"' to this gloss:

La scatologie d'abord: elle remonte à son enfance et l'on ne peut oublier qu'il a écrit, à neuf ans, 'La belle explication de la constipation'. Et puis le calembour—il en a raffolé toute sa vie. L'origine de cette festivité est *verbale*: vidange, vendanges. Quand vient l'époque du vendangeur, on fête le raisin, produit et matériau de travail; pourquoi, lorsqu'on fait la vidange, ne pas célébrer la merde, produit de l'homme et matériau d'horribles travailleurs? A partir de cet à-peu-près, Gustave se jette dans l'hyperbole et pantagruélise, la merde coule à flots, on la commande par seaux, on s'en bourre. Après l'anthropophagie, la coprophagie.[39]

The coprophile, as he had shown in his opus on Genet, can have his cake and eat it. Sartre's deprived childhood, full of lacks, was in particular starved, in his own account, of scatology. So he annexes in this passage, sniffily, some of Flaubert's gusto, his bad-taste gusto. At the same time, though with Flaubert he purloins or plants, Sartre can also coincide with him, and at such moments seems truly to speak for, or through, him in an act of empathetic ventriloquism.

For all its backhanded compliments to the power of words, *Les Mots* at times acknowledges the alien artifice of literary language: 'On parle dans sa propre langue, on écrit en langue étrangère' (p. 136). Even the spoken language can, however, be riddled with dubiousness, for instance the mystifying speech of grown-ups overheard by young children: 'La langue étrangère, en fait, c'est—comme dans le calembour—le langage saisi comme étranger'.[40] The young Flaubert and the young Sartre shared this sense of exile from the mother tongue and, like punners, became acutely aware of the mechanics of language, the separate bits which, once seen as such, appear absurd. Or excessively real. Sartre might have adduced one of Flaubert's *féeries*, in which a father catches his son boozing in a pub and exclaims: 'Tu n'es qu'un pilier d'estaminet', whereupon the lad changes into a doorpost.[41] Flesh is turned into thing in this cliché twisted by the tail; the person is made into an object, as the young Sartre often felt himself to be under the familial gaze. Sartre mechanizes even his adult self by borrowing Chateaubriand's alleged obiter dictum 'Je ne suis qu'une machine à faire des livres' (p. 137).

The other chief reason for Flaubert's frank worship of the pun is that, as well as mortifying as above, it can vivify:

> Flaubert s'y plaisait parce que chaque calembour lui redécouvrait une ambiguïé essentielle du langage et se présentait, obscurément d'abord puis de plus en plus clairement comme un grossier symbole de l'œuvre littéraire. Il s'agit en effet de miser sur une certaine imprécision des codes et, finalement, de la parole en général: un même discours a lieu sur deux plans—l'un oral, l'autre écrit, qui ne se correspondent pas exactement. Les signes graphiques et surtout leurs combinaisons sont plus nombreux que les phonèmes—en sorte que, pour une information correctement écrite, il y a, dans certains cas, plusieurs auditions possibles.[42]

The double meanings of *Les Mots* are rarely of this acoustic/orthographic sort, but they do serve likewise to multiply and to diversify the text; they beget meaning. Even if Poulou does not mishear his grandfather, he persistently misinterprets his messages, and builds a work of art on his misreadings.

'Le calembour, somme toute, nous fait découvrir le langage comme paradoxe et c'est précisément sur ce paradoxe que Gustave pressent qu'il faut fonder l'Art d'écrire.'[43] *Les Mots* itself is propelled by paradox, steered by irony (and 'tourniquet' can mean vicious circle, or paradox). Sartre's version of the dialectical method, so akin to paradox in that it operates within a closed field, is the 'progressive–regressive' shuttle between past and present, individual and class, fakery and authenticity, or rather the Lobster Quadrille ('Will you, won't you, will you, won't you, won't you join the dance?'), which characterized his relationship with the Communist Party. As well as means of having it both ways, paradox and punning are devices of economy. 'Les auteurs classiques s'inspirent du paradoxe, jeu d'idées qui est à leur style ce que le jeu de mots sera pour le style de Flaubert'.[44] Much can be crammed into a small space in puns, paradox, irony, oxymoron—that condensed paradox—('cet aveuglement lucide' (p. 209), as Sartre calls his wall-eyed perspicacity; the 'senex juvenis' (p. 54); the genuine phoniness of Poulou's grimaces): all of these modes can be densely intelligent.

The only straightforward joke in this otherwise oblique text is the one admitted and innocuous pun. The grandmother, seeking some replacement crockery with an insect-motif, is offered only the current range with a floral design. 'Personne', says the unflappable assistant, 'n'ira chercher, c'est le cas de le dire, la petite bête' (p. 202). Sartre is seldom as innocently ludic as this. He prefers the sharply pointed pun, the philosophic double-talk, as when in *L'Enfance d'un chef*, Lucien Fleurier, incensed by a chestnut-tree's unwillingness to register his misty presence, accuses it of being 'de bois'.[45] Poulou's double entendres, mentioned at the outset, are designed to impress him on the consciousness of other people who, like Lucien's hardhearted tree, rarely respond in the way that he demands. Such a roundabout code as Poulou's speaks clearly only to his accomplice-mother, and therefore counts for less. (Opponents of punning often condemn it as a form of linguistic incest, the violation of a verbal taboo; and incest is the only area of sexuality touched on in *Les Mots*.)

That other devious mode which informs the book, irony, was not available to the child at the time, for Paul Nizan, the most meaningful extra-familial presence in *Les Mots*, 'était le seul à parler de ses parents ironiquement' (p. 190). Conversely, almost the only ones to be spared the corrosive irony of the adult Sartre are the remembered schoolmates, especially those who died prematurely. Sartre's double meanings in *Les Mots* are seldom funny. They are ironical. In his own voice, Flaubert spoke of his longing to attain 'le comique arrivé à l'extrême, le comique qui ne fait pas rire'.[46] This catches well the dry *comédie* of *Les Mots*. Irony and punning both stem from bifocal vision and, like spectacles, seek to correct defective eyesight. Poulou, the voracious reader in the text, has a veritable genius for misreading everything he cons; he is conned; he is *un con*.

The major ambiguity in *Les Mots* hangs on the unanswered question, who or what is responsible for Sartre's 'neurosis'? Irony, as a double agent, enables him to squat on the barbed fence of undecidedness. He blames and refuses to blame the grandfather for his part in the grand illusion. It may be, as Sartre says of Flaubert, that 'le calembour flatte son fatalisme'—presumably because puns are accidents of language, *objets trouvés*, though you would expect this to appal the voluntarist in Sartre.[47] Sartre's declaration is only partly true, besides. It is true in the sense that some punners do simply stumble upon puns lying ready-made in their language, and as such are behaving less than proactively in their serendipity. But Flaubert also puns wilfully. If they need to defend themselves, punners cross-accuse language, saying to it: 'You thought of it first. You put the idea into my head'. Perhaps

the sublimest irony in *Les Mots*, which avowedly seeks to put words
in their place of only relative honour, is that throughout they lead
the dance. So often the metaphors seem to be self-igniting, to spread
like wildfire, and finally to consume the very object of enquiry. In
the finale, Sartre dares to hope that he has changed, that the ham can
be cured. Anyone as sensitized to words and their powers as Sartre
was is prone to end up punning, however latently, for his very life.
Although the silent cinema gets the accolade, although aspects of *Les
Mots* are literally ineffable ('the spirit of the age', class-consciousness,
unwritten social or familial protocols), this book offers a largely verbal
universe. Words come first, before the things they name, instead of
being allowed to grow from experiences. The gendarme adult books
the child-offender: *verbalization* is the name of the game.

Puns excruciate; the tourniquet hurts as it staunches.[48] Puns are
an intimate part of the painful lesson that Sartre teaches himself and,
by extension, his readers in *Les Mots*. They are not a small cranny
of his rhetoric, but sustain a philosophy and a strategy. An ageing
man discovers that he has been living back-to-front, letting the future
vocation inflect his present. This discovery entails a drawn-out double
take, and punning plays a serious role in that serious operation.
Sartre, a supremely inverted snob, makes discrete and discreet use of
this underprivileged trope. Where Flaubert clodhoppingly thumped,
Sartre insinuates: 'Glissez, mortels, n'appuyez pas'.[49] Though Sartre,
throughout *Les Mots*, acts as his own prosecutor, defence counsel,
judge and jury, he could not but recognize how indispensable a
receiver like us is to punning and its ramifications.

Can I honestly maintain that humour, in one or another of its multitudinous forms, is present in all of Sartre's fiction and drama? What
of *Les Chemins de la liberté*, with its heavy leitmotif of procrastination?
Is dithering comical? Where does that leave Hamlet? The relationship
of Brunet and Schneider/Vicarios, the high point of *La Mort dans
l'âme*, reunites Sartre and Nizan in that 'drôle d'amitié', with which
we started this essay.

Perhaps dwelling on Sartre's recurrent humours helps to make him
less of a 'monstre sacré' and more of 'ce sacré Jean-Paul'. If he had not
existed, it would have been imperative to invent him, like Diderot,
another 'wondrous necessary man'.[50]

8

Bad Jokes and Beckett

I want to look at humour in this essay from the other end of the telescope: failed humour. None of us grasps all jokes, just as none of us understands all conversations. Both jokes and conversations may be in a language we do not or barely speak, or couched in a professional idiolect to which we are not privy, or they may simply make allusions to knowledge that we as outsiders do not possess. What I judge a bad joke might send you rolling in the aisles, and an excellent one leave you stone-cold, whereupon, like the music-hall straight man, you might respond with 'I don't wish to know that'. The whole business of seeing the joke is a minefield, and, of late for some, a gold mine. Yet unarguably there are pointed, barbed jokes, and toothless ones. There are jokes pure and simple-minded, and jokes with ulterior motives, designs on us. Like poetry, jokes reveal language at its most self-aware, marvelling at its own clever navel. I am thinking here of modern-day stand-up comedians—or, in Beckett's case, supine or crawling comedians—who, in order to shatter the illusion of spontaneous wittiness, refer blatantly to their scripts and rehearsals, and thus gag about joke-making.

In a letter to Axel Kaun of 1937, Beckett spoke of 'somehow finding a method by which we can represent this mocking attitude towards the word, through words' (*Dis.*, 172). Attitude: if action in Beckett's often lunar landscapes generally seems pointless and self-defeating, the mind of his people spins on, the voices never cave in, and verbal attitudes are struck. His figments are people with attitude. With some stylishness they rearrange the remnants of meaningfulness, the loose connexions, milling around in their patchily retentive minds. Verbally, if seldom any more physically, they practise brinkmanship, as all jokers do; knowing how easy it is to come a cropper, they live on the edge. Beckett was famously taken with the 'shape of ideas'.

Jokes, like poems, need to be crafted, craftily, and placed adroitly. Notoriously, they depend on 'how you tell them'. In this respect, of course, they resemble all narratives. We all know disorganized storytellers and joke-recounters.

Surprisingly, in his study of Proust, Beckett does not see fit to make anything of Proust's highly developed sense of humour, as evidenced for example in the figure of the ineffable but continuously effing Dr Cottard. Via Cottard, Proust displays his familiarity with that common occurrence in all social interaction, the failed, or mistimed, joke. Cottard hoards up what he fondly imagines are the gems he has overheard, and reproduces them, generally on the wrong cue.[1] In his desperate urge to pre-plan his life, he plants his usually atrocious, purloined puns in infertile spots. He fails to see the tricky difference between retelling jokes (or anecdotes) and making jokes. As a receiver of humour Cottard invariably wears a knowing smile or smirk, just in case what others say turns out to have been a witticism. He does not want to be taken, as some Proustian characters do, from behind.

As existential etiolation is the constant mode in Beckett's universe, tired jokes might be thought entirely appropriate to it. A last resort, of course, is to make a joke out of a joke fallen flat: a meta-joke (like the series of pocket-sized joke-books called *Mini Ha Ha*). Beckett's humour is very often strained (and in a letter to MacGreevy he confessed he was dreading reading Proust at stool). Like all of us some of the time with jingles, Beckett cannot get bad jokes out of his head: so he repeats in *Watt* the 'stout porter' joke that I will shortly deconstruct. After all, it is perversely logical that a writer boasting that he specialized in failure should home in on failed jokes. For Bergson (whose *Le Rire*, hyped by sociologists and literary critics with no sense of or for humour, focuses essentially on clichés and existential stereotypes, without ever acknowledging its own mandarin automatisms), humour was a kill-joy gendarme, policing citizens' behaviour. For Beckett, while humour often seems all that is left by way of reaction to frustration or pain, it is not much cop. Above all, he sees life as a bad joke, to be responded to, with justifiable unkindness, in kind. As Molloy says, 'My life, my life, now I speak of it as something over, now as of a joke which still goes on' (*Moll.*, 47). Any such retaliation, what Dostoyevsky called 'joking through clenched teeth',[2] recalls the Absurdist tactic of Camus's Caligula: tit-for-tat, diamond-cut-diamond.

Time for an instance of a bad joke, from *Murphy*, whose hero, as his name suggests, is a potato, a couch-potato: '"Why did the barmaid champagne?" he said. "Do you give it up?" "Yes", said Celia. "Because the stout porter bitter", said Murphy'. Beckett plugs on, relentlessly:

This was a joke that did not amuse Celia. [...] That did not matter. So far from being adapted to her, it was not addressed to her. It amused Murphy, that was all that mattered. He always found it funny, more the most funny, clonic [...] He staggered about on the floor [...] overcome by the toxins of this simple little joke [...] The fit was so much more like one of epilepsy than of laughter that Celia felt alarm [...] The fit was over, gloom took its place. (*Mur.*, 139–40)[3]

'This was one of the Gilmigrim jokes, so called from the Lilliputian wine' (*Mur.*, 140: Beckett's, or a printer's, gremlin for Glimigrim; either way, the humour is glum). First point: this is unshared, selfish laughter (Murphy, after all, is a 'seedy solipsist' (*Mur.*, 82)). Secondly, it is a bad joke, since it contradicts itself unfruitfully: if the barmaid was bitten, she would not need to sham pain, that is, to simulate suffering. (Beckett elsewhere gainsays himself by claiming that Wylie, unlike Murphy, 'preferred the poorest joke to none' (*Mur.*, 119).) Thirdly, laughter here is equated with physico-mental illness, a bout ('clonic' means spasmic, the opposite of a tonic muscular contraction). There is not much tonic in Beckettian laughter. Murphy's Law, also known as Sod's Law, *contre-finalité* (Sartre), or Resistentialism (Paul Jennings), had not yet been named in 1938, but its wry acknowledgement of the backfiring customary in human affairs, especially in its modified version ('If anything *can't* go wrong, it will'), suits Murphy to a T.

For the sake of equity, here is a somewhat better example relayed by Beckett to MacGreevy: 'Do you know the story of the chaste centipede, who said to her suitor, crossing her thousand legs: "No, a thousand times no"?'[4] This allusion to an old music-hall ditty is almost a good joke if we subtract the first, over-anxious 'thousand', and forgive the entomological inaccuracy on centipede/millipede that we all commit. Comparably approximate (but the best kind of pun is so often the paronym, or near-pun) is this joke from *Murphy*: 'Cooper never sat, his acathisia [morbid fear of sitting] was deep-seated and of long standing' (*Mur.*, 119).[5] The French rendering is knock-kneed—'était profonde et de longue durée'—which is no joke at all.

With its abstruse references—'the socio-cultural equivalent of insider trading'[6]—some of Beckett's humour is more godawfully pedantic than any of us professional pedants persist in perpetrating. Molloy, leaning at an acute angle against a wall, talks of a 'hypotenusal posture' (*Moll.*, 9). There is, of course, an old tradition in the English (and for all I know Irish) music-hall, with its magniloquent masters of ceremony, of using long, posh words for small, run-of-the-mill things. In *Dream of Fair to Middling Women* there is a refrain of a 'private joke'. I got so little from this text that I felt it was all something of a private joke. ' "I shall write a book", he mused [...], "a book where the phrase is self-consciously smart and slick" ' (*DFMW*, 138). That sliding between recondite and idiomatic (also active in Céline and Queneau) may indeed be even more of an Irish than an English and certainly French thing, given the higher respect in Ireland for articulacy, also known as blarney.

Even though I am from Liverpool, which many Liverpudlians blasphemously christen the capital of Ireland, I have no wish to pontificate (highly suspect activity, anyway, for a 24-carat atheist) on Irishness. I cannot, for all that, resist pedantry, telling you more than you may want to know. If life is a bad joke—that is: we've heard it all before; it doesn't work; it's no laughing matter; it's a waste of breath and time—then, as the *Whoroscope* notebook informs us, 'Life is a Joe Miller'. The hero of *Murphy* thinks he knows in advance Celia's retort: 'There will be nothing to distract me from you' (*Mur.*, 65). 'Nothing', here, presumably bears the age-old positive charge that Renaissance paradoxers, Lewis Carroll (the king exclaiming at Alice's ability to 'see Nobody'), and Sartre lay upon it. The French monk Radulphus Glaber, after discovering the great Nemo in a number of biblical, Evangelical and liturgical texts, composed a *Historia de nemine*. The phrase in the Scriptures, 'nemo deum vidit', became 'Nemo saw God'. 'Thus, everything impossible, inadmissible, is, on the contrary, permitted for Nemo'.[7] The Beckett text goes on: 'This was the kind of Joe Miller that Murphy simply could not bear to hear revived' (*Mur.*, 65).

A Joe Miller is a synonym for a stale joke, an old chestnut re-roasted. A certain John Mottley (a suspiciously apt name for a clown, though he did author several plays, and the lives of Peter the Great and Catherine), compiled in 1739 a book of facetiae, which without permission he entitled *Joe Miller's jests: or the wit's vade-mecum* (the narrator of *The Unnamable* calls his stories 'facetiae' (*Unn.*, 27)); it was a childhood favourite of George Eliot. Joseph Miller (1684–1738) was a Drury Lane actor who could neither read nor write; his wife recited his parts to him. Miller was quite adept at Irish brogue. The actual 'funny' stories in *Joe Miller's jests* are mostly dire, dividing regularly between stupidity jokes, where people make laughing-stocks of themselves, and cheekiness or insult jokes, where they turn others into butts. It is as though eighteenth-century jokesters had surfeited on Thomas Hobbes and his superiority theory of humour. In the 1846 edition, the anonymous prefacer claims that the attribution was by antiphrasis, since the actual Joe Miller 'was himself, when living, a jest for dulness [...] When others told jokes Joe maintained imperturbable gravity'.[8] The jokes, then, are credited to a sort of human vacuity, which would appeal to Beckett. The prefacer also claims that few have read the jokes they allude to so knowingly and slightingly. This is a valid point, for the unknown provenance of most jokes going the rounds is, to coin an Irish Bull, well attested.

Let us turn, like desperate sinners, to God. I am miles from being the first to remark that *cosmic* and *comic* are but one letter apart.[9] The tailor-joke in *Endgame* that gives its name to *Le Monde et le pantalon* is naturally commandeered by Jewish experts on humour as one of their own.[10] The Jewish 'already' is just one indication that Jews have always heard your joke before. It features a customer complaining over a long period about the mess his tailor is making of a pair of trousers, and the inordinate time he is taking over completing them. Eventually he cites God's feat of creating the cosmos in only six days. The tailor's response: 'But look at the world, and look at my trousers' (*CDW*, 102–3). This story enacts chutzpah, brass-necked cheek, since the tailor not only compares himself to his own advantage with the Almighty, but also perseveres in boosting his own botched goods, his unspeakable bespoke strides. For his part, the narrator of *The Unnamable* speaks of having been given the low-down on God (*Unn.*, 13).[11] All the same, I am not sure Beckett ever achieved the provocative serenity of Luis Buñuel: 'Grâce à Dieu, je suis toujours athée!'[12] Robert Frost's sarcastic prayer: 'Forgive, O lord, my little jokes on Thee | And I'll forgive Thy great big one on me'[13]—and who can tell what little or great big joke Beckett plays on us readers?—is not quite matched by the less belligerent Winnie in *Happy Days*. After a play on fornication/formication, not spelt out but shared with Willie, Winnie says: 'How can one better magnify the Almighty than by sniggering with him at his little jokes, particularly the poorer ones?' (*CDW*, 150). The English version of this play quotes Thomas Gray, 'On a Distant Prospect of Eton College': 'And moody Madness laughing wild | Amid severest woe', which Winnie thinks a wonderful line; she adapts it to her own sniggering sanity. God is not a fellow of infinite jest, however, but more a jesting infinity mocking humankind. Remember Proverbs 1: 25–6: '[Because] ye have set at naught all my counsel, and would none of my reproof | I also will laugh at your calamity'. This is God the heavy father, the chastising schoolmaster, or the unrequited lover. For Baudelaire, laughter was the direct result of humanity's fallen, schizophrenic state, so that in the original confrontation at least God's creatures beat him to the draw. But He who laughs last laughs longest, and God has all eternity to play with. Less gloomy, but somehow very Beckettian, is the centenarian Abraham who, on learning that his 90-year-old spouse Sara was pregnant, 'fell upon his face and laughed' (Genesis 17: 17). Sara also laughed, but 'within herself' (Genesis 18: 12), though she has to deny having laughed: the males rule the roost. Their son Isaac's very name means 'he laughs'. In all this, God, we could say, has a funny sense of humour. As Murphy asks, a tad enigmatically, 'What but an imperfect sense of humour could have made such a mess of chaos?' (*Mur.*, 65). When Molloy chats with Father Ambrose, they find themselves in some agreement on humour, divine and other. After an analogy between a hen sitting 'with her arse in the dust, from morning to night', they laugh *seriatim*, and then the priest expatiates:

What a joy it is to laugh from time to time. Is it not? I said. It is peculiar to man, he said. So I have heard, I said [...] Animals never laugh, he said. It takes us to find that funny, I said [A truism, if only humans laugh]. Christ never laughs either, he said, so far as I know [...] Can you wonder? I said. (*Moll.*, 138)

The tailor joke, by implication, means that God was a worse botcher even than the sempster. Or, of course, that perfection is always out of reach, existing only in some Platonic form, like the narrator's hat in *The Expelled*: 'Come, son, we are going to buy your hat, as though it had preexisted from time immemorial in a preestablished place' (*Exp.*, 34). Molloy, for one, deems himself a bungler. His dangling, prototypically asymmetrical testicles might testify, he thinks, that he has 'made a balls of his life' (*Moll.*, 47).

At the outset, I spoke of attitudes. *Watt* distinguishes between various attitudes towards, or in, laughter:

The bitter laugh laughs at that which is not good, it is the ethical laugh. The hollow laugh laughs at that which is not true, it is the intellectual laugh [...] But the mirthless laugh is the dianoetic laugh [= intellectual, so why the distinction?]. It is the laugh of laughs, the *risus purus*, the laugh laughing at the laugh, the saluting of the highest joke, in a word, the laugh that laughs—silence please—at that which is unhappy. (*Watt*, 47)

I take it that the last-named involves laughing on the other side of your face (in French *le rire jaune*); you are both triumphant and beaten. Cancer is no joke, but 'you have to laugh'. Only the Homeric gods are capable of 'asbestos gelos' (inextinguishable laughter).[14] Only one of them could claim: 'I'm all right, Jack. I'm fireproof'. Mere humans cope as best they can. Lousse in *Molloy*, for example: 'She laughed. It was perhaps her way of crying. Or perhaps I was mistaken and she was really crying, with the noise of laughter. Tears and laughter, they are so much Gaelic to me' (*Moll*, 48–9).[15]

Are Beckett's jokes in some limbo area, still waiting to be definitively labelled as bad or good? Murphy has a go:

Not the least remarkable of Murphy's innumerable classifications [and Beckett is fully alert, like Rabelais, to the inherently comic nature of lists, that is: the nearness of taxonomy to taxidermy] of experience was that into jokes that had once been good jokes and jokes that had never been good jokes [...] In the beginning was the pun. And so on (*Mur.*, 65)

The pun, then, is the foundation of all things. Did Beckett think that 'Fiat Lux' was the motto of Lever Brothers? And that Goethe's dying words 'More light!' were a request not for additional *Aufklärung*, but for opened shutters? (Apparently it was the latter.) God may have given Creation a verbal fillip, but 'Let there be light' sounds pretty univocal. Ackerley picks up on 'And so on':

And so on, until the end, when 'excellent gas, superfine chaos' brings Murphy's body to its ultimate stasis, its final quiet. The pun implied in Murphy's death (*gas* creating *chaos*) may or may not be a good joke, but in Murphy's progress from young aspirant to old suspirant the puns reveal more than Beckett's imperfect sense of humour.[16]

I myself kick against the prick of associating imperfection with punning, as if it were only for mental defectives. Later, Ackerley restores the balance:

As a figure of language, the pun combines the extremes of both the rational and the irrational. Its insistence on the syzygy of ideas normally distinct offers to our rational understanding a challenge not dissimilar to that of Cartesian dualism: on the one hand, the yoked components are the 'same'; on the other, they are 'different' [...] Janus-like, the pun faces both creation and chaos.[17]

In several of Beckett's works the refrain of all things running, or limping, or hanging, together indicates the ideal territory for the punner, who is dedicated to overlap: mixing it. And, of course, anybody who, like Beckett, believes that less is more, will be attracted to the bargain-offer pun: two (meanings) for the price of one (word).

'My work', Beckett told Alan Schneider in a letter, 'is a matter of fundamental sounds (no joke intended) made as fully as possible' (*Dis.*, 109). While I might agree with Robert Desnos's wry plea, 'Pitié pour l'amant des homonymes',[18] no wordplayer should wriggle out of responsibility as in Beckett's bracket. Puns should be proudly acknowledged, their paternity shouldered. Why this sheepishness about punning? Or is it feigned, by many deliberate or accidental double-meaners? If so, this is indeed having your cake and eating it, like the coprophiliac. (This tack-on is hijacked from Christopher Ricks on Jean Genet. Ricks ludically accused me of plagiarizing this pun in my book *Puns*. He was right, except that I thought I was plagiarizing Dan Jacobson.) I take comfort in Emerson's essay 'Plato or the Philosopher': 'Every book is a quotation; and every house is a quotation out of all forests, and mines, and stone quarries; and every man is a quotation from all his ancestors'.[19]

However original Beckett fancied himself to be in writing of powerlessness, even he would have admitted to having, like all and sundry, a magpie mind. Robert Burton used the term 'apothecary' for the plagiarist who was forever mixing and remixing given elements into different compounds. In the Addenda to *Watt*, Beckett slips in a joky quote about quotes, of great ancestry: 'Pereant qui ante nos nostra dixerunt' (Aelius Donatus), which I would translate as: 'May all those who scooped our script rot in hell'. This is the pataphysical concept of 'anticipatory plagiarism', or harking forwards.

W. H. Auden wrote:

> Be subtle, various, ornamental, clever,
> And do not listen to those critics ever
> Whose crude provincial gullets crave in books
> Plain cooking made still plainer by plain cooks,
> As though the Muse preferred her half-wit sons;
> Good poets have a weakness for bad puns.[20]

We need look for corroboration of the last line no further than Shakespeare. But could the converse not also be true: bad poets have a forte for good puns? Thomas Hood? A pun disconcerts. It interrupts the euphoria (or inertia) of a text, like Stendhal's political pistol-shot in a concert. It thus draws attention to itself, and consorts happily with self-conscious writing. From *First Love*: 'Personally I have no bones to pick with graveyards. I take the air there willingly [...] when take the air I must' (*First*, 4). Here, the pun (or puns—is there a secondary one on 'musty air'?) acts as a would-be buffer-state against de rigueur gravity, as so often in the poems of Thomas Hood. In *Malone Dies*, Malone comments while watching a mule being interred: 'The end of life is always vivifying', no doubt accompanied by a horselaugh (*Mal.*, 195). Puns of course can be, and often are in Beckett, obtuse. 'The hardy laurel' (*Watt*, 253) is merely echoic, repeating famous names, but not drawing them into any interesting new relationship with the shrub. When Edgar Allan Poe maintained that 'the goodness of your true pun is in the direct ratio of its intolerability',[21] he did not specify whether 'intolerability' meant godawfulness, or terrifying pointedness. Much more to the point than that hardy laurel is the play on the magic plant moly with which Lousse/Circe tries to 'mollify' Molloy. Here, the paronomasia espouses the badgering attempt to bewitch (*Moll.*, 63, 72).[22]

Epithets mechanically applied to the pun—grinding, atrocious, excruciating (think of the verbal Chinese torture of *Finnegans Wake*) —depict it as a kind of purgatory, Beckett's place of predilection. Just before an account of Murphy's ululations at the instant of birth, Beckett mentions 'such maieutic saws as "How can he be clean that is born" [...] Murphy required for his pity no other butt than himself' (*Mur.*, 71). This tries to sound like aggressive self-pity, the kind that kicks yourself, lovingly, up the arse. At the asylum Murphy 'laboured more diligently than ever at his little dungeon in Spain' (*Mur.*, 180). Beckett loves thus playing new tunes on old musical saws, idioms, clichés. He might well have agreed with Stravinsky, who knew of what he spoke: 'The danger lies not in the borrowing of clichés.

The danger lies in fabricating them and in bestowing on them the force of law'.[23] 'Stereotype' was originally a printer's term. In clichés we run true to type. We hear ancestral voices overlaying ours. Like William Empson, Beckett could have intoned: 'And I a twister love what I abhor'.[24] Beckett everywhere resists what linguisticians call lexical institutionalization, that is the process whereby words are put in straitjackets, douched, given electroshock treatment, and generally made to behave themselves. As well as being a form of madness *in* language, puns and other verbal twists such as revitalized fixed syntagms resemble anti-psychiatry in that they loosen the straps of that straitjacket. In *Murphy* 'a person of his own steak and kidney' restores the physical sense of 'kidney' by the insertion of that unmistakable meat (*Mur.*, 192).

The macaronic mode swivels between different languages. I believe Beckett chose French against English for similar reasons to those of Jean Arp in selecting French against German: 'Je me suis décidé à rédiger directement en français parce que maîtrisant moins cette langue, je m'y dépaysais davantage'.[25] Beckett too wanted to escape the facile momentum (or inertia), the bandwagon, the contemptible cosiness of his mother tongue, its lullabying rhythms and unfree associations. Writing in French assisted him in his quest for lessness. He became a whispering barker offering amazing reductions: not great expectations, but picayune ones. The notorious Cartesian severance of mind from body was no doubt another magnet which drew Beckett to more scrawny French. The narrator of *The Unnamable* begets a splendid neologism, the 'wordy-gurdy', which thins down in French to the merely functional 'la chasse aux mots' (*Unn.*, 157; *Inn.*, 230). Once ensconced uncomfortably in a second language, Beckett could not resist the foreign speaker's instinctive catheterization (or piss-take) of a tongue not maternally his or hers. Even linguistic botching can be a spur. As *Worstward Ho* puts it: 'Fail better' (*Worst.*, 101). In *Malone meurt*, Beckett describes thus a woman's arm-movements: 'Elle les écartait de ses flancs, je dirais brandissais si j'ignorais encore mieux le génie de votre langue' (*Mal.*, 45). This sentence is inevitably omitted from the English version, though it would end something like this: 'If I were more expertly ignorant of the genius of your language'.

The macaronic mode is a gleeful acceptance that languages are not, and cannot be kept, in a state of apartheid each from the other. They overlap and contaminate each other, in a non-pejorative, beneficial sense. Whether he is composing, or decomposing, in English or French, Beckett writes in a kind of homeless language. As George Craig has said: 'The signs are that he is exploring a verbal no-man's-land where neither French nor English holds sway'.[26] French is Beckett's host-language, but of course a house is not a home. Self-evidently, French is less second nature to him than English, but he was always suspicious of what was second nature. Maybe all this is best typified by the pun, implicit in much of his work, on asylum/*asile*. As Murphy puts it: 'Asylum [...] is better than exile' (*Mur.*, 73). His creatures find that any haven is yet another madhouse, and that goes also for the brain skulking in the skull. Beckett said in a letter to Axel Kaun (written in German): 'From time to time I have the consolation, as now, of sinning willy-nilly against a foreign language, as I should love to do with full knowledge and intent against my own—and as I shall do—Deo juvante' (*Dis.*, 173). He plays across and skits both languages in this sentence from *Molloy*. Taking the set expression 'je ne sais pas à quel saint me vouer', he reshuffles it to: 'Connaître le saint, tout est là, n'importe quel con peut s'y vouer' (*Mol.*, 33–4). The English counterpart is feeble: 'Yes, the whole thing is to know what saint to implore, any fool can implore him' (p. 35). His vestigial creatures are at their wits' end (the meaning of that French idiom), and the exile's eye and ear analyse, that is break down, the impasse. But what about instances where the two languages exhibit an *entente cordiale*? In *Mercier and Camier*, the riddle 'What would we do without women? Explore other channels' (p. 188), becomes in French 'Nous prendrions un autre pli' (p. 118): we would acquire a new habit, but 'le pli' also refers to the folds of the groin.[27] In *Molloy*, the hero's legs are, in French, 'raides comme la justice' (p. 81) but in English 'stiff as a life-sentence' (p. 83). Here, idioms *are* puns, as in 'high as a kite', or 'réglé comme du papier à musique'.

The joke can also lie in a transfer of sense, a different, subversive association, as in metaphor. In *The Calmative*, a comedian is reported as —a nice case of a women's revenge-match facilitated, however

telling a funny story about a fiasco [...] He used the word snail or slug [...] The women seemed more entertained than their escorts [...] Perhaps they had in mind the reigning penis sitting (who knows) by their side and from that sweet shore launched their cries of joy towards the comic vast (*CSP*, 37) unwittingly, by a man, who was no doubt, like many comics, trying to be disarming, which is to say disempowering.

There are gentle forms of irony, such as Ariosto's, which Beckett interpreted in these words: 'The face remains grave, but the mind has smiled. The profound *risolino* that does not destroy' (*Dis.*, 89). This is poker-face. The old conundrum as to whether humour or wit undermines or preserves that which they target is perhaps most conveniently solved (or shelved) by saying that they do both. So many wisecracks seemingly damage what they set up. But, once mentioned, even under attack, can anything be altogether blotted out? Words can counter words, but not abolish them. Of the many forms of irony, so-called Romantic irony, or self-undercutting, is the one Beckett practises most, as here in *Molloy*: 'One is what one is, partly at least' (*Moll.*, 72), a joke about truisms. In this respect I recall that self-cancelling motto favoured by Montherlant (and scavenged by Camus): 'Aedificabo et destruam' (I will build and I will knock down).

Now, if we use the old criterion of someone 'protesting too much', we can see that underlined, dogged anti-sentimentality can engender just another form of mawkishness. How many writers, how many of us glossers, stand condemned by Kierkegaard's animadversion, 'His soul lacked the elasticity of irony. He had not the strength to take irony's vow of silence'.[28] Some writers, of course, out of honesty have opted for what they hoped would appear a meaningful silence.

A variety of bad jokes is the dirty joke, for the senses of 'not worth making' and 'not worthy of being made' tend to run together. For instance, 'Condom est arrosé par la Baïse' (*Moll.*, 193) is one literally converted in the English version, but minus the *tréma*, which makes it a better, if orthographically inexact, joke, albeit translingual. Sex, there, is 'un jeu de con' (p. 76): a mug's game (or a stupid cunt's game?). Some people weary, of course, of such loud or subvocal harassment. The nudge-nudge makes the mind's ribs ache, and the wink-wink becomes a neurotic tic. Orwell thought the dirty joke, at its best, 'a sort of mental rebellion'.[29] Chesterton upped the paradoxical ante: 'When you have got hold of a vulgar joke, you may be certain that you have got hold of a subtle and spiritual idea'[30] — a piously hopeful idea.

And what of gestures, rude or otherwise: kinetic puns and jokes, verbal pratfalls, the whole palaver of 'stage business'? In *Godot*, the clownish or music-hall antics of protracted attempted mastery over things (like Winnie with her parasol), including the body felt as alien presence or opponent, are recycled traditional devices to make us laugh, uneasily. 'Gag', a word of as similarly dubious or mixed parentage as 'pun' or *blague*, embraces silence, retching, and telling (or enacting) jokes. 'Gags' are also actors' interpolations into scripts, as so often practised by Beckett's narrators.

If he does not mechanically parrot Céline, Beckett is certainly at times a bird of the feather. At least at one moment, he called *Voyage au bout de la nuit* 'the greatest novel in English or French'.[31] Both writers face up to death on the never-never (*Mort à crédit*) with gallows-humour, and similarly wish that their heroes had never been born. Their protagonists experience an ageless fear and guilt for an unspecified sin; they expect the worst in 'cette farce atroce de durer'.[32] Murphy and Bardamu seek asylum in a loony-bin. Both writers find point and solace in choreography. Beckett, in *L'Innommable* especially, matches the 'métro émotif' of Céline's diarrhetoric.[33] Both writers strike the mucker-pose, by going slumming in speech. In their corners of existence, the heroes (even of the anti-Semitic Céline) take refuge in a quasi-Jewish humour: lamentations, piling it on thick. Céline and Beckett meet in limbo.

Have I been talking, as my title might suggest, of Beckett's own imperfect sense of humour? 'Bad' is an ambiguous word. Think of current slang, where 'bad' equals 'good', and Charles Lamb's paradox whereby 'the worst puns are the best'.[34] A faulty sense of humour is naturally the worst thing an English, or perhaps an Irish, person can attribute to another, almost as bad as his not having a heart. In breaking down some of Beckett's jokes, I have not sought to be a party-pooper (or wake-pooper, more fittingly). I would imagine that, by analogy with Constantine Fitzgibbon's dystopia *When the Kissing Had to Stop*, Beckett's later work could be described as 'When the joking had to stop'. In his essay on Proust, Beckett wrote: 'The whisky [Jameson's, of course] bears a grudge against the decanter' (*Proust*, 10). That which, or they who, are about to be consumed, envy and cannot forgive what will survive them. No doubt language bears a grudge against silence. But, whatever or whomsoever else I may want to eff, I do not want, as Watt says, 'to eff the ineffable' (*Watt*, 61).

This chapter is superficially 'a doctrine of scattered occasions',[35] or *disjecta membra*. Montesquieu provides a model: 'Pour bien écrire il faut sauter les idées intermédiaires'.[36] Why overvalue finition? Rabelais, Pascal, Melville, and Gide, all for their very different reasons, scorned it. Finition/finitude: if by chance anyone could say the last word on any subject, it would truly be time to die (as in 'famous last words', a phrase nowadays always used ironically). As Molloy suggests: 'Perhaps there's no whole before you're dead' (*Moll.*, 35). Is there a grave pun on whole/hole there? Beckett's prose often seems on the point of pegging out for good.

A French counterpart to 'Freudian slip' is *acte manqué*. Such slips are often, as it transpires, sure-footed: *actes manqués* can succeed. In its literal sense, we see a plethora of *actes manqués*, or fiascos, in Beckett's world. On inadvertent puns, like the possible whole/hole above, Bearn has noted:

The fact that we don't normally notice this [i.e. that all possible significances of a word are always in play whenever it is being used] is no more remarkable than the fact that we don't normally notice the size of people's ears. Inadvertent puns draw our attention to what was there all along.

He goes on to cite Austin's remark that every utterance can be used either seriously or unseriously, and concludes that 'if inadvertent puns are possible, then there is no sentence that has ever been completely understood by anyone. No wonder that punsters should be punished'. To turn the screws even further:

Most of the expressive power of our linguistic action is outside our control. Surprising as this result is, I suppose it is no surprise to discover that if you begin with inadvertent significance, you will end by denying that anyone is master of the language they speak.[37]

There is clearly, or muddily, something delirious with the logic here: words seem to have taken over, to fulfil the prophecy of this text. Nobody could actually live with this awareness to the forefront of the mind; each of us would need to watch each other's every word like a sceptical hawk. We would all be confidence-tricksters of the word. Beckett is saner: 'There is no use indicting words, they are no shoddier than what they peddle' (*Mal.*, 195). Molloy declares that 'tout langage est un écart de langage' (*Mol.*, 155).

There has been a huge amount of research, especially by sociologists, psychologists, and psychiatrists, on the therapeutic effects of humour ('Ve haff vays of making you laff!'). Adler used jokes as therapy, 'to clarify his error to the neurotic'. Contrary to Freud's grateful response to jokes arising in therapy, Adler sounds tetchy at being put, as he puts the patient, on the spot: 'Actually a large number of nervous symptoms seem like a poor joke. They try to trip us up, and sometimes surprise us as a joke does'.[38] I am reminded of the chronic mental patient who loved making incomprehensible requests for a visiting pianist to play 'Mother's Stove'. It eventually emerged that he wanted 'Home on the Range'.[39] He was pulling the sane ones' legs. No doubt, and we should be grateful for it, humour can help in alleviating distress and pain. But we often talk of 'comic relief', as if humour acted as an automatic remedy for constipation or indigestion. Humour can also rub our faces in misery, reopen old wounds, scratch at scabs. Estragon is glad to find anything that will give him the sense of being alive. In this context, joking is akin to toothache.

The cross-talk act, in Beckett's case, is primarily with language itself.

Probably my favourite proverb or cliché is 'many a true word is spoken in jest'. Humour is serious, and revelatory. As Legman said, 'Your favourite joke is your psychological signature. The "only" joke you know how to tell is you'.[40] How can I fade out except with these words from *The Unnamable*: 'Ah mother of God, the things one has to listen to, perhaps it's tears of mirth. Well, no matter, let's drive on now to the end of the joke, we must be nearly there' (*Unn.*, 102)?

Riff on Taste

I am not concerned here with 'taste' in the fashion sense.
Baudelaire drawled: 'Ce qu'il y a d'enivrant dans le mauvais goût,
c'est le plaisir aristocratique de déplaire'.[1] Elsewhere, he asks why 'le
mauvais goût ne serait-il pas aussi raffiné que le bon? Plus peut-être'.[2]
This is the dismissive view of the dandy. Finding jokes in every niche
of human activity, Freud concludes that 'the realm of jokes knows no
boundaries'.[3] This is the resigned or tolerant view. Those who bring
the charge of bad taste against certain examples of humour want to
impose censorship. Personally, I would ban prohibition.

In Auschwitz jokes, *witz* or wit skulks irremovably in the very
name. The importance of humour among inmates of death-camps
is well attested. With its reminder of a world outside hell, a sense
of humour greatly aided mental, physical, and spiritual perseverance.
Without it, many more would have committed suicide. But, some
say, is such humour understandable and acceptable only in the victims
of the Final Solution? Can those who have only hearsay experience of
the horrors have no say? If that were true, imagination and empathy
would be ruled out of human affairs. A common complaint of the
would-be censors is that such calamity-humour makes (decent) people
very uncomfortable. Tragedy, therefore, would be in bad taste, for it
aims to shake us to the core.

Can anything at all be joked about? The sane answer is: well, it
has, and is being, and will be. Realistically, nothing is sacred. The
very moralistic Malcolm Muggeridge openly admitted that 'good taste
and humour are a contradiction in terms, like a chaste whore'.[4] It
is very likely that different people laugh at the same joke or comic
situation, but for differing reasons. Indeed, there are metajokes about
such mixed responses or variant readings. If that is the case, no
humorist can control the effect of his/her humour. As with much else

in human communication, humour is a message in a bottle, destined to land somewhere unknown, and to be interpreted in various ways. To acknowledge that bad taste cannot be expurgated from humour (the world is a free country) is not to treat it as basically harmless. On the contrary, it is to recognize that, for humour to have any truth-value whatsoever, it must make house-room for the whole truth and nothing but the truth. Such a blanket-coverage, of course, can secrete lies and prejudices. Trying to restrict the field of humour is equivalent to refusing to talk or think about all aspects of human experience. While nothing is automatically risible, anything can be converted for humorous use. Those who say 'There are limits' do not see that laughter is off-limits, out of bounds, not in the sense of 'forbidden', but rather in that of 'free from rules'. We can laugh at Satan, the arch-mocker.

Humour is not squeamish; it is an agent provocateur. Elliott Oring makes the necessary contrast with euphemism: 'Jokes can get nearer the knuckles, the core of the truth, than our euphemising media, or small talk'.[5] Jokes about space disasters are often more accurate in their imagined detail than the distanced or muted pictures fed us on the screen or printed page. Of course, such black jokes are also an agent of distancing in their own way: a means of controlling our primitive emotions, our sense that the tragedy could have happened to us, if not on a spacecraft then in a car. I am not interested in bland humour, though no doubt it helps to lubricate social mechanisms and gives joy to faint hearts.

Obviously, to gainsay good taste would be to discount all tact and all taboos. That dread disease, English false modesty or self-deprecation, can be seen most charitably as a form of humour, whereby you confess to a failing while making some kind of virtue out of it.

Bad taste, in another sense: nausea in the gorge or mouth, breeds disgust. This can be physical, as so often in Céline or his alter-ego protagonists. Or abstract, as in *La Nausée*, or Tournier's story 'La Jeune Fille et la mort'. The abstract nausea is in both cases a philosophical reaction to a world that makes no philosophical sense. In *Le Roi des aulnes*, Tournier refuses the ready-to-hand disgust with Nazidom, and plunges his hero joyously into filth and monstrosity.

Political correctness, the 'nasty niceness of bowdlerisation',[6] is an effort to rescript reality along pleasanter, more anodyne lines. For Oring, it is 'ultimately a form of moral bureaucracy; an attempt to legislate hard and fast rules of social interaction rather than recognise a process in which meaning and intention are constantly being negotiated'. In other words, an attempt to replace the muddy scrum with croquet. He goes on:

'If once a man indulges himself in murder, very soon he comes to think little of robbing, and from robbing he comes next to drinking and Sabbath-breaking, and from that to incivility and joke telling'. This is a joke; it is not the moral order of things.[7]

Avner Ziv maintains, paradoxically, that 'in the name of tolerance we have to refuse those who object to politically incorrect humor'.[8] To which Arthur Asa Berger adds: 'If humor isn't "incorrect" by nature, if it doesn't violate codes of all kinds (including correctness), what is it?'[9] Byron wrote to Sir Walter Scott in 1814: 'The cant is so much stronger than the cunt now a days'. Against these libertarian commentators, and soberingly, Elaine Shafter reminds that:

People who commit atrocities can also tell jokes and can laugh and exhibit what they consider to be a sense of humour. They, however, do not become humane just because of this ability. They share the human trait of joke telling. And this makes us aware that atrocious and barbarous acts often are committed by those who seem in other ways normal.[10]

Therefore, humour is not civilizing, either for its practitioners or for their audience. It is truly democratic, for all have access to it.

Surely, some of the prejudice against cruel jokes (racist, sexist, etc.) is less against their content than against the very act of joking. For instance, hostility to sexual jokes is directed against the pleasure they afford, and the often pleasurable sex they feature. Why do we talk of near-the-knuckle humour? Why are knuckles thought of as sensitive and vulnerable, when they can be used, if bruised, in fisticuffs? If the censors succeeded in cutting the cackling, non-politically correct humour would simply go underground (where much slang starts), be privatized, less publicized.

When, for increasing numbers of people in our decreasingly emancipated age, censorship is taboo, what is then left to laugh about, except dying bogeymen? When it is easy and safe to laugh, can humour be much more than mindless self-gratification? And of course we can bandwagon on what our forebears more bravely ridiculed. We can plagiarize here as everywhere else (e.g. stereotypes, often inherited). We can, nevertheless, mock those very numerous people who cling to old, 'eternal' values that we find absurd. The persistent danger is that we might amuse ourselves to death.

Euphemism can be both a way of avoiding speaking your mind, if you have one, and of speaking it sotto voce. As John Ayto says of the politically correct words for 'mad', these are 'dispassionate technicalisms, the verbal equivalent of padded cells, to keep it [mental illness] under control'. He likens the rebaptizing of jobs to 'moving the lexical furniture about'.[11] This captures nicely the Bovarysme of vocabulary, which we do like to renew or resite periodically.

Gérard Genette couches the whole question carefully and tastefully: 'J'ai peut-être tort d'hésiter entre mauvais goût et bonne santé: c'est souvent la même chose'.[12] Probably the most honest thing Jules Renard ever wrote is this: 'Je ne réponds pas d'avoir du goût, mais j'ai le dégoût très sûr'.[13] Both sides in our argument over taste could conceivably sign this.

In dreams, you can lay to rest the heavy burden of good taste. Bad taste, after all, is where we most candidly come alive. Bad taste is what we have so often in our mouths, just as the common place is where the majority reside. It is dirty, as well as great, minds that think alike.

9

Approximating Man: Michel Tournier's Play with Language

Overripeness is all.
   After Shakespeare

Il y a des jeux de mots qui valent des théories.
                                    Tournier
Ce qui les effraie, […] la forme même du vrai, cet objet d'indéfinie approximation.
                                                    Sartre

The pun conducts a cross-talk act, within language, between different meanings of the same word, or, if you like, the straight man and the comic twister or trickster. My goal is to examine Tournier's wordplay, in the widest sense, and to see how it informs and inflects the structures, meanings, and values of his fictional world, principally in *Le Roi des aulnes* and *Les Météores*, but also in other writings.

In a text where he swings between two areas of meditation, Canada and the Sahara, Tournier concludes unabashedly with an imaginary duo and a play on words,

car je crois en la profondeur voilée d'ironie du calembour. Sahara-Canada. Ces deux mots de six lettres dont trois *a* placés aux mêmes points sont d'une saisissante analogie. Cette affinité littérale correspond à des surfaces immenses et du même ordre (7.3 millions de kilomètres carrés pour le Sahara; 9.3 millions pour le Canada), et à des climats absolument opposés. Cela fait songer à des notions complémentaires et antithétiques, comme le *yin* et le *yang* de la pensée chinoise dont la synthèse est le *tao*, principe d'ordre universel. Mais quelle serait donc la synthèse de Sahara et Canada? (EC, 52)

He might well ask. Roughly speaking, this extract epitomizes Tournier's writing strategy. He admits the approximateness of his space-link (give or take 2 million square kilometres). He exults in thus yoking the far-fetched, for this act gives him a huge field for manoeuvre. As a punner he thinks binarily.

Throughout, I will be using 'approximation' and cognate terms, both in the pejorative sense of a failure, and in the meliorative sense of a near miss. In places, some of the reprises of this highly musical writer resemble rather the scrappy darning of a holey sock, and in others his subtle weavings can enwrap us. In his prose recur constructions like 'une manière de', 'en quelque sorte', or 'n'est pas sans une lointaine affinité avec'. In *Les Météores*, women are twice quoted as saying: 'Il n'y a plus de saisons'. The implication is that the seasons are not fixed but, like language itself, are 'une suite d'approximations et d'à-peu-près' (*M*, 454). Tournier blends here as everywhere the accessory (seasonable fashions) and the momentous (the climate). His people are always situated in a large-scale environment, but ambiguously: the interconnexions are loose ones. In *Le Roi des aulnes*, the hero Abel Tiffauges, after mocking the conformist 'suradaptés', those who live like fishes in water, lauds amphibians like himself who, in his admittedly myopic eyes, show greater flexibility: 'Nous autres amphibies, toujours en porte à faux avec les choses, rompus au provisoire, à l'à-peu-près, nous savons faire face de naissance à toutes les trahisons du milieu' (*RA*, 138). Indeed, Abel's life-curve does reveal a high degree of survival-instinct, despite his readiness to go out on dangerous limbs.

Abel comes within a hair's breadth of Nazidom. Of his own rituals at Kaltenborn he boasts: 'Je les ai ordonnés selon ma double exigence de rigueur et d'aléa' (*RA*, 505): rigour and randomness, almost a definition of the paronym, or approximate pun. In *Vendredi*, Robinson all but goes native, or indeed insular, in his sexual coupling with his island. This novel's subtitle, *ou Les Limbes du Pacifique*, sketches the existential situation of Tournier's protagonists, for what is more aptly accommodating than the notion of Limbo: ambiguous, a pause before categorization, neither condemning nor forgiving? His displaced persons are at home in such clearing-houses.

As regards punning (an often ambiguous form of approximation which many people would like to consign to hellfire), Tournier distinguishes between the widespread mindless, robotic variety and his own professedly higher-order version. Among the French deportees in *Le Roi des aulnes* figures a Parisian *banlieusard*, Phiphi de Pantin, 'qui fatiguait tout le monde de ses calembours et de ses grimaces' (*RA* 259). As if to underscore the desperate nature of such verbal mechanists, Phiphi commits suicide shortly after 'un feu d'artifice d'à-peu-près' (p. 272). Clearly punning need not be a laughing matter. For his own part, Tournier puns on his relationship to his work: 'L'œuvre, l'œuvre pie, la pieuvre' (*VP*, 179). He relishes aggressive metaphors: the work gulps down its author; the reader is a vampire. If the work devours, it also of necessity excretes. He talks of 'une autogenèse de l'œuvre dont l'auteur ne serait lui-même que le sous-produit'. Robinson is likewise 'l'excrément personnel de Speranza' (*V*, 100).

Puns can support, or indeed dominate, serious comedy. The fore-word to *Vendredi* uses a Tarot-pack to plant prophecies, and notes: 'Le démiurge est aussi bateleur [buffoon]' (*V*, 7). Later, God is viewed as a divine prankster, 'un démiurge baroque poussé aux plus folles combinaisons par l'ange du bizarre' (p. 120). Tournier himself acts the part of a cosmic trickster, throwing his outsize ego over his shoulder, raffishly, if we picture it as a monster phallus. After playing on the double meaning of *grâce* (that of the saint and that of the dancer), Robinson prays: 'Soleil, délivre-moi de la gravité' (p. 217). This is itself a pun, as he wants by this stage to take off from the clogging earth, as well as to unwrinkle his puritanical brow. Similarly, Nietzsche preferred a 'dancing God' and swore that the spirit of gravity must be overcome.[1] Many good minds entertain the possibility that any God there might be must be felinely playful. Why, then, should authors, those little gods, not be ludic in their turn, in response to, in harmony with, or in protest against, the Almighty? Tournier regularly oscillates between cosmic and comic (Italo Calvino blends them in his science-fiction collection, *Cosmicomiche*) as does Gilles Deleuze commenting with paronomasia on *Vendredi*: 'C'est un étonnant roman d'aventures comique, et un roman cosmique d'avatars' (*V*, 259).

Tournier salutes in Bachelard his sense of humour: 'L'approche de l'absolu se signale par le rire' (*VP*, 148–9). He claims that when he studied philosophy, it was its concreteness which most appealed to him. The pun, too, often reminds us of the bodily in the bloodless. Puns, of course, play in the space between abstract and concrete, figurative and literal, between which there is seldom any one-way traffic. It is perhaps more a German than a French tradition. 'Nous sommes déjà avec Novalis dans ce courant qui dure encore (Heidegger) et pour lequel le calembour a valeur d'intuition métaphysique'.[2] Novalis said he was a philosopher because he loved Sophie (his fiancée) (*VV*, 68).

Tournier discriminates between three types of humour: 'rose, noir, blanc', and favours the last. Of the 'white clown' he writes: 'Le blanc cultive l'insolence, le persiflage, l'ironie, le propos à double sens' (*CS*, 73–5). By 'white', he does not mean anti-black, however, and cites as an example Kafka's wild laughter on reading aloud from *The Trial* (*TC*, 21). He has called Flaubert his master, and this kind of excruciating humour is quintessentially Flaubertian. It is also akin to that of Surrealist painting, which Tournier contrasts favourably with Surrealist writing: 'André Breton et les siens rebutent par leur compacité de pions blafards et solennels' (*VP*, 112–13).[3] With one formulation of Breton's, however, he would surely agree: 'Les mots font l'amour'.[4] Words appeal to each other, exercise a reciprocal tug. Punners love language, are true *philologers*; puns are the lovers *in* language.

Tournier's ludic slant is no doubt temperamental, but is founded also on a set of beliefs. The principal one would seem to be: 'Tout se tient, tout conspire, tout est système' (*M*, 137). It is a moot point whether this trust in an entirely meaning-full world is residually Christian (*concordiae discordes*), or Surrealist ('le hasard objectif'). A favourite of the Surrealists and a manic punner, Jean-Pierre Brisset similarly rejected the possibility of absurdity. Puns make sense, as the Metaphysical poets knew full well. The world is a book, or has the makings of a book. In their efforts to naturalize the pun, punners suggest that the ambiguity it mimics is out there in reality itself; life is a double life. This is the only kind of mimesis that Tournier himself cares to profess, for he maintains resolutely that he is not in any orthodox sense a realist writer.

The matter of wordplay is intimately bound up with the whole relationship between the author and readers. What, then, are Tournier's designs on us? Puns need someone to register them. Some kind of consensus is being convoked. It is true that Tournier often short-circuits the connexion. With his talent for self-parody, he can pre-empt our strike by playing Mine Own Executioner. Punning aids him in this, for it is both an aggressive mode and a defence mechanism. He clearly wants to trouble the vestigial morality, test the surviving shockability, of an increasingly self-permissive readership. Allusiveness, like punning, entails complicity. 'Tiffauges table sur le début sur le double sens'.[5] In *Le Roi des aulnes*, there is an urgent pun on A.T. (Abel Tiffauges), *athée*, 'à toi pour la vie'. As Baroche comments: 'Nestor reconnaît ces calembours pour ce qu'ils sont, des mots codés, des travestissements pratiques qui permettent de tout dire à l'abri d'une signification ordinaire'.[6] Taking Gide's statement that he wrote to be reread, Tournier adds that he himself requires this rereading 'dès la première lecture' (*VP*, 189). He asks in effect for a double take; he asks, with other wordplaying writers, that we read him in slow motion.

Take the case of Nestor, apparently ageless if not agelast, and a figure of much ambivalence in *Le Roi des aulnes*: an adult dwarf, or a giant baby? Physically, he is an oxymoron, another avatar of wordplay. He functions as a precursor and initiator of the hero, Abel Tiffauges, like whom he is a copious eater: ingestion, digestion, and defecation are the major rhythms of his existence. He fascinates Abel with a gyroscope, which elicits some of Nestor's more sibylline utterances (why is there not an etymological link between 'gnome' and 'gnomic'?). Nestor calls it a cosmic toy, the key to the absolute and, in a nice pun, 'mon point d'appui quand les choses tournent trop mal' (*RA*, 59–61). He is one of Tournier's herdsmen of meaning: 'Il faut réunir d'un trait alpha et oméga' (p. 63). In Greek mythology, Nestor, friend of Hercules, was granted a life of three centuries, and the roles of warrior and wise man. In Christian history, Nestorius (died AD 451), patriarch of Constantinople, is famous for denying that Christ was the son of God and for calling him 'Theophoros' (bearer of God). In James Joyce's *Ulysses*, the 'Nestor' episode takes place in a school, the subject is history, and the dominant symbol is a horse. All of these external references are internalized in Tournier's fictional character and situation. In order to become eventually a Christic figure, Abel Tiffauges needs a prophet who is to some extent a doppelgänger. Abel is a heretical Christ-figure, with both divine and human (all-too-human) components. He takes over from Nestor the vocation of bearing. I will show later how catastrophically alpha and omega are made to coincide at a historical juncture. Throughout his orchestration of Nestor, Tournier spells out some connexions and leaves others to be burrowed for by the collaborating reader.

Wordplay serves both mystification and myth-making or, more strictly, remaking. Myths, like fables, symbols, or puns, are always tantamount, suggestive rather than definitive. They offer already constituted meanings which can then be played with, rewritten. Similarly, in the adjacent field of etymology (for many myths are founded on etymological play, especially on names), Tournier can both praise its occasional accuracy ('Si profonde est parfois la sagesse que recouvre une simple parenté verbale' (*V*, 65)), and be ready to exploit its possibilities for creative falsity. Goethe's poem 'The Erl-King' ('Der Erl-König', the Alder-King) is based on an erroneous rendering by Herder (a case of folk-etymology perpetrated by a scholar) of the Danish *ellerkonge*: king of the elves. In his turn, a German professor names the corpse of one of the ancient German bog-people 'Roi des Aulnes', for it is disinterred in a grove of alders next to a body, possibly that of an emaciated child. The corpse bears a gilded, six-pointed star: a distant link between this pagan North European religion and the Judaeo-Christian tradition. In the fullness of time, Abel Tiffauges, carrying the boy Jew Ephraïm, survivor of a death-camp, will sink into a bog in their flight from the horrors of war. The ambiguous notion of *bearing* (to which I shall return) is centred on the original etymological bifurcation. *Le Roi des aulnes* is largely concerned with misuse, or deviant use.

Tournier wants us to rediscover stories that we already take as read: ogres, Robinson Crusoe, Tom Thumb. This is the wordplayer's ad hoc approach: recycle the existent. It makes Tournier, like Joyce, a 'palincestuous' writer.[7] Like puns, myths go from tops to bottoms: 'Le mythe est enfantin à sa base, métaphysique à son sommet. Voyez *Vendredi*: Antoine Vitez en a tiré un spectacle théâtral au Palais de Chaillot pour les jeunes. Gilles Deleuze en a fait une analyse philosophique'.[8] In general, Tournier opts for the carnivalesque aspect of myths rather than the socially conservative; 'Le mythe n'est pas un rappel à l'ordre, mais bien plutôt un rappel au désordre', though he recognizes a didactic element even in the ludic: 'On ne peut fabuler sans enseigner' (*VV*, 31–2, 37). One level of myths, national stereotypes, gives rise to a reversal in *Le Roi des aulnes*: Gallic *clarté* and Teutonic *ténèbres* swap sides. Perhaps because of his straddle position (the favourite posture of punners), for his part Tournier works to read the Germanic runes, and thus to speak for the traditional enemy. More generally, he believes in the mythopoeic power of wordplay, what André Clavel has termed 'le merveilleux pouvoir obstétrique des mots, qui devancent le texte et le provoquent'.[9] In *Les Météores*, for instance, Alexandre Surin links his fate to that of young Eustache because, in criminal slang, both surnames are synonyms for knife. The words come first; the justifying of their juxtaposition tags along.

Myths proceed by signs. Forced by an accident to write his diary with his left hand, the dodgy Abel inevitably entitles his entries 'Ecrits sinistres'. This changeover enables him to play between *sinistre*, *gaucherie*, *droit*, *adroit*. Tournier's left hand always knows, perhaps too well, what his right is doing, though this is not invariably true of his shortsighted visionary hero. 'Tout est signe', indeed (*RA*, 15). *Le Roi des aulnes* is a semiologist's gold mine (and minefield). In the process of scattering and bonding signs, Tournier, as befits a consistent punner, can often be excruciating. The Japanese and Venetian sections of *Les Météores* illustrate this indulged temptation. With both locales, Tournier is over-determined to make his points and thus to sign his text unmistakably. The multifaceted Venetian mirror, for instance, is 'spéculaire' and 'spectaculaire', like the city it symbolizes, which is 'une ville chiffrée' (*M*, 428, 438).

Signs, being multivalent, can be read, or misread. They can be the cautionary writing on the wall, as in the Nazi propaganda at Rominten (where, incidentally, Goethe cohabits with Hitler). In *Le Roi des aulnes*, the leitmotif of inversion (the shuttle between *inversion bénigne* and *inversion maligne*) typifies this semiotic instability. Finding that a cherished burden weighs incredibly light, that gravity yields to levity, Tiffauges comments: 'Il y a eu en quelque sorte changement de signe: le plus est devenu moins, et réciproquement' (*RA*, 133). As with myths, Tournier sports with existing bodies of signs (the Tarot pack in *Vendredi*, heraldry in *Le Roi des aulnes*), and was no doubt tickled to find that in armorial bearings right is left and vice versa. One of his stand-ins, the Kommandeur of Kaltenborn, instructs Tiffauges in the conversion of signs, the process by which a symbol is no longer carried but begins to carry the bearer, as when Christ's cross ends by bearing him: the criss-cross or chiasmus, we might add (*RA*, 473). Punning permeates this literalization of the metaphorical in which prefigurations come true. Concerning the last stages, the Kommandeur cites St John's Apocalypse and glosses: 'Ses symboles sont diaboles: ils ne symbolisent plus rien. Et de leur saturation naît la fin du monde' (ibid.). *Diabole* is a coinage, though there is a Greek word of this form meaning 'slander'.

The Kommandeur is contrasting a replete sign with its evacuated simulacrum. In addition, there is clearly a satanic undertow to *diabole*: Lucifer as the ape of God. Though the Greek prefixes *sym-* and *dis-* ('together' and 'through') are hardly antithetical, Tournier is presumably granting a propulsive sense to the parody. The symbol backfires on itself and disappears up its own foundation, just as the juvenile swordbearers finish up impaled from stern to stem. The culminating excruciation is that the Kommandeur holds out to Tiffauges the arms of an ogre ('Argent à trois *pages* de gueule dressées en *pal*'), where the puns, like signs in the disintegrating Third Reich, run riot (*RA*, 492–3).

Perhaps not too strangely, the corollary of a totally meaningful world, with its intricate networks of signs, is a diminution of individual freedom. A plethora of symbols amounts to fate. In *Les Météores*, via his homosexual safaris, Alexandre Surin hunts an impossible twinhood. His nephew Paul, one of twins, already possesses a perfect model of this desired state: 'Je trouve dans mon enfance mieux que la promesse solennelle: la préformation de l'aboutissement auquel je suis appelé' (*M*, 505). For Tournier, both in the historical events of *Le Roi des aulnes* and the geographical sequences of *Les Météores*, 'par la reconnaissance, le fatum devient amor fati' (*VP*, 234). Thus, Tiffauges says of his 'phoric' hands, made for bearing children: 'Tout cela prévu, voulu, agencé de toute éternité, et donc vénérable, adorable' (*RA*, 504). A mocking tone is sometimes directed at Abel's megalomania, which is in some ways that of the child who thinks the world revolves around him. He is very aware of the Nazi machine, 'mais il savait qu'aucune organisation n'est à l'abri d'un grain de sable, et qu'au demeurant le destin travaillait pour lui' (*RA*, 383). There are undoubtedly fissures in the apparently monolithic Reich, but Abel's grain of sand can hardly be thought to threaten the juggernaut. He collaborates with fate and with Hitler's Germany. But his only true impact on events lies in his transfiguration, his rewriting of them, whereby he deputizes for Tournier himself, who also works back-to-front.

Tournier's people, despite their submission to fate, are propelled by imperious self-affirmation, against hell and high water. He uses 'cohérence', 'logique', in an extra-ethical, Nietzschean fashion. Occasionally, he is at slight pains to disentangle himself from his creatures, as when he talks of letting them speak their fill without authorial intervention, 'pour laisser libre cours à la folie raisonneuse et systématique' (*VP*, 113). The paucity of dialogue, too, encourages solo ranting. Even Robinson alternates between claiming that the Other (Vendredi) is essential and declaring him discardable (*V*, 53, 116). Tournier can be evasive, as when he suggests that novelists do not practise what their heroes preach, but he goes on to admit 'la surcompensation fabuleuse' (*VP*, 120). He cannot, however, stay modest for long. Not only does his figment Paul wish to become 'le maître de la pluie et du beau temps' (*M*, 449), but Tournier himself candidly avows: 'Le seul être dont je revendique absolument la place, c'est Dieu'.[10] The novelist qua God is probably the grandest approximation of them all. Whether it is dwarfs or ogres, Tournier gravitates to the monstrous, the whole hog.

Like mules (puns, too, are hybrids), like Abel's gelding, a *barbe bleu* (a blatant pun on Bluebeard), monsters are sterile, which leaves them freer for other vocations. But Tiffauges longs to protect the young, and so he is defined as 'un ogre affamé de tendresse' (*VP*, 110). Here, as he habitually does, Tournier speaks metaphorically. His whole work suggests that we can do little else. Metaphors make liaisons, and these can be dangerous. Weidmann, killer of seven people, who is the same size as Abel and was born on the same day, crops up several times in the novel, by an arranged coincidence. Abel in fact attends his public execution. Where the crapulous mob howls for the guillotine, Tiffauges, hearing them, hungers for genocide (*RA*, 189). Later in the story, the Nazis bellow a *Weidmannsheil* (hunter's accolade). At Rominten, venery releases its two meanings: sex and hunting. Castrating dead stags, Goering represents 'le sacrificateur officiel de l'Ange Phallophore' (*RA*, 331). Tiffauges keeps even more grisly company; he is privy to vicious Nazi research into selective breeding. How could he keep his hands or his brain clean, when his premiss was always that purity, as against true innocence, is the real monstrosity, as in this punning list: 'Purification religieuse, épuration politique, sauvegarde de la pureté de la race' (*RA*, 125)?

In the sense of odd ones (or odd pairs) out, twins are also monsters: 'Des jumeaux vrais ne sont qu'un seul être dont la monstruosité est d'occuper deux places différentes dans l'espace' (*M*, 573). They are simultaneously split and joined. Homophones, fully or partly identical, are acoustic twins; homographs are look-alikes. (Perfect puns are as uninteresting and as tautological as clones: 'Why are red ribbons worn so much in French buttonholes? Because their name is legion'.) Two-in-one: not quite the Holy Trinity, but certainly an unholy twinnity. There is a controlling pun in *Les Météores*, which was originally to have been called *Le Vent Paraclet*. Pairs are set up: sky/heaven, religion/weather (*VP*, 252). Tournier further bridges the spatial gap by recalling that in several mythologies twins are seen as intercessors between heaven/sky (an unavoidable pun in many languages) and earth, where they command clouds and rain. They are thus associated with fertility, though, perversely as always, Tournier opts to see them as splendidly sterile in themselves. What could be more vibrantly sterile than an orgasm without ejaculation? Thomas Koussek (*coup sec*) practises this form of release (English slang, possibly with a jab at Eton's 'wet bob', calls it 'dry bob'). Discovered at one point in the missionary position on top of a crucifix, Koussek confuses throughout sacred and profane. 'Il vivait intensément l'identité étymologique de ces deux mots: l'esprit, le vent' (*M*, 47). In St John's Gospel, Thomas is called Didymus, the Greek equivalent to his Hebrew name, which means 'twin'. Koussek is a counterpart to Alexandre: their minds are in cahoots, like twins. Koussek's wilful confusion of *esprit/vent* was anticipated by Swift (the Aeolists in *A Tale of a Tub*): spirit, *afflatus*, *flatus*, and by the ancient Hebrews, whose *ruach* pictured the Holy Spirit as a wind.

All in all, for Tournier twins (human or verbal) are a bonus, and they embody the uncanny. Their other rhetorical equivalent is the zeugma: 'La tête couverte d'un bonnet de fourrure et farcie par trois millénaires de civilisation occidentale' (*V*, 144), where *tête* swivels between 'head' and 'brain', outer and inner. Meaning 'yoke', zeugma has been called 'yoke-wit'. There could, in addition, be an etymological kinship between twins and laughter. Twins are monozygotic or dizygotic; the zygomatic is the yoke-bone in the face, essential for smiling. The hyphen, or *trait d'union*, is crucial to *Les Météores*, which focuses on unions, loving or monstrous; and we have already seen how 'réunir d'un trait alpha et oméga' is Nestor's overriding goal.

'You think Oedipus had a problem,' runs the graffito; 'Adam was Eve's mother'.[11] The Adam-myth appeals to Tournier as a variant on twinhood. He rewrites to his taste the Creation story, and the account plays with itself in a far from solitary pleasure. Adam was the 'possédant-possédé [...] enceint de ses propres œuvres [...] Homme porte-femme devenu par surcroît porte-enfant, chargé et surchargé, comme ces poupées-gigognes emboîtées les unes dans les autres' (*RA*,

35). The true fall was the split-up into three of a marvellously self-contained unity. The Platonic myth of the hermaphrodite is rampant, and couchant, also in *Les Météores*. Even the ideal twins, Jean and Paul, experience the sundering from an early age and increasingly grow out of step with each other. The latter ends up legless and stationary; the former disappears, an endlessly wandering goy. Twins represent alterity in identity; they are 'frères ennemis'. Similarly, the two meanings of puns pull in differing directions semantically, while coalescing or harmonizing phonically. Nature itself begets such doubles. Witness 'syzygy' (see *M*, 419): this apparently Hungarian sport in our national lexis can mean the conjunction *or* the opposition of two heavenly bodies. Internecine fraternity (the Berlin Wall, Jacob/Esau, Cain/Abel) is the other side of the perfect twin model. After all, 'twin', like 'cleave', has meant over the years to split *or* to come together.

Twins, and not only the Siamese variety exploited by old-time funfairs, are monsters or freaks, and fated. From one angle, all humans are repressed or frustrated twins; from another most of us ogres murder the other half of ourselves (*M*, 163, 196, 384).[12] The Original Oneness, once shattered, breeds catastrophes. In the womb, twins lie *tête-bêche*, head to tail: they form an unbroken circle. They give rise to ambiguity, where we cannot make head or tail of anything. They embody a two-faced reality, and unsurprisingly Janus Bifrons is invoked in their connexion (*M*, 492), as so often in the long history of the pun. As the *frère-pareil* is valued by Tournier over the *sans-pareil*, the stereoscopic over the monocular, so puns can be elevated above single meanings. Tournier gladly courts the perils they entail.

Just as wordplay can spawn all kinds of misbegottens, so incest and homosexuality are, for Tournier, bad copies of *la gémellité* (*VP*, 247). His own substitution for the inaccessible twinhood is non-genital paedophilia, which is 'une gémellité d'élection à défaut de la gémellité naturelle. Elle satisfait un besoin de narcissisme à deux'.[13] Thus moralizes a critic. Tournier himself prefers elasticity, and puns in favour of paneroticism: 'Toutes les voies et toutes les voix lui sont bonnes' (*CS*, 106). Punners entertain possibilities. Thus, in *Vendredi*, Tournier has his imaginary cake and jokily spits it out when he describes Robinson's coitus with a tree-trunk as 'une dangereuse impasse' (*V*, 122). He would patently prefer humankind to be begotten by parthenogenesis, or rather spermless self-fecundation: 'Un serpent se mordant la queue est la figure de cette érotique close sur elle-même, sans perte ni bavure' (*V*, 12): *le coup sec* again. That in-between, the hybrid Alexandre, brings this celestial sortie down to earth by citing Ouroboros (the mythological tail-swallowing serpent) in relation to onanism. He also extends this, in a fantasy of an elephant shoving its trunk up its own rear—auto-sodomization (*M*, 137). Puns, and portmanteau words, also practise *emboîtement*, though perhaps a nearer rhetorical figure here is the palindrome.

Like his twin nephews a doomed freak or sport, Alexandre is a living pun: 'Me voilà logé à double enseigne' (*M*, 112). He dotes on double entendre: '*La morgue*, mot admirable parce qu'il désigne à la fois le poison distillé dans une âme, par une certaine forme hautaine et méprisante de l'orgueil, et le lieu où l'on expose les cadavres non-identifiés' (p. 332). His fate is precisely both to disdain his fellows and to be murdered anonymously; his wordplay is prophetic. His business, running an empire of refuse-dumps, delights him, for it affords a view of society from the underside; he can possess whole populations 'par derrière' (p. 36). *Vice a tergo*, he might have said.

One of his schoolmates, Raphaël Ganeça, matches him on a more mythological level, and attracts some of the author's more intricately allusive punning. In Indian legend, Ganesh is the elephant-headed son of Śiva, always accompanied by the same totem-animal, a rat (actually, a bandicoot, *mus giganteus*). Rats are the emblems of the *oms* (*ordures ménagères*), which Alexandre gloats over; he has in addition a blissful encounter with an elephant-keeper in the Bois de Vincennes zoo. OM, the sacred syllable of mantras, is especially associated with Ganesh, who enjoyed a virgin birth, and was often used by his mother as a living contraceptive to bar Śiva from her chamber, although, confusingly, Ganesh was reputed to be a great remover of obstacles. Thus play the criss-crosses.

Though anxious to avoid stock moralizing, or at least to hang the rest of us on a nearby hook to Tournier's, I cannot sidestep the term 'perversion'. In *Le Vent Paraclet*, the author himself complacently logs Abel's repertoire: vampirism (Nestor's wounded knee to which he presses his lips), cannibalism (munching the Host), coprophilia (I am coming to that), fetishism (shoes), paedophilia, necrophilia (the corpse of Arnim), bestialism (Barbe-Bleue). For him, this very pluralism or, we might say, omnifutuence, preserves Abel's 'innocence', for true perverts are monomaniacs (*VP*, 119). Tournier's sort are presumably just greedy. The pun is the true polymorphous perverse.

For the wordplayer, there is no such thing as waste material. Alexandre acts out the old Terence tag 'Homo sum: nihil a me alienum puto', as he scoops up the enormous tapeworm (the '*taenia solium* des éboueurs', for she too has affinities with tips) jettisoned with aristocratic nonchalance by Fabienne before her assembled guests. Like Baudelaire in many ways, Tournier makes gold from slime. 'Jetée dans la marmite romanesque, l'ontologie se transforme partiellement en scatologie'.[14] I might add that eschatology and scatology are related (and the same word serves for both in Spanish), since both have to do with the final issue of things. 'Oméga' is evoked in the vicinity of Barbe-Bleue's much-admired and shapely dung. Nestor's ambition to unite alpha and omega oscillates between spirit and defecation. Homosexual and proud of it, Alexandre expresses his pride in these scornful terms: 'Moi qui suis sujet à constipation, je serais guéri si je disposais chaque matin de la face d'un hétérosexuel pour la couvrir de ma bouse' (*M*, 141). He plays on *exprimer*: to express/to press out, and on *matière grise*: rubbish, but also brains (pp. 91, 99). He has a dirty mind.

When I think of my concentration on puns, which for many people are pure linguistic perversion, I see the point of the following quotation: 'Il n'y a sans doute rien de plus émouvant dans une vie d'homme que la découverte fortuite de la perversion à laquelle il est voué' (*RA*, 82). This is Nestor's comment, placed in conjunction with an account of the Renaissance figure Baron des Adrets, who made both Catholic and Protestant prisoners dance blindfolded to the sound of a viol on the unparapeted edge of a tower, whence they fell screaming on to lances. Power untrammelled is *viol*ation. Founded wilfully on a mistranslation, that play between words, by Herder, *Le Roi des aulnes* is ruled by deviant use, of sex, of scientific experiments, of myths. And that ill-used trope, the pun, if properly exploited, is a good tool for this deviant enterprise. The overarching pun is on 'perversion': of youth, of language, rather than more conventionally of morals. Perhaps the major excruciating approximation at work in this novel is that which superimposes Abel and the Nazis. He treads the tightrope of being suspect. Willy-nilly, he collaborates with the German war-effort. In this he leads a double life. Like Alexandre, he is an existential pun. He is forever ready to *take off* from reality (as in his encounter with the fabulous blind elk, or *élan*), and indeed often seems more at home and in tune with animals (his horse, his pigeons) than with people. In his permanently twisted situation, he is twice saved by fire (hell as salvation): at school and on the outbreak of war. His pantheon is peopled by anti-heroes: Pontius Pilate, Caligula, Rasputin, which of course prepares him for his fishy relationship with Nazidom. He is a paradox or oxymoron: in him contraries bed together. His name is a *redende Name*: Tiffauges was the village where Gilles de Rais (a later Tournier hero, in *Gilles et Jeanne*) set up residence, and where in 1435 he founded a home for the Holy Innocents, prior to murdering them. The name Tiffauges is at one time translated as *Tiefauge* ('œil profond') and at another as *Triefauge* ('œil malade') (*RA*, 406–7).

In *Le Vent Paraclet*, Tournier claims that when France was occupied, his family, because of its profound ties with Germany, was not bowled over by the invaders: 'Nous étions vaccinés contre la séduction nazie' (*VP*, 73). Is Tiffauges similarly proof? Like an ogre counting his riches, Abel loves to list and classify, which is a short step from the taxonomic lunacies of Nazi theorists. Pedantry is eroticized. In the epigraph to *Le Pied de la lettre*, Tournier juxtaposes 'au pied de la lettre' and 'prendre son pied', thus mixing up philology and orgasm.[15] When Abel meets the official ogre Goering, while he mocks this creature's tasteless, pell-mell collections, this Junker's junk, he cannot help feeling smeared by association, though he maintains that his affinities with the whole Nazi phenomenon are artificial, distant, and parodic (*RA*, 325). It is a concertina approximation which squeezes him close and away by turns, but such raucous melodies, such cacophonous sirens, need to be resisted.

Misuse, overuse: playing with language leads in this direction, too: piling things on thick. In *Les Météores*, Alexandre adopts a hyperbolic dog, Sam, which he credits (playing on *cynos*, dog) with *cynisme*.[16] Sam sodomizes a male dog already copulating with a bitch. This spectacle *edifies* Alexandre, 'au double sens du mot, augmentant ma vertu, ma moralité, mais aussi ajoutant comme un étage au château de mes rêves par cet acte d'amour en seconde position' (*M*, 225). Sam is *un corniaud*, a hefty cross-breed and a mutt, and his sexual doubling or squaring is a pun in action. Cynicism clearly contains the idea of pushing beyond normal limits, conventions, or measure. Jankélévitch is also pondering cynicism when he talks of 'l'homéopathie de la surenchère'.[17] This stresses a self-regulating factor in such apparent excess, a check on the escalation. Likewise, Tournier's provocation often reminds me of the fail-safe, pulled-punch variety of Jewish imprecation: 'May he go blind—God forbid!' Abel's inflation, however, knows no such bounds. Convinced of the allegorical status of East Prussia and its people, he is resolved to celebrate this, 'de porter toutes leurs vertus à incandescence' (RA, 282–3). But words have two faces and forked tongues. He will ultimately have to confront the Nazi version of 'incandescence': the death-camp furnaces and the hellfire of war.

These verbal modulations indicate how much Tournier's word-playing is itself 'une inversion maligne'—a clever, controlled, often malicious twist. Punning and ethical distortion can consort. Tournier has said of his experiences as a translator (and *traductio* is one of the several terms in rhetoric for punning): 'Il y a de grandes ressources pour le style—en prose et plus encore en poésie—dans la distorsion des locutions usuelles' (VP, 160). Abel finds it easier to say certain things in German than in his mother tongue, though of course even in going native he remains a linguistic exile. Despite his loathing for France, he nevertheless adores French. Tiffauges seeks to impart home truths from abroad. In a provocative page, Tournier argues that writers, whatever their politics, are truer patriots than anyone else, because of their guardianship of the national language (VP, 85–6).

It is in the predominant and equivocal image of *phorie*, focused on Tiffauges, that Tournier's child-centred world view finds its fullest expression. This is a pun-idea. Bearing can obviously be inner (gestation) or outer (carrying on shoulders or in the arms); the second can substitute for the first. There is a link between *phorie* and *métaphore*, for the latter, too, bears extra meaning and conveys across a gap. Tournier spells out the resonances: 'Le fond de la phorie est équivoque [...] Saint Christophe porte, tel une bête de somme, l'enfant-Dieu. Le Roi des aulnes emporte, tel un oiseau de proie, l'enfant vers la mort' (TC, 22). Tournier wants to convince us of 'la portée humaine et universelle' of Abel's obsession (VP, 122). He is at his most dubious when he generalizes in this fashion. It is simultaneously a form of opportunism and a loss of nerve, in that it seeks to make Abel's weirdness more orthodox. Tournier calls in the bearers Atlas, Hercules, St Julian the Hospitaller, and the Portuguese conquistador Albuquerque as sureties for his sermon on the *mount*. This gives 'le sens de la grande récompense de Saint Christophe: pour avoir porté sur ses épaules l'enfant-Dieu, sa perche soudain fleurie et chargée de fruits' (*RA*, 524). Bearing a child precedes ejaculation.

As well as travesty of religion, there is parody of the value, *la phorie*, which replaces it. Market-porters, *les forts des Halles*, are just a gross version of the *phore* Abel, as *Les Halles* themselves are a crude counterpart to his taste for *crudités*: they offer 'une phorie trivialisée' (*RA*, 135). At the other extreme, the horse represents, when its rider carries a child in his arms, 'une superphorie' (p. 469). Barbe-Bleue gives Abel effortless lessons in defecating, and Abel amplifies these in musing on the hunting of stags on horseback and practising one of his many switch-arounds: 'La persécution de l'Ange Phallophore par l'Ange Anal, le pourchas et la mise à mort d'Alpha par Oméga'. He loves this inversion, 'qui dans ce jeu meurtrier faisait de la bête fuyarde et fessue un principe agressif et exterminateur, et dans le roi des forêts, à la virilité épanouie en buisson capital, une proie forcée, pleurant vainement sa merci' (pp. 353–4). The rump attacks the phallus; passivity rules. More gently, Abel bends the etymology of *euphorie* from 'se porter bien' to 'porter bien' (p. 132). Bearing others helps him to bear up, to be borne up, to be reborn.

The doubts persist. The Atlas-figure apparently holding up part of the structure at Kaltenborn is only *un trompe-l'œil* (*RA*, 361). When Abel gradually takes over control of the *napola*, he begins dangerously to parody and corrupt his own good instincts. He preserves the shorn locks of his golden boys, as Nazis did in extermination-camps; his communal showers recall the murderous subterfuge practised on the Jews; his anal fixations refer him cruelly to Auschwitz, the 'Anus Mundi'. *Phorie* can be black: the carrying of a decapitated child is far more onerous than that of a whole one. The infamous Mengele, too, was obsessed by twins. Abel is made to see by Ephraïm that 'toutes ses inventions, toutes ses découvertes se reflétaient dans l'horrible miroir, inversées et portées à une incandescence d'enfer' (p. 560). Even more guilty, however, are the accursed tribe of grown-ups for, by a particularly malignant inversion, they have perverted kids' non-lethal wargames into homicidal battles. The child is father to the man, who betrays him/her. Perhaps the most cheering of the inversions is that Abel the prisoner becomes a boss in the imprisoning country. The downfall of the Reich is offset by the apotheosis of Tiffauges. Behind all these changes of sign lurk the Christian notions of exchange, reversibility of merits, compensation.

Can humour coexist with death-camps (as the *napola* turns out to be)? Opinions are polarized. You instinctively believe either that a sense of humour helps people to survive any horror, or that some areas are no-go to humour. Even if it cannot be proved to effect real change, surely humour can bolster that which refuses and those who refuse to change, to renege on their humanity.

The Kommandeur refers to 'la mécanique des symboles', and Abel acknowledges a parallel tendency in his own usage and misuse (*RA*, 457, 473). For his or her part, any reader might well find that there is in Tournier's work a surplus of signs: semiology shades into the semaphore; the discreet boats into the blatant.

Il n'est pas étonnant que les trois préoccupations majeures de Tiffauges, la *phorie*, la *densité* et l'*inversion* [...] se nouent et trouvent leur parodie à la faveur du jeu de mots: le portage [...] s'inverse diaboliquement dans la *déportation*, la densité [...] dans la concentration des camps de la mort.[18]

Punning tightens the screws.

Like Abel, Tournier could say: 'J'ai toujours porté le plus grand intérêt aux opérations d'inversion, de permutation, de superposition' (*RA*, 452). Like Queneau, Tournier rhymes, and puns, situations. He imagines analogically. One such pattern is the chiasmus. As little children, the identical twins of *Les Météores* used to swap their name-tags, so that not only others but they themselves would not know who was who. Later, after separation, it is not clear, in this couple of 'frères intervertis', who is pursuing whom. This transposing betokens the lust for osmosis and total merger. Tournier's people are forever twisting and turning. Playing again with the notion of gravity (and traditionally lead and feathers are invoked in scientific experiments on this phenomenon), Tournier describes a black storm-cloud over Prussia releasing a heavy snowfall: 'Inversion spectaculaire du noir au blanc, en accord avec ce paysage sans nuances. Ainsi le nuage de plomb n'était qu'un sac de plumes'. An oxymoron enables him to play between opposites: 'Quel est donc le cosmologue grec qui a parlé de la "secrète noirceur de la neige"?' (*RA*, 410). Thus some of the nuances missing in the landscape are restored in this glossing text. Tournier often tries to attenuate the menacing rigidity of his pattern-making by stressing not abrupt contraries but overlap, continuum, as for example in the survival of Jean's *tête-bêche* position into his heterosexual affair with Sophie. Another kind of overhang, or hangover, is intertextuality. Tournier/Fournier, *aulnes*/Meaulnes, the piggyback fight in both novels (though how chaste in the earlier): is this thieving or phonic memory? Tournier's head buzzes with other literature. Patterns, parodies, pastiches, quotations—he favours such doublings, because he likes laying it on with a trowel: *débauche, surenchère*. So like Gide in many ways, he chooses to differentiate himself from his master's 'binary classification', for his own 'trousseau de clefs binaires' are 'tempérées par ce qu'il faut de scepticisme et d'esprit ludique' (*VV*, 212): the let-out, the sanity-clause.

He is totally unabashed by repetitiveness. Is it a sign of musical ambitions, or merely sub-Homeric anxiety, or pedantry (and the last two are often identical)? Why does he yank together distant and disparate elements? There is in *Le Roi des aulnes* a relentless imposition of patterns, reminiscent of Joyce's Stakhanovite punning in *Finnegans Wake*. The mentally handicapped Franz in *Les Météores* is quite literally murdered by Tournier's systematizing of signs and reversals. Obsessed with calendars and seasons, hungering for regularity, Franz ends up being killed by unpredictable nature, when his stolen boat founders on a reef. The author's imagination, too, can be a death-camp where the unfittest do not survive. At one stage, Paul says: 'L'analogie s'impose, oui. Et elle va dans mon sens' (*M*, 449). This is too often the case with Tournier himself. He is prone to use reflexive verbs ('s'impose, here, or 'se forme') to introduce his etymological punning, thereby abdicating personal responsibility, by implying that language has a will of its own. Alexandre confesses: 'Tout cela est fort bien, mais ne s'agit-il pas d'une simple construction de l'esprit?' (*M*, 382). All literature is a mental construct, but readers prefer not to collide with the scaffolding.

Tournier's defence would no doubt be that the patterns, signs, and puns he scatters in his work were already there in reality. Hence (and the pun is an acoustic fortuity) his naked and unashamed use of coincidences, all of which are planted pointedly, like efficient puns. Nothing is random in his universe, nothing wasted. Far more than Alexandre who has access to reclamation, he is dedicated to recuperation. He is a prolific spinner of yarns, and his stories often proceed by lurches, *rebondissements*, dependent on metaphorical swings and roundabouts. Just as puns are a turn on words, so whole stories can hinge on a pun: for example, 'Le Coq de bruyère', which pivots round the phrase 'fermer les yeux'—psychosomatic blindness and refusal of awareness, a potent duality. This is a generative pun. In 'Les Suaires de Véronique', Tournier exploits a mythopoeic literalization of the idiom 'avoir la peau' (figuratively, to skin someone alive). This story concerns a fanatical female photographer who obtains extraordinary effects by dunking her dumb male model in chemical fluids before capturing this complex new image on paper, thereby hospitalizing him, and transforming photography into 'dermography'. Perhaps the prime example of eddying meanings comes with the multiple suggestions of the verb *couvrir*, so essential to a novel like *Les Météores*, which is so taken up with space: 'parcourir (à pied), protéger (d'un manteau), combler (de prévenanccs), défendre (avec des troupes), munir d'un toit, cacher, déguiser, excuser, justifier, compenser, féconder' (*M*, 572). This is the key switch-pun, the verbal fillip, for the whole novel. Perhaps, like Carroll's Humpty Dumpty, Tournier should pay this word overtime.

'Variations on a theme' is the most suitable musical analogy for his procedure. Fear of boring himself or others leads him to proliferate analogies, fables, myths, allusions, parodies, puns, for it cannot be denied that wordplaying often stems from an incapacity for patience or dullness, an inability to look tedious facts straight in the face. As soon as Abel learns of Martine's three sisters, he dies to know them: 'Je retrouve là mon étrange incapacité à m'enfermer dans une individualité, mon irrépressible inclination à rechercher, à partir d'une formule unique, des variations, une répétition sans monotonie' (*RA*, 183). Now, variation can easily be merely decorative, the same thing in different dress, whereas double meanings are different things in the same dress. A concerted attempt is made in *Le Roi des aulnes* to make everything slot together, to fabricate a perfect, or infernal, machine. This author works to convince us that ogres, complicity with destiny, density, inversion, bearing, all cohere. For, like the founding fathers of the United States of America, if they do not hang together, assuredly they will all hang separately.

Many readers have found something pungently 'decadent' in Tournier's language and themes. Religion, for instance: 'Fastueuse, subtile, érotique, telle est l'Église initiatrice dont je rêve' (*VP*, 62). The pomp of the Catholic Church is the devil's part. In a splendid passage of scatological, belittling *amplificatio*, the Holy See is metamorphosed into a lavatory-seat, and a cathedral organ into a steam-organ (with its *soupapes*, no doubt) (*RA*, 117−18). Parody is the dubious homage that vice pays to virtue. The theological doctrines of the communion of saints and the reversibility of merits are converted for use in the punishment system of Abel's college. Having achieved his goal of sleeping with four hundred boys simultaneously, Abel travesties Pascal: 'Joie, pleurs, pleurs de joie' (*RA*, 512).

Alexandre provides almost a thumbnail parody of French intellectual 'decadentism' when he proclaims: 'L'idée est plus que la chose, et l'idée de l'idée plus que l'idée'. Infinite regress, 'en vertu de quoi l'imitation est plus que la chose imitée' (*M*, 101). 'Roi et dandy des gadoues', he bears an aristocratic coat-of-arms: six gold medallions filled with compacted rubbish from his dumps, kept in the pockets of his silk waistcoat. His surname recalls allusive arms. *Surin*, means, first, a Parisian apache's knife (he carries a swordstick and mixes, fatally in the end, in rough-trade company), and, secondly, young apple-tree stock. He has in fact no stock, no possibility of self-furtherance, but he is drawn to apple cheeks. He is especially fond of equivocal words like *folie*, 'qui désigne à la fois un rendez-vous galant caché sous des feuillages et la perte du sens commun' (*M*, 125−6). We see here the bondage of punning and High Camp. Though professionally involved in recycling garbage, Alexandre is predominantly concerned with gloating over it as a secret information source (*un grimoire*) on a city's life, and with shaping it aesthetically (landscaping). This is in keeping. If he is not cut out for generation, so must he be for regeneration; he himself never expects to be saved. He is in fact derisive towards his brother Gustave's term of 'répurgation' (Gustave dies accidentally under three tonnes of domestic rubbish): 'Cela semblait échappé d'un traité de médecine digestive ou d'une étude de casuistique religieuse' (*M*, 35). The lofty and the low again conjoined; the sport Alexandre is anti-utilitarian.

Tournier calls himself proudly a thieving magpie. Although the very term 'eclecticism' enrages postmodern theorists, choosers are not beggars (nor buggers). For his own obituary, Tournier suggests: 'S'il fallait un ancêtre et une étiquette, on pourrait songer à J. K. Huysmans et à celle de *naturaliste mystique*. C'est qu'à ses yeux tout est beau, même la laideur; tout est sacré, même la boue' (*CS*, 194). *A rebours*: Alexandre works 'à rebrousse-poil' (*M*, 40). Books written so wilfully against the grain naturally resort to wordplay, since they aim for excruciation. This goes from the particularized ('Jumo', *jumeaux*, *jumelles*) to the generalized, where the author worms his way through all the so-significant details of a situation, rubbing our noses in it, like a bitch trying to school a tyro puppy. Teeth set on edge and sickly grins must be a not uncommon response. There is a reader's *phorie*, too: we have to bear a great deal. I am not whinging about bad taste, whatever that is, but about overtaste, glut.

Tournier's sign language can have this effect on our sensibilities and bodies. Throughout his work, signs are made flesh. The Mistral, in *Les Météores*, is the Holy Spirit in a truly apocalyptic mood. Wild but not woolly is Tournier's world. Are we, as examiners, to grant magisterially the lordly Tournier, author of these dexterous, sinister, ambidextrous books, a *proxime accessit*? After all, interpretation and evaluation are themselves approximate. Punning, with its myriad offshoots, informs the themes, structures, and values of Tournier's fiction. Likewise, just as he has to find ways to pull together *phorie*, *densité*, and *inversion*, so I in this essay have sought to juxtapose: approximation, straddle, hybrid, monster, twins, zeugma, sex, perversions, twists, hinges, patterns, paradox, and ambiguity. A tall order. I wear baggy trousers; I prefer loose fits, like Tournier's fetishist, who steals bras too big for his wife's petite breasts. In a rough-and-ready way, I have done what my subject does. I am fascinated by what the neo-Irishman Hugh Kenner calls 'large-scale punning, whose unit is a whole literary convention, the pun being mightier than the sword'.[19] This is what I have termed the 'overarching pun'. Punning acts as a bonding agent for the disparate materials of Tournier's universe.

Le Roi des aulnes stinks, and is a feast (an obsolete meaning of 'symbol' is 'a contribution to a banquet'). A sight for sore eyes, a refresher of tired minds, a cloyer of the palate. Manna or manure? I could find no etymological link between these two words, although one meaning of 'manna'—a sweetish exudation from some species of ash, of a laxative nature—seems apt, for what goes in must surely squeeze out. 'Manure' may be a corruption of 'manoeuvre'. (The reader, of course, like e.e. cummings's glad and big Olaf, might decorously retort: 'There is some s. I will not eat'.[20]) Though one is a luxury and the other an essential, both are useful; even the miraculous manna needs manure, albeit heavenly. Playing translingually, we might say that 'une manne' is Tournier's ideal creature. Changing sex, Tournier might be called 'un allumeur', for he teases the reader protractedly, but also 'un sage-homme', for he delivers in the end. A plethora of nourishment and wayward taste are his twin possibilities, as when in *Gaspard, Melchior et Balthazar* a feast (*un balthazar*) of sugary sweets is offered to the starving kids of Bethlehem while the Massacre of the Innocents is going on. Tournier's spendthrift pen throws out riches like a drunken sailor, but this very generosity makes him at times an opinionator, a barrack-room lawyer, a bar bore.

Just as, in sexual terms, self-penetration seems to be the imaginary ideal, so perhaps myths are meant in Tournier's work to back-fire on themselves, to autodestruct. We should not forget that as well as reminding us that myths contain our oldest, deepest stories, he suggests, by his practice, that we need to defeat our own mythologizing urges. Aptly, in his war book *Le Roi des aulnes*, he deploys the strategy of saturation bombing. He is his own de-constructionist, and thus seeks to outstrip his critical pursuers. He privileges paradox. 'Paradox', of course, is itself paradoxical, self-contradictory, for it can mean a statement that seems false but is true, or which seems true but is false. He plays dangerous games, and wordplay aids this initiative. Playing with words is dangerous for the player (it antagonizes many receivers), for the receiver (be-dazzlement), and the stability or self-satisfaction of language. *Chic* and *chicane*, two words of doubtful provenance, are a permanent temptation.

What is perhaps most alienating is the movement in Tournier's fiction from I to It: the decentring of the first person, the weariness of being human at all. To pun can be quintessentially human, but it can veer to the inhuman. Robinson couples with his island. Tiffauges sinks gratefully into the bog. Paul opens himself to the sky, his compensation for the amputation both of his limb and of his twin brother. When Paul argues that the ubiquity pursued in travel must give way to a more imaginative, static variety, we may wonder whether he is now seeking nusquamity. *Porosité* will be his step towards 'un corps barométrique, pluviométrique, anémométrique, hygrométrique' (*M*, 610). Man reduced to a weather-box; the outlook is gloomy. This Aeolian harps jinglingly. Can his sense of God-power, 'maître de la pluie et du beau temps', be other than an impious hope?

The real poser with Tournier is not how to decipher what is in his works, which house all kinds of internal or external commentaries from him, but how to decide what to make of all the separate or converging elements: the difference between studying a knitting-pattern and the

finished, syncretistic, technicoloured dreamcoat. Language itself is
naturally, as well as artificially, double-dealing. Take 'secrete' for
example: to retain and to expel. Tournier does both. He projects and
explicates a world, but it remains something of a mystery. I may have
exhausted readers, but I am under no illusions that I have exhausted
Tournier. That would be unlikely, for he is forever doubling up,
multiplying himself. 'On n'oublie pas—quand on l'a entendu dans son
enfance—le sinistre *nunquam duo* (jamais deux) des anciens internats
religieux où le couple est a priori suspect' (*VD*, n.p.). All Tournier's
efforts since then have gone towards reinstating that duo, and the
maligned pun (with its copulation of ideas) is a boon companion in
the enterprise. The deaf, cantankerous Mélanie in *Les Météores*, though
illiterate, writes a book she keeps from everyone's sight. This is her
grimoire: a wizard's book of spells, a black book, or an undecipherable
scribble? Mystery and nonsense coexist. Unlike Thomas Pynchon or
J. D. Salinger, and although living in an ex-presbytery, Tournier offers
to many an open house, and readily confesses in public. His solution
is a clever form of hermit-crab behaviour. He uses the confessional
mode as a bargepole. He has a mortal dread of appearing edifying and
an irresistible urge to moralize (deviantly). Like the defrocked abbé
Prelati in *Gilles et Jeanne*, he aims at concocting specious but irrefutable
arguments (*GJ*, 75).

   Tournier is a heretic. He believes, but he deviates. He is a metaphysical playboy, reminiscent at times of Musset's Fantasio, who claimed
to be turning the world upside down to make an acrostic.[21] The
punner is forever turning words upside down, but Tournier's French,
like any other's, has its quota of inertia words, unexamined values
(like 'initiation'), as though he forgets that wordplay is useful also
for subverting the automatism of one's own language. Do Tournier's
texts, which go so debonairly against the grain of orthodoxy, offer
any resistance to the author of their days? That is: does Tournier ever
think against himself, against his idiosyncratic political correctness?
One critic, Jeffress, argues that much of Tournier's myth-making
results in an 'exchange of stereotypes for archetypes'.[22] It is indeed
true that Tournier's values, even if the outcome of reshuffling, remain
frozen into categories. No doubt he knows as well as anybody that all
writing, and speaking, and silence, are ultimately approximative. We
never do justice to anyone or anything. Yet he does strive to loosen
those categories by interplay. Abel Tiffauges says at one point: 'C'est

de cette ouverture du thorax que dépend le degré d'inspiration de tout l'être. Ici, on ne joue pas sur les mots. Il est logique qu'à ce niveau, le sens propre et le sens figuré se confondent' (*RA*, 483). As well as confusing literal and figurative levels, Tournier wants to confound us. Abel suggests at another point that if his fellow-men 'me connaissaient parfaitement, ils m'aimeraient infiniment. Comme fait Dieu' (p. 202). It is excessively agreeable for readers to be placed on celestial thrones, especially if what they are entreated to evacuate there is their moral discrimination.

I hope that it is by now obvious that in calling Tournier a punner, I do not mean that he is unserious, though he is treacherous. A writer so alert to the ambiguity of everything, the pattern-making and the pattern-breaking, must cherish punning. Robinson writes in his log-book, when his rhetorical superstructure falls away, leaving a taste only for concreteness: 'Je ne puis plus parler qu'à la lettre' (*V*, 68). This is the last thing Tournier could say of himself, and it shows how conscious or self-conscious he is about wordplay.

Inconclusion

Without having researched this except minimally, I suspect that cross-talk acts are quite rare in the French equivalent of music-hall/vaudeville or in comic films. Is this monologuing bent yet another consequence of the Jacobin, centralizing tradition that frowns on distractions? Besides, it is difficult to imagine any writer worth his salt being willing to act, in a cross-talk routine, the part of the stooge, the straight man, the foil, the fall-guy. My leitmotif works only in a loosely interpreted sense.

Perhaps another, better mind than mine could pull all my thread(worm)s together into some significant pattern. For myself, my definition of humour is the sum total of the discrete things I have said about humour in the course of this book. It is a variegated patchwork, or crazy paving. Naturally, there are constants, or hobbyhorses. Serious, pointed punning; calculated exaggeration; the sense of priorities, of proportion, which is not in conflict with hyperbole; certain kinds of irony, but especially self-irony; distancing, new perspectives or slants. Sartre and Tournier twist and turn ideas and words. Céline whips lexis and syntax into paroxysms. Diderot philosophizes ludically. Flaubert, as he tells us endlessly, but stoically jokily, suffers agonies over language. Sade was forcibly constrained for much of his life to erect a verbal substitute universe, as, in a more wilful way, was Brisset. Huysmans kept the unloved world at bay with sumptuous words. Rousseau fails to see the joke, and Beckett enjoys telling bad ones. Vallès, militantly, keeps his sunny side up. Flaubert's dream, to leave the reader unsure whether he/she is being had, chimes in with the general fact of life that we all have difficulty deciding whether certain oral or graphic statements are meant to be funny or not; whether we listeners or readers are the real butt of the joke; if not, why lead us up the garden path so often? More widely, is God's masterplan for us the biggest joke, the longest shaggy-dog story, of them all?

When many of us swear that we value, in everyday relationships, a sense of humour in those we respect, like, or love, how can we ignore, or meanly sniff at, its active presence in writers?

Have I lived up to my title? Are my cross-talk acts any more than odd couples? Perhaps not, except intermittently. I have arranged some shotgun marriages or at least cohabitations in which the partners, while far from seeing eye to eye, still communicate, after a fashion. It would be grotesque self-flattery for me to ennoble my zapping between authors, themes, modes, by calling it contrapuntal. It resembles more an enthusiastic, raucous, far from disciplined jam session. Readers with stamina will have noticed that I do not possess an overarching theory of humour. In fact, I prefer the ancient plural 'humours', which places the comic instinct in our very core. Humour proper never forgets (for words and concepts have memories, too) its origins in the body as well as in the psyche. None of my authors ever neglects the body and its imperious needs. I am not, it is plain to see, a deconstructionist or a postmodernist, but a fragmentarist. God lies in the details (and economizes on the truth elsewhere, too). As in that old notion of the humours, each of us has his/her own set of permutations. We can touch each other at times; we do not overlap completely. In this syncopated book, some pairings are (I contradict myself) less a series of shotgun marriages than a scatter-gun fusillade by a fallible marksman.

Humour proliferates; it refuses bounds (except leaps of imagination). You have to keep on the move, by associations of ideas, loose connexions, in order to cope with this moving target, this *perpetuum mobile*, humour. I have my own private, small-scale internet. I find links that others may not think were missing. All I can hope is that my pieces of eight have not struck readers, who will of course rap me on the counter of plausibility, as counterfeit currency, funny money.

Lacking a theory, I have an atheist's credo. We have seen Diderot shaking his existential dice. Pascal was right. Everything, all belief, is a lottery. Chance rules. Guesswork is the nearest we get to thinking. If any of this credo is correct, then a sense of humour is crucial; anything less would miss the point. Why are we so often like lawyers, terrified of the open-ended, and nervously trying to tie everything down? To come clean: I have concentrated on the writers I find rewarding and intriguing; I am fascinated by humour. Any other justification for this book would be a bonus.

Gravity desperately needs its (false) antonym, levity. Without levity, there is no true gravity, and overcoming gravity has been a persistent, and now intergalactically realizable, dream of humankind. The best humour works its passage, earns its keep.

I have committed self-plagiarism, but not the other-directed kind. It has been an act of ecological recycling. Intertextuality (or plagiarism, pastiche, or parody) all practise the juvenile (later parent with child) game of piggybacking. This action is also used on battlefields to get a wounded colleague to safety, and then it is anything but a frivolous game.

At its best, humour is an end in itself, as well as a means to other ends. We want to be transitive verbs, but so often we are intransitive, passive, reflexive, or defective. Humour is internutritional. We feed off each other, as the comedian feeds off the straight man, or the audience. At the very least, humour gives us some elbow room, space for manoeuvre. It can force us to rethink, to view from another angle, to reject the lazily obvious. As such, it acts against cliché, which is where we slump much of the time. Even when it resorts to stereotypes, it gives them a new extension or twist. Reanimating a word or phrase's meaning is giving it mouth-to-mouth. It is no good telling a joke about the operation of the stock market to someone who has never heard of it. The best jokes are dissolute solvents, upsetting the apple-cart of inertial discourse.[1]

The verdict on the heroine of *La Dame aux camélias* is that she will be greatly forgiven because she loved intensely. If only she had laughed a lot, too. 'Love' and 'laugh' are phonetic cousins. The kind of humour that most interests me is not now-and-then, *ponctuel*, but informs and inflects the whole text, giving it vision, colour, flavour, sound, and tact. The ludic is not the opposite of the serious, but one of its modes. When we play, we can bluff or cheat—gamesmanship instead of sportsmanship; we can play double games. Play does not exclude pomposity, or gravity.

A major *dada* of mine is the pun, wordplay, which includes the twist, or more modestly the tweak. Many distrust, disavow, or would even like to abolish punning. Some are overjoyed by phonic coincidences, while others are suspicious or appalled. It is true that puns, originally bright ideas, can become clichés through overuse. As the arch-punster James Joyce puts it: 'Once current puns'.[2] Given the strong metaphorical bent of languages, especially English, speaking literally, plain speech, is not easy. Speaking literally is not the same as taking literally, a favourite tactic of the punner. A mindless set phrase I loathe is: 'X has a weakness for puns'. I prefer: 'Puns give him strength'. I also abominate the false humility of the sheepish punster. Humour should be coterminous with the message, and in pointed puns it certainly is. The vehicle and the load are inseparable. Being in this as in nought else a perfectionist, I favour pointed puns, a tiny percentage of humanity's mass production. I do understand the widespread disdain for the vast majority of bad, anodyne, echoic ones. Punners are inventors only in the old sense of finders. You have either to be blessed with linguistic serendipity (the more reactive kind of finding), or proactively seek out temptations, occasions. Or is it six of one and half a dozen of the other? Freud noted: 'language meets us halfway by linguistic compliance'.[3] Puns lie around in languages, like hitch-hikers or streetwalkers, waiting to be picked up.

There is something sexy in punning: (fore-)playing with words, meanings on top of each other, rubbing up against each other. As Viola in *Twelfth Night* says, not at all judgementally: 'They that dally nicely with words quickly make them wanton'.[4] Sceptics see in puns irreconcilable differences (anomalies), where believers see, hear, and value resemblances (analogies). In the pun lie attraction and repulsion: tension. The pun brings together, serioludically but forcefully, parts normally kept distinct, e.g. 'beer' and 'bier', depending on whether we order from an off-licence or a mortician. It melds formal similarity, whether graphic or acoustic, with semantic variance (divergence, conflict, or overlaying). It looks and sounds the same, or as near as dammit, but means different. Puns stem from, and incite, mental agility. They can be blatant, upfront, or nonchalant and submerged. They bring home to us that we are to a significant extent at the beck and call of language.

What can Lacan contribute to the survey of punning?

One of Lacan's theoretical tenets is that in a single act the child accepts both the name of the father (in French, *le nom*) and the father's saying 'no' to the child's sexual attachment to the mother (in French 'le non'). So, when he called his 1973 seminar 'Les Non-Dupes Errent' (those who are not duped are in error), he was playing on the other two ways of hearing these sounds as 'the father's *name*' and as 'the father's *no*'.[5]

The fact that the sounds quoted are homophonic in French alone should have given pause for thought to Lacan, before he erected a theory on such a gratuitous and flimsy basis. For him, this wordplay was not just a frill, but was at the heart of what he considered the objective of psychoanalysis. Thus he enacted analysis in his public seminars, rather as Ponge enacts the goat.[6]

If the pun is an in-game, what of irony? Classically, irony says the opposite of, or something different from, what you mean. Thus, like the pun, it works on two levels simultaneously. It too serves a dual purpose: of communion or excommunication. It too secretes coincidence. Is coincidence pure chance and therefore meaningless, or can it suggest something meaningful, especially when we talk of 'life's little ironies' or the 'irony of fate'? These betoken a mocking of our efforts, a backfiring, a resistance to our will. How does this sort of general irony, or *dérision*, link up with double-meaning, oblique irony? Irony is clearly a passepartout. The stock definition cannot possibly be true of all ironic statements. What is the opposite of eating babies? Eating adults? Does the suggestiveness of irony, like the 'wanton' pun, bear largely a sexual overlay today?

We must always entertain opposites. Can we think of comedy without invoking tragedy? Watching or reading a tragedy, we let ourselves be persuaded to feel small. Unless of the Hobbesian superiority-model kind, humour, while not enabling us invariably to walk tall, can make us feel successful, or at least adequate. Is tragedy the opposite of comedy? The latter is often heavily loaded, like the trickster's dice, but so is tragedy. Each genre piles it on thick, is naturally hyperbolic. Tournier's Mélanie dies laughing; she pushes comedy as far as it will go. Comedy can thus blend the most trivial and the terminal, whereas tragedy relies on the lofty, the exceptional. 'Mourir en riant n'est pas mourir de rire'.[7] Both genres depend on disparity, and in either case absurdity cannot shed its comic overtones. Comedy offers catharsis rather more frequently than does tragedy, where we are browbeaten to be on our best behaviour, on our high horse, on our honour as thoughtful and sentient beings.

There is a depressing tendency to see humour as a disjunction, as in 'comic relief'. If it is a relief, it is in the aesthetic sense—underlining, adding another dimension (bas-relief, high relief, standing out from flatness). 'Gelotherapy' sounds like a dismal infant diet. Humour is not a respite, a separate activity, from seriousness. It is its companion, twin, or at least enemy brother. It is not a spice or a condiment, not an aspirin or a bandage. Like football for Bill Shankly, it is more important than life or death. Many see humour as exclusively companionable, feel-good. It can, however, install a feel-bad factor which is good for you. It can not only settle its audience, but also unsettle them, shame them, make them question their unreflective reflexes.

Neurological research indicates that the higher functions of our brains are connected with the allegedly lower forms of wit (puns, sarcasm). When such functions are damaged, people cannot detect these forms.[8] Yet scientists have so far (thankfully) not discovered any evidence for a humour centre in the brain. Much the same is true of the soul, similarly elusive. As the humorist E. B. White remarked: 'Humour can be dissected, as a frog can, but the thing dies in the process and the innards are discouraging to any but the pure scientific mind'.[9]

Nietzsche, who believed that all books could usefully be telescoped into one sentence, and the Desert Father who defined good sermons as having a beginning and an end, with the two as close together as possible, alike pursue the impossible dream of packed brevity.[10] It has taken me tens of thousands of words to get thus far. These are now my last words, in this book at least, on humour. But neither I nor anyone else can have the last word on humour. Humour is inescapable, *incontournable*, even though it twists and turns, and favours volte-faces and upendings. If we think we have tied it down, it will always wriggle free. Ideally, this book wishes to release a message in a bottle or a flock of carrier pigeons. Whether either will eventually come home to roost, God alone knows and, as usual, he is giving nothing away.

'Le rire [est] ce qui, par un dernier tour, délivre la démonstration de son attribut démonstratif'.[11] Or, in other words (not those of Barthes's jammed record), if there is nothing to laugh about, laugh anyway. If, as some gloom-mongering cultural commentators maintain, we humans have grown fundamentally unserious, totally ruled by the urge to find every single thing ludicrous and amusing, then presumably we will tire of laughter. Then, truly, we will be tired of life itself, and better off dead. I believe that, if I ever grow disillusioned with humour,

I will be tired of life. As it is, I have written this book, as well as academically and pedantically, jokily, ironically, gleefully. Let no one conclude that I am not in deadly earnest. Is humour the ultimate refuge of the would-be non-dupe? Rather the willing dupe. Humour is language with attitude.

Notes

PROMISES, PROMISES

1. Anthony Burgess, *Language Made Plain* (London: Fontana/Collins, 1975), 110.
2. Gérard Genette, *Figures V* (Paris: Seuil, 2002), 180.
3. Jacques Prévert, 'Je suis comme je suis', *Paroles* (Paris: Gallimard, 1949), 96.
4. Dominique Noguez, *L'Arc-en-ciel des humours* (Paris: Hatier, 1996), 15.
5. Voltaire, *Lettres philosophiques*, ed. R. Naves (Paris: Garnier, 1956), 125. In an addendum of 1756, he writes: 'et un commentateur de bons mots n'est guère capable d'en dire' (p. 255). I cannot agree with this.

I THE LAUGHING PHILOSOPHER: DIDEROT

1. Michel Delon, *Notice* on *Mystification*, in Delon (ed.), *Diderot: Contes et romans* (Paris: Gallimard, 2004), 1038.
2. W. B. Yeats, 'Anima Hominis', section 5, *Essays* (1924).
3. Though Diderot commissioned the notorious pun-machine, the Marquis de Bièvre, to contribute the entry 'Kalembour' to the *Encyclopédie*, he himself was not much of a punner, though he was certainly a champion of the free play of the intellect, the imagination, the tongue, and the writing fingers. He is one of the few funny men in my Pantheon who rarely puns.
4. We will see thinking as whoring in *Le Neveu de Rameau*.
5. Gershon Legman, *No Laughing Matter*, vol. ii of *The Rationale of the Dirty Joke* (London: Hart-Davis, MacGibbon, 1978), 999.
6. Nobody is sure where *mentula* comes from. A diminutive of *menta*: mint seems pointless. Why not *mens*: mind?
7. Eve Ensler, *The Vagina Monologues* (London: Virago, 2002), 72.
8. Eva Russo, 'The Burlesque Body in Diderot's *Les Bijoux indiscrets*', in Angelica Goodden (ed.), *The Eighteenth-Century Body* (Berne: Lang, 2002), 95–106.
9. Ibid. 95.
10. *Sarbacane* had an older meaning of mouthpiece or conduit.
11. Steven Connor, *Dumbstruck: A Cultural History of Ventriloquism* (Oxford University Press, 2000), 198–9.
12. Montaigne, *Essais*, ed. M. Rat (Paris: Garnier, 1958), iii. 7.
13. *Les Bijoux indiscrets*, in *Œuvres romanesques*, ed. H. Bénac (Paris: Garnier, 1959), 108–9.

14. Diderot, *Lettre sur les aveugles*, in *Œuvres philosophiques*, ed. P. Vernière (Paris: Garnier, 1956), 97.
15. Aram Vartanian, 'La Mettrie, Diderot and Sexology in the Enlightenment', in Jean Macary (ed.), *Essays on the Age of Enlightenment in Honor of Ira O. Wade* (Geneva: Droz, 1977), 356.
16. Diderot, *Essai sur la peinture*, in *Œuvres*, ed. A. Billy (Paris: Gallimard, 1951), 1143–4.
17. Christopher Ricks, *Beckett's Dying Words* (Oxford University Press, 1995), 65.
18. Diderot, *Correspondance*, ed. G. Roth, xi (Paris: Minuit, 1956), 97.
19. Diderot, *Réfutation d'Helvétius*, in *Œuvres philosophiques*, 575.
20. Diderot, *Le Rêve de D'Alembert*, in *Œuvres philosophiques*, 283.
21. Juvenal, *Satire*, I. 30.
22. Ross Chambers, *Loiterature* (Lincoln, Nebr.: University of Nebraska Press, 1999), 184.
23. Diderot, *Salons*, in *Œuvres esthétiques*, ed. P. Vernière (Paris: Garnier, 1959), 511–12.
24. Diderot, *Le Neveu de Rameau*, ed. J. Fabre (Geneva: Droz, 1950), 3. Subsequent page references to this edition appear in brackets after quotations. Cf. Novalis: 'The organs of thought are the world's reproduction system, the sexual parts of nature as a whole'. *Schriften*, ed. S. R. Samuel et al. (Darmstadt: Wissenschaftliche Buchgesellschaft, 1968), 476.
25. Cf. the description of Jacques Vingtras's mother as a composite rhetorical figure, in Ch. 5 on Vallès.
26. Virgil, *Aeneid*, vi. 743.
27. Champfleury, *Les Excentriques* (Paris: Lévy, 1852), 9.
28. Diderot, *Lettre sur les sourds et muets, à l'usage de ceux qui entendent et qui parlent*, ed. P. H. Mayer, in *Diderot Studies*, 7 (1965), 52.
29. The 'comédien de nature' has also to work hard as well as rely on natural gifts. He has to build on his birthright by observation and the study of great models. More volatile than lesser actors, he is prone to failure. The Nephew often shoots himself in the foot.
30. After Dustin Hoffman had rehearsed the exhaustive Stanislavski methodology to him while making the film *Marathon Man*, Laurence Olivier allegedly commented: 'Dear boy, you should try acting'. In the film *Charade*, a policeman watching Punch belabour a *flic*, replicates all the wincing movements of the victim, out of fellow feeling. Diderot would call this: 'la singerie dans les organes'. *Éléments de physiologie*, ed. J. Assézat (Paris: Garnier, 1875), 354.
31. Cf. the film *Funny Bones*, where Lee Evans gives a disjointed but troubling performance of a manic body-artist. The link of comedy and madness is strongly communicated.
32. 'Why should the Devil have all the good tunes?' Ascribed to the originator of the penny post, Rowland Hill.
33. Michel Serres, *Le Parasite* (Paris: Hachette, 1997), 56.

34. Thomas Middleton and William Rowley, *The Changeling*, v. i.
35. The term 'parasite' is in fact multi-layered. It embraces: social behaviour, biological intruders, interference in communication-systems, and
computer-bugs. Parasites can be lodged in the brain, the flesh, machines,
or the household.
36. Manic comic actors like Jerry Lewis or Lee Evans have achieved an
approximation to such a performance, a simulated St Vitus's dance.
37. Though Stendhal envied the ability of music to impart simultaneity, in
fact music is sequential like writing. Perhaps only painting offers all at
once, though the eye cannot cope with it.
38. Leo Spitzer, 'The Style of Diderot', in *Linguistics and Literary History: Essays
in Stylistics* (Princeton University Press, 1974 [1948]), 135–91. Subsequent
page references appear in brackets after quotations.
39. Vladimir Nabokov, *Lolita* (London: Transworld, 1961), 35.
40. Diderot, *Éléments de physiologie*, 354.
41. Iris Murdoch, *The Sandcastle* (Harmondsworth: Penguin, 1960), 67.
42. Pataphysically, too, this text practises 'plagiat par anticipation'. Diderot's
labile mind-set foreshadows that of Raymond Queneau.
43. The edition of *Jacques le fataliste* used is by S. Lecointre and J. Le Galliot
(Geneva: Droz, 1976). Subsequent page references to this edition appear
in brackets after quotations.
44. Cf. Vigny: 'Je ne suis pas toujours de mon opinion'. *Les Consultations du
docteur Noir* (Paris: Garnier, 1970), 15 (also 'à l'insu de son plein gré').
45. Arthur Koestler, *The Yogi and the Commissar* (London: Cape, 1945),
227. And Thomas Vaihinger, *The Philosophy of As-If*, tr. C. K. Ogden,
(London: Kegan Paul, Trench, Tubner, 2nd edn. 1935), p. xli: ' "As-If",
i.e. appearance, the consciously false, plays an enormous part in science,
in world-philosophies and in life'.
46. Diderot, *Réfutation d'Helvétius*, 619.
47. 'Buck', in this sense, is derived from a term in poker, a game of chance,
though expert players think they are in charge.
48. Diderot, *De la poésie dramatique*, in *Œuvres esthétiques*, 219.
49. See Ch. 4 on parrots for further variations on this name. In the *Réfutation
d'Helvétius*, Diderot had dismissed the ageing Voltaire as the parrot of the
younger (p. 607). Voltaire himself had admitted: 'J'ai ignoré absolument
pendant le quart de ma vie les raisons de tout ce que j'ai vu, entendu et senti,
et je n'ai été qu'un perroquet sifflé par d'autres perroquets'. 'Ignorance',
in *Dictionnaire philosophique* (Paris: Baudoin, 1826), 133. Characteristically,
Voltaire spreads, like psittacosis, psittacism to others apart from himself,
and thus seeks to attenuate his crime.
50. Laurence Sterne, *The Life & Opinions of Tristram Shandy*, ed. G. Petrie
(Harmondsworth: Penguin, 1967), 137.
51. Hillel Schwarz, *The Culture of the Copy* (New York: Zone, 1996),
362.

52. Hence authors like Queneau in *Le Vol d'Icare*, or Unamuno in *Niebla*, feign to let protagonists escape their grasp and take off.
53. Henry James, 'The Art of Fiction', in *Partial Portraits* (London: Macmillan, 1911), 379.
54. Diderot, *Lettres à Sophie Volland*, ed. A. Babelon (Paris: Gallimard, 1930), ii. 273.
55. Baudelaire, *Mon Cœur mis à nu*, in *Le Spleen de Paris*, ed. Y. Le Dantec (Paris: Colin, 1958), 155.
56. Diderot, *Éléments de physiologie*, 418.
57. Malraux, *La Condition humaine* (Paris: Livre de poche, 1946), 46–7.
58. Plagiarism is usually not physical theft, for the original stays undiminished. Of course, the plagiarized one can feel robbed, violated, but really the literary burglar has simply photographed his/her jewels, leaving them in place.
59. Sterne, *Tristram Shandy*, 282. Sterne was himself, in the 19th century, taxed with plagiarism, e.g. a passage lamenting the lack of originality in contemporary writers was lifted from Robert Burton's *Anatomy of Melancholy*, in its turn the epitome of the omnium-gatherum.
60. Valéry: 'L'Idée fixe', in *Œuvres*, ed. J. Hytier (Paris: Gallimard, 1960), ii. 206.
61. Milan Kundera, *Jacques and his Master* (London: Faber, 1986), 11.
62. *Éléments de physiologie*, 428.

RIFF ON LAUGHTER

1. According to L. Molinier, 'Quand le malin fait de l'esprit: le rire au Moyen-Âge vu depuis l'hagiographie', *Annales, Histoires, Sciences sociales*, 3 (1997), 470–1. He refers to Hildegard's treatise *Causae et curae*, ed. P. Kaiser (Leipzig: Teubner, 1903), 148.
2. Sartre, *Les Mots* (Paris: Gallimard, 1964), 88–9. This may be a twist on Baudelaire's aphorism: 'La femme est naturelle, c'est-à-dire abominable'. *Le Spleen de Paris*, ed. Y. Le Dantec (Paris: Colin, 1958), 130.
3. 'Rictus' is the past participle of *ringi*: to open wide, gape. 'Jehan Rictus' was the macabre pseudonym of Gabriel Randon de Saint-Amand, who went, despite his *particule*, slumming in his verse (e.g. *Le Soliloque du pauvre* (1897)).
4. T. S. Eliot: 'Whispers of Immortality', *Collected Poems, 1909–1962* (London: Faber, 1974), 55.
5. Anthony Ludovici, *The Secret of Laughter* (London: Constable, 1932).
6. My father's less classical version, when offered a rare treat, was to say: 'It'd be like giving a donkey strawberries'.
7. Nietzsche, *Thus Spake Zarathustra*, tr. R. Hollingdale (Harmondsworth: Penguin, 1971) 201.
8. Diderot, *Éléments de physiologie*, 307. Think of the difficulties of breathing during a fit of coughing or laughing.

9. For details, see Howard Jacobson, *Seriously Funny* (London: Viking, 1997), 28.

10. Lord Chesterfield, *Letters to his Son*, 9 Mar. 1748.

11. See Joë Friedemann, *Victor Hugo, un temps pour rire* (Saint-Genulph: Nizet, 2002), 15. Hugo, *L'Homme qui rit*, in *Œuvres complètes: Romans III* (Paris: Laffont, 1985).

12. William Empson, 'Let it Go', *Collected Poems* (London: Hogarth, 1984), 81.

2 THE QUESTION OF HUMOURLESSNESS

1. Rousseau, *Les Rêveries du promeneur solitaire*, ed. R. Niklaus (Manchester University Press, 1952), 29–30.

2. Rousseau, *Dialogues*, ed. E. Leborgue (Paris: Garnier-Flammarion, 1999), 184.

3. Cocteau, 'Rousseau', *Tableau de la littérature française* (Paris: Gallimard, 1939), 267. The mooning is in *Les Confessions*, ed. Ad. Van Bever (Paris: Garnier, 1946), i. 120.

4. Freud, *Jokes and their Relation to the Unconscious*, tr. J. Strachey and A. Richards (Harmondsworth: Penguin, 1976), 62–3.

5. Rousseau, *Les Confessions*, ii. 132.

6. Ibid. i. 201.

7. Michèle Crogiez, *Rousseau et le paradoxe* (Paris: Champion, 1997), 231. Subsequent page references appear in brackets after quotations.

8. Frances Gray, *Women and Laughter* (Basingstoke: Macmillan, 1994), 5.

9. Huysmans, *A rebours* (Paris: Fasquelle, 1929 [1894]), 99.

10. Rousseau, *Rêveries*, 57.

11. Camus, *La Chute* (Paris: Gallimard, 1956), 141.

12. Woody Allen, in the film *Annie Hall* (1977).

13. Rousseau, *Émile*, in *Œuvres complètes*, iv. (Paris: Gallimard, 1969), 496.

14. *Les Confessions*, in *Œuvres complètes*, i. (Paris: Gallimard, 1959), 109.

15. Robin Howells, *Playing Simplicity: Polemical Stupidity in the Writing of the French Enlightenment* (Berne: Peter Lang, 2002), 300.

16. Isaiah Berlin, *Observer*, 9 Nov. 1952.

17. Crogiez, *Rousseau et le paradoxe*, 221.

18. George Steiner, *Lessons of the Masters* (Cambridge, Mass.: Harvard University Press, 2003), 26.

19. Jean Sareil, *L'Écriture comique* (Paris: PUF, 1984), 27.

20. Philippe Sollers, 'Lettre de Sade', *Tel Quel*, 61 (1975), 20. Lacan, that humourless joker, on the other hand found Sade totally devoid of humour. 'Kant avec Sade', *Ecrits II* (Paris: Seuil, 1999), 266.

21. Sade, *Les Cent Vingt Journées de Sodome*, in *Œuvres*, i, ed. M. Delon (Paris: Gallimard, 1990), 64.

22. Sade, *Français, encore un effort si vous voulez être républicains* (Paris: Pauvert, 1965), 87. And *Justine* (Paris: Union générale d'éditions, 1969), 75.

23. George Steiner, *After Babel* (Oxford University Press, 1975) 38.

24. John Phillips, *Sade* (London: Granta, 2005), 37.

25. Sade, *La Philosophie dans le boudoir* (Paris: Union générale d'éditions, 1972), 299.

26. John Phillips, ' "Laugh? I nearly died!" Humour in Sade's Fiction', in John Parkin and John Phillips (eds.), *Laughter and Power* (Oxford: Lang, 2006), 81–3.

27. A rare printed jest book, the *Hundred Merry Tales*, antedated the first printed English Bible by ten years.

28. Mark Twain, *Following the Equator* (New York: Dover, 1989), 119.

29. Diderot, *Addition aux Pensées philosophiques*, in *Œuvres philosophiques*, ed. P. Vernière (Paris: Garnier, 1956), 60.

30. Heinrich Heine, on his deathbed, according to Alfred Meissner, *Heinrich Heine: Erinnerungen* (1856), ch. 5. This maxim had earlier been attributed to Catherine the Great, in the form: 'Moi, je serai autocrate: c'est mon métier. Et le bon Dieu me pardonnera: c'est son métier'—a rather better formulation in its balance of two powers, earthly and heavenly.

31. Beckett, *Endgame*, in *CDW*, 119.

32. Nietzsche, *Thus Spake Zarathustra*, tr. R. Hollingdale (Harmondsworth: Penguin, 1971), 68.

33. Nietzsche: Motto called 'Over the Door to my House'. *The Gay Science*, tr. W. Kaufmann (New York: Vintage, 1974), 31.

34. Ibid. 207.

35. While I think on, the subjects of the rest of this book line up thus on God: Diderot (materialist: God is superfluous); Huysmans (a wayward Catholic, who seemed to lose his sense of humour after conversion); Vallès thought Christ greatly overrated; Céline and Sartre (atheists); Tournier (a rogue vestigial Catholic); and Beckett (angry with God for not existing).

36. Gide, *Les Caves du Vatican* (Paris: Livre de poche, 1956), 205. On Amédée.

37. Gérard Genette, *Figures V* (Paris: Seuil, 2002), 216.

38. Readers whose interest in Brisset may have stirred itself can consult, for a full-length account of this phenomenon, my *All Puns Intended: The Verbal Creation of Jean-Pierre Brisset* (Oxford: Legenda, 2001).

39. The original title of Sartre's *La Nausée* was *Melancholia*.

40. Maria Yaguello, *Les Fous du langage* (Paris: Seuil, 1984), 16.

41. André Breton, *Anthologie de l'humour noir* (Paris: Pauvert, 1968), 16–17. Subsequent page references appear in brackets after quotations.

42. Paul Éluard and André Breton, *Dictionnaire abrégé du surréalisme* (Paris: Corti, 1980), 5.

43. André Breton, *Les Pas perdus* (Paris: Gallimard, 1924), 170–1.

44. Robert Desnos, *Domaine public* (Paris: Gallimard, 1963), 43, and *Corps et biens* (Paris: Gallimard, 1980), 50. Desnos figures in a list in Breton's *Anthologie de l'humour noir* (pp. 311–12) that juxtaposes Brisset's humour with Jarry's Pataphysics (or 'science of imaginary solutions'),

Dalí's 'activité <u>paranoïa</u>-critique', Roussel, Duchamp, Léon-Paul Fargue, Leiris, Michaux, James Joyce, 'et la jeune école américaine' (presumably Gertrude Stein).

45. Michel Pierrsens, 'Les Aventures du Bon Dieu et de la fille-mère: une lecture de *La Science de Dieu*', *L'Icosathèque 1*, *Le Siècle éclaté* (1974), 122 (author's stress in first quotation).

46. Paul Jennings, *I Said Oddly, diddle I?* (London: Max Reinhardt, 1961).

47. André Blavier, *Les Fous littéraires* (rev. edn. Paris: Éditions du Cendre, 2000), 106 (Blavier's stress).

48. Ronald R. Koegler, 'In Defense of the Pun', *American Imago*, 16 (1959), 234.

49. Brisset, *Le Mystère de Dieu est accompli* (Paris: Navarin/Seuil, 1984), 102.

50. Brisset, *La Science de Dieu* (Paris: Tchou, 1979), 256. Re 'plagiat par anticipation', see *Atlas de la littérature potentielle* (Paris: Gallimard, 1981), 167.

51. *Le Mystère de Dieu*, 52.

52. Elliott Oring, *Jokes and their Relations* (Lexington: University Press of Kentucky, 1992), 2.

53. Brisset, *La Science de Dieu*, 251. Subsequent page numbers appear in brackets after quotations. I revisit *la blague* in Ch. 5 on Vallès.

54. *Le Mystère de Dieu*, 75.

55. Maurice Réja, *L'Art chez les fous: Le Dessin, la Prose, la Poésie* (Paris: Mercure de France, 1908), 205.

56. Brisset, *Les Origines humaines* (Paris: Baudoin, 1980), 109.

57. Ibid. 145.

RIFF ON DREAMS

1. Freud, *The Interpretation of Dreams*, tr. J. Strachey et al. (Harmondsworth: Penguin Freud Library, 1976), iv. 129, 130, 405–6.

2. Iris Murdoch, *The Black Prince* (Harmondsworth: Penguin, 1975), 81.

3. Freud, *Interpretation*, 262, 84.

3 HUYSMANS

1. 'Joris-Karl Huysmans par A. Meunier', in *Cahiers de l'Herne*, 'Huysmans', ed. P. Brunel and A. Guyaux (1985), 27, 29.

2. *A rebours* (Paris: Fasquelle, 1925 [1884]), 9. Subsequent page references to this edition appear in brackets after quotations.

3. In Proust, Legrandin's snobbery is visible only to the microscopic gaze of the narrator, but Mme Verdurin's variety is plain to see to all but her purblind, dominated *fidèles*.

4. Roger Kempf, *Dandies: Baudelaire et Cie* (Paris: Seuil, 1977), 10.

5. Rae Beth Gordon, *Why the French Love Jerry Lewis: From Cabaret to Early Cinema* (Stanford University Press, 2001), 278.

6. Think of the irresistibly comic Victor Meldrew, curmudgeon *extraordinaire*, in the TV series *One Foot in the Grave*. Cf. also Sade's punishing recitals of self-boosting sexual boasting, or Flaubert's relentless flogging of dead horses in *Bouvard et Pécuchet*.

7. Anthony Burgess, *Joysprick* (London: Deutsch, 1973), 146.

8. William Empson, 'The Beautiful Train', *Collected Poems* (London: Hogarth, 1984), 64.

9. See Robert Burac, *Le Sourire d'Hypatia: Essai sur le comique de Charles Péguy* (Paris: Champion, 1999), 13.

10. Jean Borie, *Huysmans: Le Diable, le célibataire et Dieu* (Paris: Grasset, 1991), 246.

11. Baudelaire, *Curiosités esthétiques*, ed. H. Lemaître (Paris: Garnier, 1962), 258.

12. Thoreau, *Walden* (New York: New American Library, 1960 [1854]), 213.

13. Nietzsche, *Human, all too Human*, tr. M. Faber and G. Lehmann (Harmondsworth: Penguin, 1994 [1878–9]), 259.

14. 'Cohibé' is an alchemist's term: distilled to a high degree of concentration.

15. Borie, *Huysmans: Le Diable*, 98–9.

16. Ibid. 196.

17. Ibid. 44–5.

18. Huysmans, *La Retraite de Monsieur Bougran*, in *Un dilemme, Sac au dos et La Retraite de Monsieur Bougran* (Toulouse: Éditions Ombres, 1994).

19. William Empson, 'This Last Pain', *Collected Poems* (London: Hogarth, 1984), 33.

20. Breton, *Anthologie de l'humour noir* (Paris: Pauvert, 1966), 247–8.

21. Ibid. 249

22. Zola, *Correspondance*, ed. B. H. Bakker (Presses de l'Université de Montréal/Paris: CNRS, 1987), vi. 445.

23. Sartre, *Qu'est ce que la literature?*, in *Situations II* (Paris: Gallimard, 1948), 122–3.

24. Montaigne, 'D'un enfant monstrueux', *Essais*, ed. M. Rat (Paris: Garnier, 1962), ii. 118.

25. Tournier, 'Entretien avec des élèves du lycée Montaigne', cited by Arlette Bouloumié, 'Rire, humour et ironie dans l'œuvre de Michel Tournier', in Jean-Bernard Vray (ed.), *Relire Tournier* (Publications de l'Université de Saint-Étienne, 2000), 223.

26. Oscar Wilde, *The Picture of Dorian Gray* (Oxford University Press, 1981 [1891]), 127. Subsequent page references to this edition appear in brackets after quotations. Huysmans's section on Gustave Moreau's *Salome* in *A rebours* in part inspired Wilde's play on that subject.

27. Wilde, quoted in André Gide, 'In Memoriam', *Oscar Wilde* (Paris: Mercure de France, 1910).

4 A LITTLE BIRD TELLS US

1. Sartre, 'Qu'est-ce que la littérature?', *Situations II* (Paris: Gallimard, 1948), 313.
2. Midas Dekkers, *Dearest Pet: On Bestiality*, tr. Paul Vincent (London: Verso, 2001 [1994]), 60. 'From' should read 'via'.
3. Buffon, *Histoire naturelle des animaux* (Paris: Robert, 1985). Buffon kept an African grey, which he let fly freely about the house. He celebrated its humanoid qualities like a convinced fancier.
4. See Terence Cave, 'Des perroquets', in *Pré-histoires II: Langues étrangères et troubles économiques au XVIe siècle* (Geneva: Droz, 2001), 34, 39, 43.
5. Diderot, *Jacques le fataliste* (Paris: Livre de poche, 1959), 180.
6. Antti Aarne, *The Types of the Folktale*, tr. Stith Thompson (Helsinki: Soumalainen Tiedakatemia, 1961), 77. See also Gershon Legman, *Rationale of the Dirty Joke*, i (London: Panther, 1973), 205. François George called another self-deifier, Jacques Lacan, 'le père Hoquet', by reason of his jamming on certain sounds. See *L'Effet 'yau de poêle* (Paris: Hachette, 1979), 148.
7. *L'Opinion nationale*, 20 June 1863. In *Bouvard et Pécuchet*, i (Paris: Club de l'Honnête Homme, 1972), 313. In Boccaccio, *De Genealogia deorum Gentilium* (IV. xlix), Psittacus, son of Deucalion and Pyrra, is linked with wisdom, before and after his request to the gods to transform him into a parrot. No compendium of mythology I have conned backs up this notion. Boccaccio invented other bizarre, variant lineages, often punning on a name. (The edition of *Un Cœur simple* that I use is in *Trois Contes* (Edinburgh: Nelson, 1945). Subsequent page references to this edition appear in brackets after quotations.)
8. Flaubert, letter to Madame Brainne of 28 July 1876, in *Correspondance*, iv (Paris: Club de l'Honnête Homme, 1975), 476. All subsequent references to Flaubert's correspondence are to this edition.
9. According to Cave ('Des perroquets', 32), 'l'interprète était regardé habituellement comme une sorte de perroquet, un être parleur'. In *Salammbô*, where the Babel of mutually unintelligible tongues is in dire need of interpreters, Flaubert mentions 'la légion des interprètes, coiffés comme des sphinx, et portant un perroquet tatoué sur la poitine' (Paris: Pocket, 1995), 95. This is presumably where Louis Guilloux, an assiduous reader of Flaubert, derived his belief that 'l'insigne des interprètes, dans les armées de l'antiquité était, paraît-il, le perroquet' (*Absent de Paris* (Paris: Gallimard, 1952), 193). A classical expert on ancient armies informed me that this practice is probably apocryphal. Guilloux acknowledged his own

facility at imitation, which helped him to acquire English and Spanish, and indeed to act as interpreter in US Army rape-trials after the Second World War. 'Talent de perroquet', he concluded (*Absent de Paris*, 193). Elsewhere, in spite of his criticism of priests as parroters of divine scripts, Guilloux knew as well as Diderot, Nietzsche, or Thomas Mann that the artist is ineluctably a copycat ape, a hairy parrot.

10. I recall an ignorant or knowing student essay which claimed that 'Félicité had no love-life, so she stuffed her parrot'.

11. See François Fleury (ed.), *Plans, notes et scénarios de 'Un Cœur simple'* (Rouen: Lecerf, 1977), 33.

12. It has been maintained that *perroquet* derives from the Italian *parrochetto*, diminutive of *parroco*: parish priest. *Parrocchetto* is a parakeet. Close, obviously. But what to make of it? Are parrots chaste clerics, preaching against the vices of their flocks? But traditionally parrots are foul-mouthed. Unless sermons are seen as psittacism. See n. 9 for Guilloux's take on this question. The 'parrotdise' pun is from Hillel Schwarz, *The Culture of the Copy* (New York: Zone Books, 1996), 149.

13. See Fleury (ed.), *Plans*, 30.

14. Letter of Flaubert to Louise Colet of 8 Oct. 1846, *Œuvres diverses. Correspondance*, i (1974), 547.

15. Letter to Louis Bouilhet of 24 Aug. 1853, *Correspondance*, ii (1974), 395.

16. Robert Louis Stevenson, *Memories and Portraits* (London: Chatto and Windus, 1898), 59. He is talking of his youthful efforts to impersonate in his writings other authors. To ape: *singer* (French), *nachäffen* (German), *scimmiottare* (Italian). Spanish has no equivalent.

17. Proust, *Les Plaisirs et les jours*, in *Jean Santeuil*, ed. P. Clarac (Paris: Gallimard, 1971), 110.

18. Letter to Louise Colet of 12 Sept. 1853, *Correspondance*, ii. 407.

19. Letter to Mme Roger des Genettes, end of July 1876, ibid. 478.

20. Possibly an *obiter dictum*, applied to himself when cited by Sartre in *Les Mots* (Paris: Gallimard, 1964), 137.

21. Letter to Louise Colet of 1 Feb. 1852, *Correspondance*, ii. 165.

22. Flaubert, *Par les Champs et par les grèves*, in *Œuvres complètes*, ii, ed. B. Masson (Paris: Seuil, 1964), 484.

23. Guilloux, *Carnets II* (Paris: Gallimard, 1982), 51.

24. Philippe Bonnefis, 'Exposition d'un perroquet', in *Mesures de l'ombre* (Presses universitaires de Lille, 1987), 77.

25. Ibid. 99.

26. Queneau, *Les Fleurs bleues* (Paris: Gallimard, 1978), 102.

27. Flaubert, letter to Alfred Le Poittevin of 16 Sept. 1845, *Correspondance*, i. 463.

28. Queneau, *Zazie dans le Métro* (Paris: Livre de poche, 1964), 37. Subsequent page references to this edition appear in brackets after quotations.

29. Jules Vallès, *La Rue*, in *Œuvres complètes*, ed. R. Bellet (Paris: Gallimard, 1975), i. 799.

30. Queneau, *Les Fleurs bleues*, 46. Queneau was also familiar with the *Arabian Nights* and, probably, with the poem *The Language of the Birds*, a masterpiece of Persian literature by Farid al-Din Attar (*fl. c.*1180–*c.*1220).

31. Aristotle, quoted by Strabo, in his *Geography*, ix (London: Heinemann, 1929), 7. The reference is to a certain wall in Homer's poem. Aristotle is expressing his doubt whether such a wall ever existed in fact, or whether it was merely a poet's fabrication which, being made solely of words, could be verbally abolished (unlike the Panthéon, which looms up on the city tour in *Zazie*, and is confused by the guide with the Gare de Lyon).

32. Queneau, interviewed by Marguerite Duras: 'Uneuravek'. *L'Express*, 22 Jan. 1959, p. 27.

33. Did Queneau know of Flaubert's genial but confused idea of ending *Madame Bovary* with a scene in which Homais realizes that he is a character in a novel, 'le fruit d'une inspiration en délire, l'invention d'un petit paltoquet que j'ai vu naître et qui m'a inventé pour faire croire que je n'existe pas'? There is a double-bind here. Homais both doubts his own reality, except as a reflection in multiple mirrors, and yet claims he was born before his certifiably real creator, Flaubert. See *Madame Bovary: Nouvelle Version*, ed. J. Pommier and G. Leleu (Paris: Corti, 1949), 129. Naturally, blowing the gaff on the craft, or craftiness, of fiction was hardly news in 1959, or even 1857.

34. I might translate *bavardage* as 'gas-baggage'. After all, the French invented the hot-air balloon.

35. Queneau, *Pierrot mon ami* (Paris: Livre de poche, 1943), 123.

36. See Rae Beth Gordon, *Why the French Love Jerry Lewis: From Cabaret to Early Cinema* (Stanford University Press, 2001), 238.

37. Lewis Carroll, *The Hunting of the Snark*, in *The Annotated Snark*, ed. M. Gardner (Harmondsworth: Penguin, 1979), 46.

38. Franc Schuerewegen and Liliane Tasmowski-De Ryck, 'Ecriture et répétition dans *Zazie dans le Métro*', in Christian Plantin (ed.), *Lieux communs, topoï, stéréotypes, clichés* (Paris: Kima, 1993), 18.

39. Queneau, *Les Fleurs bleues*, 69.

40. See *OED* under 'echolalia'. Perhaps only a dictionary, the alleged home and fount of meanings, could so confidently define what is meaningless.

41. Balzac, *Le Père Goriot*, (London: Nelson, 1954), 61.

42. Camus, 'Pierrot mon ami', *Essais* (Paris: Gallimard, 1965), 1929.

43. See Queneau, 'L'Humour et ses victimes', *Voyage en Grèce* (Paris: Gallimard, 1973), 80–8. Subsequent page references appear in brackets after quotations. Queneau provocatively asserts (p. 87) that 'le genre le plus voisin de l'humour véritable, c'est la fable (mais oui, mais oui)', for, like the Aesopian fable, humour is not hogtied by verisimilitude.

44. Queneau, unpublished note, cited by Claude Debon-Tournadre, 'Présence d'Apollinaire dans l'œuvre de Queneau', *Revue d'histoire littéraire de la France*, 81 (1981), 75.

45. Queneau, *Les Œuvres complètes de Sally Mara* (Paris: Gallimard, 1962), 349.

46. Queneau, *Le Chiendent* (Paris: Gallimard, 1974), 267.

47. In London, Casanova bought a parrot and taught it to say: 'La Charpillon est plus p[utain] que sa mère': double blasphemy—the mistress and her sainted mother degraded. The bird accompanies its accusation with a burst of laughter, which it has not been taught. Casanova sells it at quintuple profit. When La Charpillon hears of this, she is amused, her mother not. Can a bird commit libel? See *Mémoires de Jacques Casanova de Seingalt* (Paris: Garnier frères, n.d.), vii. 3–5.

48. Robert Louis Stevenson, *Treasure Island* (Oxford University Press, 1992 [1883]), 55. Subsequent page references to this edition appear in brackets after quotations.

49. See n. 16. Here, 'My First Book', in *Essays in the Art of Writing* (London: Chatto and Windus, 1905), 120.

50. Daniel Defoe, *Robinson Crusoe* (Harmondsworth: Penguin, 1970), 131, 152.

51. Bruce Boehrer, 'Men, Monkeys, Lap-Dogs, Parrots, Perish All! Psittacine Articulacy in Early Modern Writing', *Modern Language Quarterly*, 59/2 (1998), 177.

52. *Mal.* 71. Cf. Turandot succeeding Laverdure in its cage. The full phrase is 'nihil in intellectu quod prius non fuerit in sensu' (There is nothing in the mind that was not first in the senses). Leibniz added to this empiricist motto 'except the intellect itself'. See Leibniz, *New Essays on Human Understanding* (Cambridge University Press, 1996), 111. As Steven Pinker remarks in quoting this, something in the mind must be innate, for 'a blank slate can do nothing'. *The Blank Slate* (London: Penguin, 2003), 34. Is this argument applicable to parrots? Even if they were purely echoers, how come they often refuse to play ball sonically? Natural echoes are garbled or truncated. Parrots' echoes, when they are in the mood, are passably accurate reproductions.

53. *Merc.*, 27.

54. Pliny, *Natural History*, x. lviii (London: Heinemann; Cambridge, Mass.: Harvard University Press, 1940), 367–8. This Loeb translation is not brilliant.

55. Beckett, *Textes pour rien*, in *No's Knife: Collected Shorter Prose 1945–1966* (London: Calder & Boyars, 1967), 104.

56. Stevenson, *Treasure Island*, 54–5.

57. Attributed to Nelson Moe by Ross Chambers, *Loiterature* (Lincoln, Nebr.: University of Nebraska Press, 1999), 171.

58. 'We have already lost another [language] whose last recorded speaker was a parrot (though I reckon the Amazonian natives were pulling Alexander von Humboldt's leg in this one).' Chris Lavers, review of M. Abley, 'Spoken Here: Travels among Threatened Languages', *Guardian (Review)*, 7 Feb. 2004, p. 10.

59. Howard Jacobson, *Seriously Funny* (London: Viking, 1997), 37, in the course of a book-long argument that the more outrageous the comedy, the closer it gets to the core of human reality.
60. *The Poems of Thomas Sheridan* (Newark: University of Delaware Press, 1994), 96. No amount of sleuthery on my part could unearth a factual source for this claim.
61. *American Speech*, 48 (1973), 265.
62. Valéry, 'L'Idée fixe', in *Œuvres*, ed. J. Hytier (Paris: Gallimard, 1960), ii. 238.

5 *BLAGUE* HARD!

1. F. Letessier, 'Blague, blagueur, blaguer', *Le Français moderne*, 12 (1944), 306–7.
2. *SEP*, 84. Vallès relishes the idiom 'brosser le ventre', to go without food, as he often did in his bohemian days/daze.
3. See P. T. Barnum: *Humbugs of the World* (New York: Carleton, 1865), 20. Such a showman is not an impostor or hypocrite, but one who puts on 'glittering appearances—outside show—novel expedients by which to suddenly arrest public attention'.
4. Vladimir Jankélévitch, *La Méconnaissance, Le Malentendu* (Paris: Seuil, 1980), 207.
5. 'La Caricature', in *Œuvres*, i (1975), 583.
6. Two different poles of euphemism: young Jacques watching his scrumptious cousin Polonie dressing, and feeling 'tout chose' (all of a doodah); and his mother substituting 'chose de bouteille' for 'cul'. *Enf.*, 154, 301.
7. *La Dompteuse* (Paris: Livre Club Diderot, 1970), iii. 326.
8. *Les Réfractaires*, in *Œuvres*, i. 294.
9. Vallès, quoted in Gaston Gille, *Jules Vallès* (Paris: Flammarion, 1941), vol. i, pp. v–vi. Contrast Lamartine, in the days when caricaturists had to ask their model for permission to publish: 'Je ne puis autoriser sur ma personne une dérision qui, si elle n'offense pas l'homme, offense la nature et prend l'humanité en moquerie'. Quoted in M. Melot, *L'Œil qui rit: Le Pouvoir comique des images* (Paris: Bibliothèque des Arts, 1975), 14. Lamartine takes himself for every man Jack of us.
10. Beckett, *Endgame*, in *CDW*, 101.
11. *La Rue*, in *Œuvres*, i. 710.
12. Réjean Ducharme, *Les Enfantômes* (Paris: Gallimard, 1976), 85.
13. See article, *Œuvres*, ii. 812.
14. *Le Testament d'un blagueur,* in *Œuvres*, i. 114.
15. *La Rue*, 818.
16. Camus, *La Chute* (Paris: Gallimard, 1956), 77.
17. 'Les Victimes du livre', in *Œuvres*, i. 238.
18. Julien Sorel plays with such possibilities, but with quivering seriousness.

19. *La Rue à Londres*, in *Œuvres*, ii. 1135.
20. *La Rue*, in *Œuvres*, i. 720.
21. *Œuvres*, i. 120.
22. Ibid. 138.
23. All of these plays on sack/*sac* are available also in French.
24. Philippe Hamon, *L'Ironie littéraire* (Paris: Hachette, 1996), 142.
25. Baudelaire, *Œuvres*, ed. Y. Le Dantec (Paris: Gallimard, 1951), ii. 664. Walter Benjamin, *Charles Baudelaire: A Lyric Poet in the Era of High Capitalism*, tr. H. Zahn (London: NLB, 1973), 14.
26. Flaubert, *Correspondance* (Paris: Conard, 1927), iii. 37. Flaubert cannot escape *bêtise* even in his publisher's name.
27. Ibid., i. 79.
28. Ibid., ii. 407.
29. Edmond and Jules de Goncourt, *Manette Salomon* (Paris: Librairie internationale, 1868), 40–1.
30. Henri Bergson, *Le Rire* (Paris: PUF, 1975 [1900]), pp. vi, 82. Subsequent page references appear in brackets after quotations.
31. Arthur Koestler, *The Act of Creation* (London: Hutchinson, 1964), 47. For Koestler, humour is creative, like poetry, or scientific hypotheses.
32. *La Rue à Londres*, 1161.
33. Louis Veuillot, *Les Odeurs de Paris* (Paris: Crès, n.d.), 68–9.
34. Louis Guilloux, 'A propos de Jules Vallès', *Nouvelle Revue française*, 35 (1930), 438, 440.
35. Mallarmé, 'Le Tombeau d'Edgar Poe', *Poésies* (Paris: Gallimard, 1945), 129.
36. J. R. Klein, *Le Vocabulaire des mœurs de la 'vie parisienne' sous le Second Empire* (Louvain: Nauwelaarts, 1976), 173.
37. Gershon Legman, *No Laughing Matter* (London: Granada, 1978), 16.
38. Pierre Larousse, *Grand Dictionnaire universel du XIXe siècle* (Paris: Larousse, 1866–76).

RIFF ON BLACK HUMOUR

1. Surprising how many shades of black there are.
2. Vladimir Jankélévitch, *L'Ironie* (Paris: Flammarion, 1964), 113.
3. Elliott Oring, *Jokes and their Relations* (Lexington: University Press of Kentucky, 1992), 38.
4. Lautréamont, *Œuvres complètes*, ed. M. Saillet (Paris: Livre de poche, 1963), 222–3.
5. John Irving, *The Fourth Hand* (London: Black Swan, 2002), 344.

6 UPPING THE ANTI/E

1. Jean-Paul Sartre, '*La Conspiration* par Paul Nizan', *Situations I* (Paris: Gallimard, 1947), 29.

2. All references to *Mort à crédit*, henceforth in brackets after quotations, are to the Pléiade edition (Paris: Gallimard, 1981), vol. i. Here, p. 572.
3. David Lacey, *Guardian (Sport)*, 30 Oct. 2004, p. 7.
4. Nathanael West, *The Dream Life of Balso Snell*, in *Complete Works* (New York: Farrar, Straus & Cudeby, 1957), 28.
5. Céline, *Bagatelles pour un massacre* (Paris: Denoël, 1937), 61.
6. Roland Barthes, 'Léon Bloy', *Tableau de la littérature française* (Paris: Gallimard, 1974), iii. 47.
7. William Blake, 'Proverbs of Hell', *The Marriage of Heaven and Hell*, in *Complete Works*, ed. G. Keynes (Oxford University Press, 1984), 150.
8. Léon Bloy, *Journal* (Paris: Mercure de France, 1963), iii. 314.
9. Henry Thoreau, *Walden* (New York: New American Library, 1960), 215. *Walden* is full of punning. 'Yard' is a long-attested, and hopeful, word for the penis. Thoreau's contemporary P. J. Barnum similarly lauded his own notorious ballyhoo.
10. Pierre Fontanier, *Les Figures du discours* (Paris: Flammarion, 1977 [1821–7]). His English opposite number, George Puttenham, on the other hand, talks (tautologously) of 'too much surplusage' as a rhetorical vice. See *The Art of English Poesie*, ed. E. Arber (London: Alex. Murray & Son, 1869), 264.
11. Céline, letter to N of 30 Sept. 1932, *Cahiers Céline*, 5 (1979), 73.
12. Céline, letter to Milton Hindus of 12 June 1947. 'Céline', *Cahiers de l'Herne*, 2 (1965), 80.
13. Julia Kristeva, *Pouvoirs de l'horreur: Essai sur l'abjection* (Paris: Seuil, 1980), 157, 240, 240–1.
14. For more on *la blague*, see Ch. 5 on Vallès.
15. Jean Cocteau, *Le Coq et l'Arlequin*, in *Le Rappel à l'ordre* (Paris: Stock, 1948 [1926]), 2.
16. George Santayana, *Dialogues in Limbo* (New York: Scribner, 1925), 5.
17. Cf. Céline's dedication of *Bagatelles pour un massacre*: 'A mes potes du théâtre en toile'.
18. Céline, letter to Pierre Monnier. See Pierre Monnier, *Ferdinand furieux* (Lausanne: L'Âge d'homme, 1979), 113.
19. Georges Darien, *Le Voleur* (Paris: Union générale d'éditions, 1955), 35.
20. Darien, *Bas les cœurs!* (Paris: Pauvert, 1957), 273–4.
21. Roland Barthes, *Le Degré zéro de l'écriture* (Paris: Seuil, 1972), 20.
22. Zola, letter to Henry Céard of 22 Mar. 1885, in *Correspondance*, ed. H. Bakker, vol. v (Presses de l'Université de Montréal/Éditions du Centre national de la recherche scientifique, 1985), 249.
23. Darien, *L'Épaulette* (Paris: Union générale d'éditions, 1978), 324.

RIFF ON POLITICS

1. Jules Vallès, letter to the editors of *L'Almanach du socialisme*, in *Les Amis de Jules Vallès*, 5 (1987), 78.

2. Steve Murphy, Preface to Jean Richepin, *Les Étapes d'un réfractaire* (Seyssel: Champ Vallon, 1993), 37.
3. Pierre-Joseph Proudhon, *Les Confessions d'un révolutionnaire* (Paris: Rivière, 1922), 291–2.
4. Anthony Burgess, *1985* (London: Arrow, 1984 [1978]), 44.
5. George Orwell, *Nineteen Eighty-Four* (Harmondsworth: Penguin, 1956 [1949]), 47.
6. Arthur Koestler, *Darkness at Noon*, tr. D. Hardy (London: Four Square, 1959 [1940]), 39–40, 99.
7. Ramón Gómez de la Serna, *Greguerías, 1940–1945* (Buenos Aires: Espasa Calpe, n.d.), 73.
8. See Ch. 4 on parrots for Queneau's take on this question: 'littérateur'.
9. Laurie Taylor, *Times Higher*, 8 Nov. 2002, p. 29.
10. Allen Douglas, *War, Memory, and the Politics of Humor: The 'Canard enchaîné' and World War 1* (Berkeley and Los Angeles: University of California Press, 2002), 21. Subsequent page references appear in brackets after quotations. Other references built into *canard* are (1) a speculum, used to introduce food into the mouths of soldiers with severe facial wounds, and (2) *canarder*: to snipe.
11. Francis Debyser, 'Les Avatars de l'humour dans une Europe postmoderne', in M. Abramowicz et al. (eds.), *L'Humour européen* (Lublin: Université Marie Curie-Skłodowska; Sèvres: Centre international d'études pédagogiques, 1993), i. 167.

7 DRÔLE DE PHILOSOPHIE

1. Daniel Lagache, quoted in Claude Bonnefoy, 'Rien ne laissait prévoir que Sartre deviendrait "Sartre"', *Arts*, 11–17 June 1961, 14.
2. Sartre, *L'Être et le Néant* (Paris: Gallimard, 1943), 721. Subsequent page references to this edition appear in brackets after quotations.
3. Ibid. 95.
4. Sartre, *Carnets de la drôle de guerre* (Paris: Gallimard, 1983), 380.
5. Yet compare Sartre's notorious squelching of Mauriac in 'M François Mauriac et la liberté', in *Situations I* (Paris: Gallimard, 1947), 36–57.
6. *La Nausée* (Paris: Livre de poche, 1956 [1938]), 15. Subsequent page references to this edition appear in brackets after quotations. I must recall e.e. cummings: 'My soul a limp lump of lymph', 'Light Cursed Falling in a Singular Block', *Complete Poems, 1904–1962*, ed. G. Firmage (London: Liveright and Norton, 1993).
7. 'Rencontre', here, means 'randomness'. An older sense was 'pun', a meeting-place of meaning.
8. Sartre, *L'Idiot de la famille*, ii (Paris: Gallimard, 1971), 1443. Sartre contrasts such forced laughter with the authentic togetherness of revolutionary groups, which, however, he does not present as ever laughing.

9. Paul Valéry, 'L'Idée fixe', in *Œuvres*, ed. J. Hytier (Paris: Gallimard, 1960), 224.
10. *L'Idiot de la famille*, ii. 1244. Cf. Flaubert's rewrite 'l'hénaurme'.
11. Cyril Connolly, *Enemies of Promise* (Harmondsworth: Penguin, 1961), 54.
12. Sartre, 'Qu'est-ce que la littérature?', *Situations II* (Paris: Gallimard, 1948), 313.
13. Quoted by N. Malcolm, *Ludwig Wittgenstein* (OUP, 1958), 29.
14. Robert Escarpit, *L'Humour*, (Paris: PUF, 1960), 70–1.
15. W. J. Harvey, *Character and the Novel* (London: Cape, 1966), 170.
16. Mary McCarthy, *On the Contrary* (New York: Farrar, Straus & Cudaby, 1961), 287.
17. Jean Borie, *Huysmans: Le Diable, le célibataire et Dieu* (Paris: Grasset, 1991), 22.
18. Sartre, *L'Idiot de la famille*, ii. 1440.
19. On these two points, see 'Notice', by Michel Contat and Michel Rybalka, to *La Nausée*, in *Œuvres romanesques* (Paris: Gallimard, 1982), 1661, 1669.
20. 'Le Mur', in *Le Mur* (Paris: Livre de poche, 1954 [1939]), 32. Subsequent page references to this and other stories appear in brackets after quotations.
21. William Empson, 'Just a Smack at Auden', *Collected Poems* (London: Hogarth, 1984), 62.
22. Sartre, *L'Idiot de la famille*, ii. 1443. Sartre himself makes the link with Clamence in *La Chute*.
23. Sartre, *Un Théâtre de situations*, ed. M. Contat and M. Rybalka (Paris: Gallimard, 1973), 77.
24. See *Situations IX* (Paris: Gallimard, 1972), 35.
25. Sartre, *Huis clos*, suivi de *Les Mouches* (Paris: Gallimard, 1972 [1947]), 42.
26. Sartre, *Les Mains sales*, ed. W. D. Redfern (London: Methuen, 1985 [1948]), 180.
27. See my *Sartre: 'Huis clos' and 'Les Séquestrés d' Altona'* (London: Grant & Cutler, 1995), *passim*.
28. *Les Séquestrés d'Altona* (Paris: Gallimard, 1960), 25. Subsequent page references to this edition appear in brackets after quotations.
29. Christina Howells, *Sartre: The Necessity of Freedom* (Cambridge University Press, 1988), 15.
30. Sartre, *Saint Genet, comédien et martyr* (Paris: Gallimard, 1952), 549.
31. Sartre, *Les Mots* (Paris: Gallimard,1964), 17. The twist is on La Fontaine: 'Le Bûcheron et Mercure', *Fables* (Paris: Crès, n.d.), 141 (… 'à cent actes divers').
32. Sartre, *Situations VIII* (Paris: Gallimard, 1972), 448. From a 1965 lecture in Japan.
33. *Les Mots,* 170. Subsequent page references to this edition appear in brackets after quotations.
34. The jackdaw duet of Sartre and Camus is notorious: *La Chute* riposting to *Saint Genet*, and *Les Mots* yodelling to *La Chute*. Both *Les Mots* and *La*

Chute are written in the classical French Maxim-gun mode, which sprays humour in a high-speed, condensed way.

35. *Saint Genet*, 275.
36. Sartre, *L'Idiot de la famille*, ii. 1244.
37. Queneau, *Les Œuvres complètes de Sally Mara* (Paris: Gallimard, 1962) 349.
38. Sartre, *L'Idiot de la famille*, ii. 1974.
39. Ibid. 1316.
40. Ibid. 1978.
41. See M.-J. Durry, *Flaubert et ses projets inédits* (Paris: Nizet, 1950), 60–1.
42. *L'Idiot de la famille*, ii. 1974.
43. Ibid. 1975.
44. Ibid. 1985.
45. Sartre, *Le Mur*, 143.
46. Flaubert, *Correspondance* (Paris: Conard, 1928), ii. 407.
47. *L'Idiot de la famille*, ii. 1974.
48. In French, *un tourniquet* is also *un garrot*, which is a variant for garrotte. The garrot, then, saves lives from haemorrhaging, or chokes the life out of the prisoner. *Tourniquet* is, furthermore, a revolving door, an image suitable for much of the tail-chasing activity of *Les Mots*.
49. This favourite saying of the grandmother derives from a poem about skating by Pierre-Charles Roy (1693–1764), appearing under an engraving by Lancret, *Le Patinage*. Fontenelle said Roy was the stupidest man he had ever met.
50. Thomas Middleton and William Rowley, *The Changeling*, v. ii.

8 BAD JOKES AND BECKETT

Like handles on old French trains, I use Beckett's English or French versions, *indifferently*, as suits my purpose.

1. The incomparable Gershon Legman describes the opposite of the miscued joke as the equivalent of a 'three-cushion carom in billiards'. *No Laughing Matter* (London: Granada, 1981), 859.
2. F. Dostoyevsky, *Notes from Underground*, tr. A. MacAndrew (New York: New American Library, 1961), 115.
3. In the French version, most of this passage is jettisoned, no doubt because deemed untranslatable.
4. I should like to thank Edward Beckett and the Board of Trinity College Dublin for permission to re-cite the centipede joke from Beckett's letter to Tom MacGreevy (TCD MS 10402/72).
5. The *OED* quotes *Murphy* at the entry for 'acathisia'.
6. J. Campbell, 'Allusions and Illusions', *French Studies Bulletin*, 53 (1994), 19.
7. M. Bakhtin, *Rabelais and his World* (Cambridge, Mass.: MIT Press, 1968), 413.
8. *Joe Miller's jests* (London, 1846 edn.), n.p.

9. And the same in Greek, Latin, French, Spanish, Italian, and German. Michel Tournier makes great sport with this verbal near-incest, and calls the offspring 'white laughter', which he locates in Thomas Mann among others, as well as practising it brazenly himself. See Ch. 9 on Tournier.

10. Letters to me from D. Katz, Oxford Institute for Yiddish Studies, and J. Cohen, All Souls, Oxford, 24 Jan. 1996 and 17 Dec. 1996, respectively.

11. In the French version, 'ils m'ont affranchi sur Dieu', an even greater liberating effect is conveyed (*Inn.*, 21).

12. Buñuel, interviewed by Jean de Baroncelli in *Le Monde*, 16 Dec. 1959, p. 13, in answer to the question whether his *Nazarin* represented a return to Christianity.

13. R. Frost, Untitled, in *The Poetry of Robert Frost*, ed. E. C. Lathem (London: Vintage, 1971), 428.

14. *Iliad*, i. 599.

15. A twist on 'Greek', or 'Hebrew' in the French usage. Queneau invented the useful blend 'pleurire'.

16. C. J. Ackerley, ' "In the beginning was the pun": Samuel Beckett's *Murphy*', AUMLA 55 (1981), 16.

17. Ibid. 19.

18. R. Desnos, *Corps et biens* (Paris: Gallimard, 1930), 40.

19. R. W. Emerson, *Collected Works* (London: Bell & Daldy, 1866), i. 290.

20. W. H. Auden, 'The Truest Poetry is the Most Feigning', *Collected Poems*, ed. E. Mendelson (London: Faber, 1994), 619.

21. E. A. Poe, 'Preface to Marginalia', in *Collected Works of Edgar Allan Poe*, ed. T. O. Mabbutt (Cambridge, Mass.: Harvard University Press, 1978–9), 1116.

22. In Homer, it is Odysseus who uses the moly to resist Circe's spells.

23. I. Stravinsky, *The Poetics of Music* (OUP, 1947), 79.

24. W. Empson, 'The Beautiful Train', *Collected Poems* (London: Hogarth, 1977), 64.

25. J. Arp, quoted in L. Peeters, *La Roulette aux mots* (Paris: La Pensée universelle, 1975), 163.

26. G. Craig: 'The Voice of Childhood and Great Age', *TLS*, 27 Aug. 1982, p. 921.

27. Even an author's self-translation can often be improved upon (a verb which also means 'upped' ...). 'Sur le demi-qui-vive' in *Oh les beaux jours* breeds 'on the semi-alert', whereas 'keeping your weather-eye half-open' might have been better. Or not.

28. S. Kierkegaard, *Repetition* (OUP, 1942), 27.

29. G. Orwell, 'The Art of Donald McGill', *Collected Essays* (Harmondsworth: Penguin, 1970), ii. 193.

30. G. K. Chesterton, 'Cockneys and their Jokes', *All Things Considered* (London: Methuen, 1908), 12.

31. Quoted in D. Bair, *Samuel Beckett* (London: Cape, 1978), 275.

32. Céline, *Voyage au bout de la nuit* (Paris: Livre de poche, 1952), 335.
33. Céline, *Entretiens avec le professeur Y* (Paris: Gallimard, 1955), 102.
34. One of Lamb's 'Popular Fallacies', *The Essays of Elia* (London: Moxon, 1840), 353.
35. The title of J. P. Stern's study of Lichtenberg.
36. Montesquieu, 'Mes pensées', in *Œuvres complètes* (Paris: Gallimard, 1949), i. 1220.
37. G. C. F. Bearn, 'The Possibility of Puns: A Defense of Derrida', *Philosophy and Literature*, 19/2 (1995), 331, 333, and 334.
38. *The Individual Psychology of Alfred Adler*, ed. H. and R. Ansbacher (London: Allen & Unwin, 1958), 252.
39. J. Levine: 'Humor and Psychopathology', in C. Izard (ed.), *Emotions in Personality and Psychopathology* (New York: Plenum, 1979), 59–60.
40. Legman, *No Laughing Matter*, 16.

RIFF ON TASTE

1. Baudelaire, *Le Spleen de Paris*, ed. Y. Le Dantec (Paris: Colin, 1958), 121.
2. Quoted in Pierre Guiraud, *Les Jeux de mots* (Paris: PUF, 1976), 116.
3. Freud, *The Interpretation of Dreams* (Harmondsworth: Penguin Freud Library, 1976), iv. 262.
4. Malcolm Muggeridge, *The Times*, 14 Sept. 1953.
5. Elliott Oring, *Jokes and their Relations* (Lexington: University Press of Kentucky, 1992), 36.
6. Robert O. Foote, 'Who was Joe Miller?', in Louis Untermeyer (ed.), *Treasury of Laughter* (New York: Simon and Schuster, 1946), 246.
7. Elliott Oring, 'Round Table on Political Correctness', *Humor*, 10/4 (1997), 469, 472.
8. Avner Ziv, ibid. 473.
9. Arthur Asa Berger, ibid. 475.
10. Elaine B. Shafter, ibid. 509.
11. John Ayto, *Bloomsbury Dictionary of Euphemisms* (rev. edn., London: Bloomsbury, 2000), 212, 259.
12. Gérard Genette, *Figures V* (Paris: Seuil, 2002), 137–8.
13. Jules Renard, quoted by Pierre Schneider, *Jules Renard par lui-même* (Paris: Seuil, 1956), 114.

9 APPROXIMATING MAN

1. *The Portable Nietzsche*, ed. W. Kaufmann (New York: Viking, 1975), 53. Tournier praises the notion of a dancing God (*CS*, 33).
2. Heidegger's puns are of the etymological variety, as are many of Tournier's. See *V*, 129: *exister* = *être dehors* (*sistere ex*).

3. *Compacité* means compactness, but surely Tournier's inner ear heard *compassé*: starched.

4. A. Breton, *Les Pas perdus* (Paris: Gallimard, 1924), 171.

5. C. Baroche, 'La Matière première', *Sud*, special no. (1980), 76.

6. Ibid, 79. (Compare the secret language of some twins.)

7. A. Burgess, *Joysprick* (London: Deutsch, 1973), 146: 'The piling on of extra connotations is of the essence of the palimpsestuous—or palincestuous—technique'.

8. Tournier quoted by J. J. Brochier: 'Dix-huit questions à Michel Tournier', *Magazine littéraire*, 138 (1978), 11.

9. A. Clavel, 'Le Corps Météo', *Sud* (1980), 135.

10. Tournier, preface to *Le Fétichiste*, in *La Quinzaine littéraire*, 1290 (1974), 30.

11. Construction-wall, Philadelphia, 1969, quoted in R. Reisner and L. Wechsler, *Encyclopaedia of Graffiti* (New York: Macmillan, 1971), 256.

12. See *Guardian*, 1 Feb. 1983, for a report on the Fourth International Congress on Twin Studies: 'A mother can absorb into her own body one twin that has already been diagnosed or it can be swallowed up by the other twin in the womb'.

13. M. Mansuy, 'Trois Chercheurs de paradis: Bosco, Tournier, Cayrol', *Travaux de Linguistique et de Littérature* (Strasbourg), 16 (1978), 229.

14. Brochier, 'Dix-huit questions', 12, quoting Tournier. Swapping 'marmite' for 'creuset', Tournier repeats this formula in *VP*, 257.

15. Tournier, *Le Pied de la lettre* (Paris: Mercure de France, 1994).

16. Compare Queneau, *Chêne et chien* (Paris: Gallimard, 1969), 81: 'Le chien est chien jusqu'à la moelle, | il est cynique, indélicat'.

17. V. Jankélévitch, *L'Ironie* (Paris: PUF, 1950), 95.

18. D. Bougnoux, 'Des métaphores à la phorie', *Critique*, 301 (1972), 541.

19. H. Kenner, 'The Jokes at the Wake', *Massachusetts Review*, 22 (1981), 733.

20. e.e. cummings, *selected poems* (Harmondsworth: Penguin, 1963), 25.

21. A. de Musset, *Fantasio*, in *Théâtre complet*, ed. M. Allem (Paris: Gallimard, 1958), 300.

22. L. C. Jeffress, 'The Novels of Michel Tournier', Ph.D. thesis (University of Oregon, 1981), 255.

INCONCLUSION

1. Interestingly, but maybe irrelevantly, 'apple-cart' used to mean the human body, as well as plans.

2. James Joyce, *Finnegans Wake* (London: Faber, 1975), 183.

3. *The Freud—Jung Letters* (London: Hogarth/Routledge & Kegan Paul, 1974), 220. See also Ernst Gombrich's comments in *Tributes* (Oxford: Phaidon, 1984), 106.

4. Shakespeare, *Twelfth Night*, III. i.

5. Sherry Turkle, *Psychoanalytic Politics* (London: Burnett/Deutsch, 1979), 55.
6. See my 'Ponge Enacting the Goat', *Romanic Review*, 62/4 (1981), 482–8.
7. Gérard Genette, *Figures V* (Paris: Seuil, 2002), 138.
8. As reported in the *Guardian* of 23 May 2005, p. 6.
9. E. B. White and Katherine S. White (eds.), *A Subtreasury of American Humor* (New York: Coward-McCann, 1941), p. xvii.
10. Nietzsche, *Twilight of the Idols*, tr. R. Hollingdale (Harmondsworth: Penguin, 1972), 104. The Desert Father, quoted in Georges Minois, *Histoire du rire et de la dérision* (Paris: Fayard, 2000), 131.
11. Roland Barthes, *Roland Barthes par Roland Barthes* (Paris: Seuil, 1975), 84.

Bibliography

I have decided on a pell-mell listing, as befits my theme of cross-talk acts. I have kept, however, to an alphabetical order.

Abramowicz, Maciej, et al. (eds.), *L'Humour européen*, 2 vols. (Lublin: Université Marie Curie-Skłodowska; Sèvres: Centre international d'études pédagogiques, 1993).

Acevedo, Evaristo, *Teoría e interpretación del humor español* (Madrid: Editora Nacional, 1966).

Anzieu, Didier, 'Une passion pour rire: l'esprit', *Nouvelle Revue de Psychanalyse*, 21 (1980), 161–79.

Apte, Mahadev L., *Humor and Laughter: An Anthropological Approach* (Ithaca: Cornell University Press, 1985).

'Armées d'humour: Rires au féminin', eds. Judith Stora-Sandor and Elisabeth Pillet, *Humoresques*, 11 (2000).

Attardo, Salvatore, *Linguistic Theories of Humor* (Berlin/New York: Mouton de Gruyter, 1994).

Austin, James C., *American Humor in France* (Ames: Iowa State University Press, 1978).

Autrand, Michel, *L'Humour de Jules Renard* (Paris: Klincksieck, 1978).

Baecque, Antoine de, *Les Éclats de rire: La Culture des rieurs au XVIIIᵉ siècle* (Paris: Calmann-Lévy, 2000).

Baldick, Robert, *The Life of J.-K. Huysmans* (Oxford: Clarendon, 1955).

Barreca, Regina (ed.), *New Perspectives on Women and Comedy* (Philadelphia: Gordon and Breach, 1992).

Baudin, Henri, *Les Métamorphoses du comique et le renouvellement littéraire du français de Jarry à Giraudoux (1896–1944)* (Lille: Atelier Reproduction des thèses, 1981).

Benayoun, Robert, *Le Rire des Surréalistes* (Paris: La Bougie du Sapeur, 1988).

Bennett, Gillian (ed.), *Spoken in Jest* (Sheffield Academic Press, 1991).

Berger, Arthur Asa, *An Anatomy of Humor* (New Brunswick: Transaction, 1993).

—— *Blind Men and Elephants* (New Brunswick: Transaction, 1995).

—— (ed.), *The Postmodern Presence* (Walnut Creek, Calif.: Altamira, 1998).

Bernstein, Michel André, *Bitter Carnival: 'Ressentiment' and the Abject Hero* (Princeton University Press, 1992).

Bertrand, Denis (ed.), 'Sémiotique et humour', *Humoresques*, 4 (1993).

Bertrand, Dominique, *Dire le rire à l'âge classique* (Aix-en-Provence: Publications de l'Université de Provence, 1995).

——(ed.), 'Humour et société', *Humoresques*, 7 (1996).

——(ed.), 'L'Horrible et le risible', *Humoresques*, 14 (2001).

Bertrand, Jean-Pierre, et al. (eds.), *Huysmans à côté et au-delà* (Louvain: Peeters/Vrin, 2001).

Besant, Walter, *The French Humourists from the Twelfth to the Nineteenth Century* (London: Richard Bentley & Son, 1873).

Bleu, Albert, 'Huysmans humoriste', *Bulletin de la Société J.-K. Huysmans*, 25 (1953), 265–74.

Blondel, Eric, *Le Risible et le dérisoire* (Paris: PUF, 1988).

Boehrer, Bruce, ' "Men, Donkeys, Lap-Dogs, Parrots, Perish All!" ' Psittacine Articulacy in Early Modern Writing', *Modern Language Quarterly*, 59/2 (1998), 171–93.

Bonnefis, Philippe, 'Exposition d'un perroquet', in *Mesures de l'ombre* (Presses universitaires de Lille, 1987), 77–110.

Bonnet, Gilles, *L'Écriture comique de J.-K. Huysmans* (Paris: Champion, 2003).

Borie, Jean, 'La Blague', *Cahiers du chemin*, 26 (1976), 58–71.

——*Huysmans: Le Diable, le célibataire et Dieu* (Paris: Grasset, 1991).

Bouloumié, Arlette, 'Rire, humour et ironie dans l'œuvre de Michel Tournier', in Jean-Yves Vray (ed.), *Relire Tournier* (Publications de l'Université de Saint-Étienne, 2000).

Breton, André, *Anthologie de l'humour noir* (Paris: Pauvert, 1966).

Brunel, Patrick, *Le Rire de Proust* (Paris: Champion, 1997).

Cahen, Gérald (ed.), 'Humour: Un état d'esprit', *Autrement*, 131 (1992).

Cahiers de l'Herne, 'Huysmans', ed. P. Brunel and A. Guyaux (1985).

Cameron, Deborah, *Verbal Hygiene* (London: Routledge, 1995).

Carpenter, G. D. H. and Ford, E. B., *Mimicry* (London: Methuen, 1933).

Cave, Terence, 'Des perroquets', in *Pré-histoires II: Langues étrangères et troubles économiques au XVIe siècle* (Geneva: Droz, 2001), 29–44.

Cazamian, Louis, 'Pourquoi nous ne pouvons définir l'humour', *Revue germanique* (1906), 601–34.

Cazeneuve, Jean, *Du Calembour au mot d'esprit* (Monaco: Éditions du Rocher, 1996).

Chambers, Ross, *Loiterature* (Lincoln, Nebr.: University of Nebraska Press, 1999).

Chanfrault, Bernard, 'The Stereotype of "Deep France" in the *Almanach Vermot*', *Humor*, 1–2 (1992), 7–32.

Chard-Hutchinson, Martine (ed.), 'L'Humour américain', *Humoresques*, 15 (2002).

Chartier, Pierre, 'Diderot, ou le rire mystificateur', *Dix-huitième Siècle*, 32 (2000), 145–64.

Chaulet-Achour, Christiane, and Sylvos, Françoise (eds.), 'Humour et esthétique', *Humoresques*, 8 (1997).

Chénieux-Gendron, Jacqueline, and Dumas, Marie-Claire, *Jeu surréaliste et humour noir* (Paris: Lachenal & Ritter, 1993).

Clapier-Valladon, Simone, 'L'Homme et le rire', in Jean Poirier (ed.), *Histoire des moeurs II*, vol. i. (Paris: Gallimard, 1991).

Cohn, Ruby, *Samuel Beckett: The Comic Gamut* (New Brunswick, NJ: Rutgers University Press, 1962).

Connon, Derek, *Diderot's Endgames* (Berne: Peter Lang, 2002).

Conrad, Peter, *Shandyism: The Character of Romantic Irony* (Oxford: Blackwell, 1978).

Conway, Daniel W., and Seery, John E. (eds.), *The Politics of Irony: Essays in Self-Betrayal* (New York: St Martin's Press, 1992).

Dariosecq, Luc, 'A propos de Loulou', *French Review*, 4 (1958), 322–4.

Davies, Christie, *Ethnic Humour around the World* (Bloomington: Indiana University Press, 1996).

Debailly, Pascal, et al. (eds.), *Le Rire de Voltaire* (Paris: Éditions du Félin, 1994).

Debon, Claude, 'Le Langage des animaux dans l'œuvre de Raymond Queneau', in *Études sur Raymond Queneau* (Paris: Presses de la Sorbonne nouvelle, 1998), 181–9.

Dekkers, Midas, *Dearest Pet: On Bestiality*, tr. P. Vincent (London: Verso, 2000).

Desmeules, Georges, *La Littérature fantastique et le spectre de l'humour* (Quebec: L'Instant même, 1997).

Drachline, Pierre (ed.), *Le Grand Livre de la méchanceté* (Paris: Le Cherche Midi, 2001).

Elgozy, Georges, *De l'humour* (Paris: Denoël, 1979).

Emelina, Jean, *Le Comique* (Paris: SEDES, 1991).

Escarpit, Robert, *L'Humour* (Paris: PUF, 1960).

Fabre, Lucien, *Le Rire et les rieurs* (Paris: Gallimard, 1929).

Fabrice, Antoine, and Wood, Mary (eds.), 'Traduire l'humour', *Ateliers*, 15 (1998).

Favre, Robert, *Le Rire dans tous ses éclats* (Presses universitaires de Lyon, 1995).

Feinberg, Leonard, *The Secret of Humor* (Amsterdam: Rodopi, 1978).

Feuerhahn, Nelly (ed.), 'Humour et politique', *Humoresques*, 5 (1994).

Friedemann, Joë (ed.), 'Rire et littérature', *Humoresques*, 9 (1998).

Genette, Gérard, 'Morts de rire', in *Figures V* (Paris: Seuil, 2002), 134–225.

Gordon, Rae Beth, *Why the French Love Jerry Lewis: From Cabaret to Early Cinema* (Stanford University Press, 2001).

Gray, Frances, *Women and Laughter* (Basingstoke: Macmillan, 1994).

Gripari, Pierre, *Du rire et de l'horreur: Anatomie de la 'bien bonne'* (Paris: Julliard/L'Âge d'homme, 1984).

Grojnowski, Daniel, *Aux commencements du rire moderne: L'Esprit fumiste* (Paris: Corti, 1997).

——and Sarrazin, Bernard, *L'Esprit fumiste et les rires fin de siècle* (Paris: Corti, 1990).

Gruner, Charles R., *The Game of Humor* (New Brunswick: Transaction, 1997).

Gutwirth, Marcel, *Laughing Matter* (Ithaca: Cornell University Press, 1993).

Haig, Stirling, *Flaubert and the Gift of Speech* (Cambridge University Press, 1986).

Hale, Jane Alison, *The Lyric Encyclopedia of Raymond Queneau* (Ann Arbor: Michigan University Press, 1989).

Hamon, Philippe, *L'Ironie littéraire* (Paris: Hachette, 1996).

Hanrez, Marc, 'Céline et Vallès', *Les Amis de Jules Vallès*, 18 (1994), 47–52.

Henriot, Jacques: *Sous couleur de jouer: La Métaphore ludique* (Paris: Corti, 1989).

Holland, Norman N., *Laughing: A Psychology of Humor* (Ithaca: Cornell University Press, 1982).

'Humor', *Yale French Studies*, 23 (1959).

'L'Humour', *Revue française de psychanalyse*, 37/4 (1973).

'L'Humour d'expression française', *Humoresques*, 2 (1990), 2 vols.

'Humour et traduction', *Contrastes* (1986).

'L'Humour juif', *Humoresques*, 1 (1990).

Hyers, Conrad, *The Spirituality of Comedy: Comic Heroism in a Tragic World* (New Brunswick: Transaction, 1996).

Jameson, Fred, 'The Laughter of Nausea', *Yale French Studies*, 23 (1959), 26–32.

Jankélévitch, Vladimir, *L'Ironie* (Paris: Flammarion, 1964 [1950]).

Jardon, Denise, *Du comique dans le texte littéraire* (Brussels and Paris: De Boeck-Duculot, 1988).

Jeanson, Francis, *Signification humaine du rire* (Paris: Seuil, 1950).

Jones, Baird, *Sexual Humor* (New York: Philosophical Library, 1987).

Jones, Louise, 'The Comic as Poetry: Bergson Revisited', *Nineteenth-Century French Studies*, 2/1–2 (1974), 75–85.

Jourde, Michel, *La Voix des oiseaux et l'éloquence des hommes*, 3 vols. (Thèse de doctorat, Université Michel de Montaigne-Bordeaux 3, 1998).

Kaufman, Will, *The Comedian as Confidence Man: Studies in Irony Fatigue* (Detroit: Wayne State University Press, 1997).

Kofman, Sarah, *Pourquoi rit-on? Freud et le mot d'esprit* (Paris: Galilée, 1986).

Kundera, Milan, *Jacques and his Master*, tr. Simon Callow (London: Faber, 1986).

Kundera, Milan, *L'Art du roman* (Paris: Gallimard, 1986).

Laffay, Albert, *Anatomie de l'humour et du nonsense* (Paris: Masson, 1970).

Lalo, Charles, *Esthétique du rire* (Paris: Flammarion, 1949).

Latta, Robert L., *The Basic Humor Process* (Berlin and New York: Mouton de Gruyter, 1999).

Le Juez, Brigitte, *Le Papegai et le Papelard dans 'Un Cœur simple' de Gustave Flaubert* (Amsterdam: Rodopi, 1999).

Levin, Harry (ed.), *Veins of Humor* (Cambridge, Mass.: Harvard University Press, 1972).

Lewis, Paul, *Comic Effects* (Albany, NY: State University of New York Press, 1989).

Lipman, Steve, *Laughter in Hell: The Use of Humor during the Holocaust* (Northvale, NJ: Jason Aronson, 1991).

Lipovetsky, Gilles, 'La Société humoristique', in *L'Ère du vide* (Paris: Gallimard, 1983), 153–93.

Lloyd, Christopher, 'Huysmans auteur comique', in Jean-Pierre Bertrand et al. (eds.), *Huysmans à côté et au-delà* (Louvain: Peeters/Vrin, 2001), 361–78.

Louette, Jean-François, and Viegnes, Michel (eds.), 'Poésie et comique', *Humoresques*, 13 (2001).

Maistre, Xavier de, *Voyage autour de ma chambre*, in *Œuvres complètes de Xavier de Maistre* (Plan de la Tour, 1984).

Maloux, *L'Esprit à travers l'histoire* (Paris: Albin Michel, 1977).

Mauron, Charles, *Psychocritique du genre comique* (Paris: Corti, 1985).

Mayer, Tony, *L'Humour anglais* (Paris: Julliard, 1961).

Mayoux, Jean-Jacques, 'Beckett et l'humour', *Cahiers Renaud-Barrault*, 53 (1966), 33–41.

Melot, Michel, *L'Œil qui rit: Le Pouvoir comique des images* (Paris: Bibliothèque des Arts, 1975).

Ménager, Daniel, *La Renaissance et le rire* (Paris: PUF, 1995).

Ménard, Maurice, *Balzac et le comique dans 'La Comédie humaine'* (Paris: PUF, 1983).

Mendel, Werner M. (ed.), *A Celebration of Laughter* (Los Angeles: Mara, 1970).

Michelson, Bruce, *Literary Wit* (Amherst: University of Massachusetts Press, 2000).

Minois, Georges, *Histoire du rire et de la dérision* (Paris: Fayard, 2000).

Monro, D. H., *Argument of Laughter* (University of Notre Dame Press, 1963 [1951]).

Morreall, John, *Taking Laughter Seriously* (Albany, NY: State University of New York Press, 1983).

Mulkay, Michael, *On Humour: Its Nature and its Place in Modern Society* (Cambridge: Polity, 1988).

Murray, Jack, *The Proustian Comedy* (York, SC: French Literature Publication Co., 1980).

Nash, Walter, *The Language of Humour* (London: Longman, 1985).

Noguez, Dominique, *L'Arc-en-ciel des humours: Jarry, Dada, Vian, etc.* (Paris: Hatier, 1996).

——*L'Homme de l'humour* (Paris: Gallimard, 2004).

Normand, Jean, 'L'Humour des poètes', *Thalia*, 4/1 (1981), 62–70.

Olbrechts-Tyteca, Lucie, *Le Comique du discours* (Éditions de l'Université de Bruxelles, 1974).

Olds, Marshall C., *Au pays des perroquets: Féerie théâtrale et narration chez Flaubert* (Amsterdam: Rodopi, 2001).

Oring, Elliott, *The Jokes of Sigmund Freud* (Northvale, NJ: Jason Aronson, 1997 [1984]).

——*Jokes and their Relations* (Lexington: University Press of Kentucky, 1992).

Pagnol, Marcel, *Notes sur le rire* (Paris: Nagel, 1947).

Palmer, Jerry, *Taking Humour Seriously* (London: Routledge, 1994).

Parkin, John, *Humour Theorists of the Twentieth Century* (Lewiston: Mellon, 1997).

——and Phillips, John (eds.), *Laughter and Power* (Oxford: Lang, 2006).

Paulhan, Francis, 'Le Sens du rire', *Revue philosophique de la France et de l'étranger*, 111 (1931), 5–47.

Paulos, John Allen, *I Think, therefore I Laugh* (New York: Columbia University Press, 1985).

'Les Petits Maîtres du rire', *Romantisme*, 75 (1992).

Phillips, John, ' "Laugh? I nearly died!" Humour in Sade's Fiction', in Parkin and Phillips (eds.), *Laughter and Power*, 63–84.

Pintard, René, 'L'Humour de Rousseau', in *Jean-Jacques Rousseau et son œuvre* (Paris: Klincksieck, 1964).

Pouilloux, Jean-Yves, *'Les Fleurs bleues' de Raymond Queneau* (Paris: Gallimard, 1991).

Pratt, Alan R., *Black Humor* (New York/London: Garland, 1993).

Preiss, Nathalie, *Pour de rire! La Blague au XIXe siècle* (Paris: PUF, 2002).

Prince, Gerald, 'Le Comique dans l'œuvre romanesque de Sartre', *PMLA*, 87/2 (1972), 295–303.

Quesnel, Alain, *Premières leçons sur 'Les Fleurs bleues' de Raymond Queneau* (Paris: PUF, 1999).

Redfern, Walter (ed.), 'Vallès ridens', *Les Amis de Jules Vallès*, 20 (1995).

Revue des Sciences humaines, 'Huysmans', 170–1 (1978).

Richardot, Anne, *Le Rire des Lumières* (Paris: Champion, 2002).

Ricks, Christopher, *Beckett's Dying Words* (Oxford University Press, 1995).

'Rire et rires', *Romantisme*, 74 (1991).

'Le Rire, le Comique, l'Humour', *Revue d'Esthétique*, 3/3 and 4 (1950).

'Rires', *Revue d'Esthétique*, 38 (2001).

Roberts, David, 'Is de Sade funny? Or the Prison of Parody', in P. Petr, *Comic Relations* (Frankfurt: Lang, 1985), 227–37.

Royle, Peter, 'Hidden Word-Play in the works of Jean-Paul Sartre', Conference paper (2005); (shorter version in Royle, *L'Homme et le néant chez Jean-Paul Sartre* (Presses de l'Université de Laval, 2005).

Royot, Daniel, *L'Humour américain: Des puritains aux Yankees* (Presses de l'Université de Lyon, 1980).

Ruch, Willibald (ed.), *The Sense of Humor* (Berlin and New York: Mouton de Gruyter, 1998).

Sangsue, Daniel (ed.), *Stendhal et le comique* (Grenoble: ELLUG, 1999).

Sareil, Jean, *L'Écriture comique* (Paris: PUF, 1984).

Sarrazin, Bernard, *Le Rire et le sacré* (Paris: Desclée de Brouwer, 1991).

——— *La Bible parodiée* (Paris: Cerf, 1993).

Sauvy, Alfred, *Aux sources de l'humour* (Paris: Odile Jacob, 1988).

Schaeffer, Neil, *The Art of Laughter* (New York: Columbia University Press, 1981).

Schutz, Charles E., *Political Humor, from Aristophanes to Sam Ervin* (Cranbury and London: Associated University Presses, 1977).

Seery, John Evan, *Political Returns: Irony in Politics and Theory from Plato to the Antinuclear Movement* (Boulder, Colo.: Westview, 1990).

Serpell, James, *In the Company of Animals* (Oxford: Blackwell, 1986).

Slater, Maya, *Humour in the Works of Proust* (Oxford University Press, 1979).

Sollers, Philippe, *Le Rire de Rome* (Paris: Gallimard, 1992).

Spitzer, Leo, 'The Style of Diderot', in *Linguistics and Literary History* (Princeton University Press, 1974 [1948]), 135–91.

Sternberg, Jacques (ed.), *Un siècle d'humour français* (Les Productions de Paris, 1961).

Szafran, A. Willy, and Nysenholt, Adolphe (eds.), *Freud et le rire* (Paris: Métailié, 1994).

Topsfield, Valerie, *The Humour of Samuel Beckett* (Basingstoke: Macmillan, 1988).

Turier, Claude, *L'Humour de l' 'Almanach Vermot', de 1886 à 1900* (Paris: Le Cherche Midi, 1989).

Vartanian, Aram, 'La Mettrie, Diderot, and Sexology in the Enlightenment', in Jean Macary (ed.), *Essays on the Age of Enlightenment in Honor of Ira O. Wade* (Geneva: Droz, 1977), 347–67.

Wagg, Stephen (ed.), *Because I Tell a Joke or Two* (London: Routledge, 1998).

Wechsler, Robert (ed.), *Savoir Rire: The Humorists' Guide to France* (London: Robson, 1989).

Werner, Stephen, *The Comic Diderot* (Birmingham, Ala.: Summa, 2000).

——— *The Comic Philosophes: Montesquieu, Voltaire, Diderot, Sade* (Birmingham, Ala.: Summa, 2002).

Wickler, Wolfgang, *Mimicry in Plants and Animals*, tr. R. D. Martin (London: Weidenfeld and Nicolson, 1968).

Woodrow, Alain, *Et ça vous fait rire!* (Paris: Éditions du Félin, 2000).

Zimmerman, Laurent, 'De l'humour dans la théorie littéraire', *Littérature*, 132 (2004), 100–11.

Ziv, Avner, *Personality and Sense of Humor* (New York: Springer, 1984).

—— (ed.), *National Styles of Humor* (New York: Greenwood, 1988).

—— and Diem, Jean-Marie, *Le Sens de l'humour* (Paris: Dunod, 1987).

Index

West, Nathanael 122–3
White, E.B. 209
Whitman, Walt 8
Wilde, Oscar 78–9, 218n
Wittgenstein, Ludwig 144–5

Yaguello, Marina 54
Yeats, William Butler 9

Ziv, Avner 178
Zola, Emile 70, 76, 130